JOHN CHRYSOSTOM

The second half of the fourth century was a turbulent time. Bishops came and went, monks rioted and Christianity struggled to gain a foothold against competing religions as increasingly it came to exert its influence. Just as often Christian group fought against Christian group for power and influence. From the midst of this turmoil a number of outstanding figures arose to dominate the ecclesiastical and political landscape. One of the most remarkable was John Chrysostom.

This book examines John Chrysostom's role as a preacher and his pastoral activities as presbyter and bishop. The authors draw together the latest research on preaching, the preacher's audience and pastoral care in a comprehensive introduction. They also provide fresh and lively translations of a key selection of sermons and letters which allow John Chrysostom to speak on these topics in his own words.

John Chrysostom presents a valuable introduction to the processes of Christianisation, the roles of elites in the church, the offices of presbyter and bishop, and the place of the church in late antique society.

THE EARLY CHURCH FATHERS
Edited by Carol Harrison
University of Durham

The Greek and Latin Fathers of the church are central to the creation of Christian doctrine, yet often unapproachable because of the sheer volume of their writings and the relative paucity of accessible translations. This series makes available translations of key selected texts by the major Fathers to all students of the early church.

Already published:
MAXIMUS THE CONFESSOR
Andrew Louth

IRENAEUS OF LYONS
Robert M. Grant

AMBROSE
Boniface Ramsey OP

ORIGEN
Joseph W. Trigg

JOHN CHRYSOSTOM

Wendy Mayer and Pauline Allen

London and New York

First published 2000
by Routledge
11 New Fetter Lane, London EC4P 4EE

Simultaneously published in the USA and Canada
by Routledge
29 West 35th Street, New York, NY 10001

Routledge is an imprint of the Taylor & Francis Group

Typeset in Garamond by BC Typesetting, Bristol
Printed and bound in Great Britain by
St Edmundsbury Press, Bury St Edmunds, Suffolk

British Library Cataloguing in Publication Data
A catalogue record for this book is available from the British Library

Library of Congress Cataloging in Publication Data
Mayer, Wendy, 1960–
John Chrysostom/Wendy Mayer and Pauline Allen.
p. cm. – (Early church fathers)
Includes bibliographical references and index.
1. John Chrysostom, Saint, d. 407. 2. Theology, Doctrinal.
I. John Chrysostom, Saint, d. 407. Selections. 1999. II. Allen,
Pauline. III. Title. IV. Series.
BR65.C46M39 1999
270.2′092–dc21 99–17709
[B] CIP

ISBN 0–415–18252–2 (hbk)
ISBN 0–415–18253–0 (pbk)

CONTENTS

CONTENTS

PREFACE

In the case of John Chrysostom no single volume can do justice to a father of the church whose output was so prolific and is so well preserved. Indeed, it is unwise to try. What we aim to present through the carefully selected sermons and letters translated in this volume is rather a snapshot of two important aspects of John's life – his experiences as a preacher and his involvement in the pastoral care offered by the Nicene Christian church in the cities of Constantinople and Antioch in his time. Over the centuries many biographies and accounts of the life and times of this famous preacher have appeared (in English: Stephens 1880; Attwater 1939; Baur 1959–60, orig. publ. in German 1929–30; Kelly 1995), yet in few has either aspect received more than a superficial treatment. In general, too, critical assessment of John as preacher, analysis of the character, composition and behaviour of his audience, and nuanced discussion of John's involvement in pastoral care, is scarce (with the exception of Rentinck 1970 and MacMullen 1989). Also rare is the firm situation of these three aspects within the two distinct urban environments in which John and his parishioners lived and worked, and within which interaction between them of a homiletic and pastoral nature necessarily occurred. It is these deficiencies that we hope in some small part to address.

The detail which we offer in the introduction to the volume derives largely from the intensive, systematic assessment to which we have been subjecting John's homilies in the course of the past eight years (Allen and Mayer 1993) – a process which we are now applying to his correspondence also. The research which we conducted for the recently released handbook on Greek preaching (Cunningham and Allen 1998; Allen 1996, 1997; Mayer 1997a, b, 1998b) is likewise reflected. This research has been supported generously and continuously by the Australian Research Council. Without its funding none of the painstaking reading and analysis upon which this work is based could have been undertaken. Thanks are due also to the Society for the Promotion of Byzantine Studies (UK) and the A.G. Leventis Foundation, which assisted the contributors to the above volume to meet in Oxford in 1996 to discuss at first hand the finer points of what occurred between the Greek preachers of the first millennium and their audiences. With regard to the book itself, we are grateful to the editors for allowing us to incorporate a longer than usual bibliography containing a greater than usual number of items in foreign languages. The literature on John Chrysostom is extensive and there is no single up-to-date bibliography available for this author. In addition, while much is written in English, the majority of the scholarship relevant to the two areas upon which we focus appears in other languages. The comments and advice of Carol Harrison, the General Editor of this series, have been most helpful.

Finally, it is with considerable appreciation that we acknowledge the efficient and cheerful assistance of Fran Wilkinson, Secretary of the Department of Theology; Pam Ackroyd, Secretary of the Centre for Early Christian Studies; and Elaine Mortimer, Interlibrary Loans Librarian – all at McAuley Campus, Australian Catholic University. Without their support this volume could not have reached fruition.

Wendy Mayer and Pauline Allen
Feast day of blessed Philogonius
20 December 1998

ABBREVIATIONS

ACW	*Ancient Christian Writers*
a.i.	*ab imo*
CPG	*Clavis Patrum Graecorum*
EEC	*Encyclopaedia of the Early Church* (ed. A. Di Berardino)
HE	*Historia ecclesiastica*
HR	*Historia religiosa*
LSJ	Liddell and Scott, *A Greek-English Lexicon*
OCD	*The Oxford Classical Dictionary*
ODB	*The Oxford Dictionary of Byzantium*
ODJR	*The Oxford Dictionary of the Jewish Religion*
PG	*Patrologia Graeca*
PLRE	*The Prosopography of the Later Roman Empire*
SC	*Sources Chrétiennes*

Introduction

1

JOHN'S LIFE AND TIMES

THE SECOND HALF OF THE FOURTH CENTURY

At Antioch in Syria in c.349[1] John was born into a world that was at once both stable and caught up in the inexorable momentum of change. By the time that he died on 14 September 407 his life would span the greater part of a remarkable period, during which the boundaries of power and thought within the Roman empire shifted and the world of antiquity was irrevocably changed.[2] Christianity, while by no means as yet the dominant religion, was in the ascendant; yet, at the same time, it struggled to compete with the older pagan religions, the imperial cult and Judaism, each of which had a strong and tenacious hold on the public space and upon the public mind. In cities where Christianity did have a strong hold it was scarcely homogeneous. John himself grew up in a place in which there resided three Christian bishops, all claiming legitimate authority – a figure which swelled in one memorable year to four (Wilken 1983: 10–16). Throughout the fourth century the call to a life of *askēsis*, the exercise of self-denial, grew attractive for a number of reasons and there was a dramatic increase in the number of men, young and old, who abandoned secular life for communities of monks or for a solitary life as a holy man. Women too in increasing numbers avoided childbearing or second marriages by declaring themselves celibate and in many cases devoted their lives to charitable works.[3] At this same time the idea that the bones or ashes of those who had died for the faith had special powers gained credence and such mortal remains were considered to sanctify the place where they resided. These associations led to the first translations of saints' and martyrs' remains, a practice which rapidly gained momentum.[4]

In the secular world the empire became divided permanently into east and west, each with its own emperor and administrative centre. After residing at Antioch for much of the middle part of the fourth century for military reasons, from Theodosius onwards the emperors in the east became permanently domiciled at Constantinople. In association with this shift the ecclesiastical see of Constantinople rose dramatically in status, being declared at the Second Ecumenical Council of 381 second in standing after Rome. This declaration accelerated an already emerging shift in the balance of power in the east between the see of Constantinople and its more prominent rivals Antioch and Alexandria. Throughout this same period at Constantinople the new aristocracy, promoted by Constantine and successive emperors as the senatorial class of the new Rome, consolidated its position. In association with all of these developments bishops, monks and pagans flooded into Constantinople in increasing numbers and began to reside there for lengthy periods in order to seek influence and favour. They were vibrant times in which, in the east, the two cities between which John divided his life and career played roles that were prominent.

It was a world in which much was changing; and yet much remained the same. Despite the growing influence of Christianity and the increasing presence of distinctive ascetic men and women, the larger cities of the late antique world remained uniform havens of Hellenistic culture. In many ways, to travel from one such city to another was to journey from the usual into the familiar. Greek was spoken everywhere, trade and administration continued as it had before, and the pagan festivals that had defined civic life for centuries were celebrated with continued enthusiasm. As in the past the male children of the upper classes were trained in classical rhetoric and fixed their sights on careers in law or the civil service. At Antioch, as we shall see in *Against the Jews oration 1*, citizens continued to solemnise business contracts in the local synagogue and to seek healing at local pagan or Jewish shrines according to the sacred location's speciality or reputation. It was to pagan priests that they turned, as they had always done, when a valuable animal had strayed and they were anxious to locate it (*In 2 Tim. hom. 8*: PG 62,650 16–24).[5] The norms of daily life were scarcely altered.

JOHN'S LIFE

It was such a world into which John was born and within which he lived out his life. With regard to his family background, it is generally agreed that his mother at least was Christian and that his father was a successful civil servant in the bureau of the commander of military operations in the diocese of Oriens, the *magister militum per Orientem*. His mother was widowed young and, as was the growing custom for Christian women of independent means at the time, chose not to enter into a second marriage. Kelly (1995: 4) speculates that the family, while not of the uppermost echelon, was well connected and very comfortably off. This conclusion may overstate the case slightly since there is no clear evidence that in the period of his priesthood at Antioch or while he was bishop of Constantinople John exploited family connections or operated on the basis of a private income.[6] Nonetheless it is certain that he came from a family of some means and status since he was sent to school and received the full education that was standard for the male children of the families which belonged to the more elevated classes.

Little is known about the earliest stage of John's childhood and the twelve or so years during which he passed through the various phases of his schooling. What is certain is that he finished his training under the tutelage of a professional orator – probably the renowned pagan rhetorician Libanius, a prominent citizen of Antioch – graduating in *c*.367 when he was eighteen. The young John was at that point most probably destined for the civil service, perhaps as one of the clerks of the *sacra scrinia* (Kelly 1995: 15–16). At some point within the year following his graduation John presented himself for baptism by the pro-Nicene bishop Meletius and, turning away from a secular career, spent the next three years in that bishop's service as an aide. As Kelly points out (1995: 16–17), the Christian faction to which he attached himself was not in imperial favour at this time and was obliged to assemble for worship outside of the city walls across the river on the military exercise ground. In his *Historia religiosa* Theodoret of Cyrrhus twice describes these assemblies and refers to the difficulties faced by Meletius' followers (HR 2.15, 8.5–8: SC 234, 226–8, 382–92). At this same time John seems to have began to frequent an ascetic school or *askētērion* run by Diodore (a priest ordained by Meletius; subsequently bishop of Tarsus) and a certain Carterius. In an encomium preached when Diodore was later visiting Antioch John suggests that this instruction too was conducted across the river (*Laus Diodori*: PG 52,764 26–8). Kelly (1995: 18–20) speculates that the form of ascetic life with which he experimented at this time involved the renunciation of marriage, the adoption of a distinctive style of dress and meetings with like-minded young men for the purposes of prayer. At this point he was still living at home.

In c.371, not long before Meletius again departed from Antioch for exile in Armenia, John was brought into the official ranks of the Meletian clergy through his appointment as lector (*anagnōstēs*). The duty of this office was the reading of the Old Testament and epistle lessons during worship.[7] Not long after he was installed as lector John abandoned those duties and his other activities within that Christian community and left Antioch to try out a more rigorous ascetic life in the mountains that abutted the city. There he spent four years learning to control his passions under the tutelage of an elderly Syrian ascetic. At the end of the four years he withdrew to a cave in the mountains and spent a further two years continually standing, scarcely sleeping, and learning the Old and New Testaments by heart. As a consequence of the extreme practices he followed during this latter period his stomach and kidneys were permanently damaged (Palladius, *Dial.* 5; ACW 45: 35). At the conclusion of those six years, perhaps driven by his failing health, perhaps enticed by the possibility of the return of bishop Meletius from exile,[8] John returned to Antioch and resumed his duties as lector in a Christian faction which now received the support of the new emperor. He continued as lector for some two years before receiving ordination to the rank of deacon. After five years in that role he was promoted and ordained to the priesthood by Meletius' successor, Flavian.[9] Meletius had died shortly after John's ordination as deacon, while attending the Second Ecumenical Council in Constantinople. It is at this point that John's career becomes of special interest to us in terms of his experiences as a pastoral carer and preacher.[10]

We know surprisingly little about the twelve years (386–97) during which John served the dominant Christian faction at Antioch as a presbyter. For Palladius and the church historians Socrates and Sozomen the events that overtook his life once he had been elevated to the throne of the church of Constantinople hold greater interest. As a consequence there is much speculation about John's activities throughout this period. Most of the opinion put forward, however, has yet to be verified. Kelly (1995: 57), for instance, promotes John rapidly to the position of personal assistant to bishop Flavian, and has him following Flavian around in the course of that person's duties. He further supposes that in the final stages of his presbyterate John took over more and more of Flavian's episcopal duties as a consequence of the bishop's advanced age (Kelly 1995: 103).[11] The same evidence which he cites in support of John's attachment to Flavian, however, indicates that John was at that point assigned to his own congregation,[12] a circumstance which leads one to question whether he spent the greater part of the twelve years accompanying his bishop. On the contrary, it may be that for much of that time he had particular duties to perform in a specific congregation, regardless of whatever additional tasks he was obliged to undertake at his bishop's behest. We have adduced this example in order to point out just how imprecise our knowledge of this phase of John's life is at present. The only fact of which we can be absolutely sure is that, as presbyter, he preached a great deal in addition to pursuing a number of less readily defined activities.

We know that John preached a great deal because of the over nine hundred sermons which survive (by no means the original total). The majority of these can be presumed to stem from the period of his priesthood at Antioch, when there are taken into account the far fewer years − only five and a half compared to twelve − that he subsequently spent at Constantinople.[13] Among these sermons there is one group which does provide insight into an important event that occurred early in John's tenure as presbyter. This group consists of twenty-two sermons preached from immediately prior to Lent until Easter in the year 387[14] − the same period during which the people of Antioch feared retribution at the hands of the emperor Theodosius in response to the overturning of the imperial statues.[15] The effects of this event upon the city were dramatic. Various persons, children included, were executed immediately following the insurrection. In a subsequent trial the decurions were arrested and sentenced variously to capital punishment or exile. In a number of waves many of Antioch's citizens − working class and wealthy, women, children and students − fled the city for the mountains and uninhabited places. More than a few of the fugitives encountered death along the way. In the city itself the baths and theatre were shut; the usually bustling market-place was empty. Only the churches were full. Throughout this period John preached on Saturdays and Sundays in the morning and on weekdays in the afternoon.[16] His sermons reflect the fear which permeated the city at that time and provide us with much valuable information about the second trial, the rumours and more concrete news which periodically swept through the city, and the behaviour of Antioch's citizens as they anxiously awaited the decision of the emperor.

Ten and a half years later, in October or perhaps November 397, John's life was to undergo a dramatic change. On 26 September of that year the bishop of Constantinople, Nectarius, suddenly died.

With the elevation of the see of Constantinople in 381 to second in status after Rome and with the emperor in the east now permanently residing in that city, the death of Nectarius left vacant a position that had rapidly become strategic and highly desirable. Various parties favoured their own candidates and nomination for the position was hotly contested. It appears that without his knowledge John was put forward as a candidate by the imperial eunuch Eutropius. Allegedly through the judicious use of blackmail,[17] Eutropius was successful in having his nomination preferred and John was duly elected by a synod of bishops in the east summoned specially for that purpose. In the meantime, instructed by the *comes Orientis* (Count of the East) Asterius to meet him at the martyrium near the Romanesian Gate of Antioch, John found himself carried off en route to Constantinople. Palladius implies that this tactic was adopted because there were fears that the populace would make its displeasure felt if it was given advance warning of John's removal (*Dial.* 5; ACW 45: 36).

In the five and half years which followed his consecration on 26 February 398, John was to spend almost as much time dealing with the various interest groups that vied for power at Constantinople as he was to devote to his episcopal duties. Periodic contact with the emperor and his wife and court added to his commitments. At times the different spheres became inseparable. When John made a move to combat the nocturnal processions which the Arians conducted within the city on the eve of Saturdays and Sundays and of certain liturgical festivals, it was the empress Eudoxia who donated the large silver crosses which helped to distinguish the Nicene counter-processions. It was she also who lent the services of her chamberlain, the eunuch Brison, to train and conduct the choir needed to counter the provocative hymns sung by the Arians as they moved through the city (Soc., HE 6.8; Soz., HE 8.8). As we shall see in *Hom. delivered after the remains of martyrs etc.*, on occasion she herself took an active role in liturgical processions. John's encounters with the palace and its officials were not always so pleasant, however. In the homily *On Eutropius* it becomes clear that Eutropius' effecting of John's promotion did not guarantee cordial relations between them. At the time that the homily was preached, however, their lives had become enmeshed in a way that neither could have anticipated. Eutropius suddenly found himself in need of John's pastoral care; while for John the opportunity to draw a moral lesson from the consul's plight was too convenient to pass over.

8

Other political developments – both secular and ecclesiastical – interfered directly with the bishop's more ordinary duties. Twice in 400 John, who had a close interest in the Gothic community both in Constantinople and elsewhere (Kelly 1995: 142–4), was obliged to suspend his other activities while he spent time (first at Chalcedon, second in Thrace) negotiating with the hostile Gothic general Gainas over the fate of the political hostages Saturninus, John and Aurelianus (Kelly 1995: 151–62). A little over a year later, possibly in early January 402 (Kelly 1995: 163–74), John chose to place the administration of the see in the hands of his archdeacon Serapion and to entrust his preaching duties to the visiting Syrian bishop Severian while he made a lengthy journey to Ephesus to sort out a number of disciplinary matters. Whether, as bishop of Constantinople, John had the authority to interfere in the affairs of the churches in Asia Minor is questionable; certainly he could not have done so without imperial backing (Kelly 1995: 178–80). As we observe in the homily *On his return*, he was absent for so long (almost four months) that he missed out on presiding at the baptisms conducted that Easter and was obliged to soothe those who felt put out by this circumstance when he returned some weeks after the festival.

By this stage significant political events which touched upon John's life and office were beginning to occur concurrently and his stress levels were increasing. Whereas the original request for John to involve himself in affairs at Ephesus had been put forward in 400 at a time when Gainas' activities were proving an acute distraction, the arrival of a group of Nitrian monks in dispute with the bishop of Alexandria, Theophilus, only a few months prior to his actual departure for Ephesus was to cause him further anxiety. To offer overt support for their cause, as they requested, would have placed John in conflict with a powerful and hostile fellow prelate. Because of the delicacy of dealing with their needs in a way that would not compromise his own position, his lack of action in the matter led to their residence at Constantinople for the better part of two years (Kelly 1995: 191–202). In addition to the constant anxiety caused by the monks' presence in the capital, John was also faced with the unpleasant discovery that while he had been absent in Asia Minor his substitute homilist Severian had been securing his own position at court and among the aristocracy at the expense of that of his host bishop. John's relations with a portion of his clergy, with the majority of the local monks and ascetics, with certain women at court, with a growing number of the aristocracy, and with certain visiting bishops were in any case poor or deteriorating.[18]

It was in this climate that a number of factors converged, resulting in the now famous Synod of the Oak in autumn 403. In a twist indicative of the fragile state of politics in the capital at the time Theophilus, himself summoned to Constantinople to stand trial over charges relating to the Nitrian monks, suddenly became one of the members of the tribunal at a synod before which John was now summoned as the accused. The synod, stacked with bishops from Egypt whose loyalties lay with Theophilus and with individual bishops known for their hostility towards John, found him guilty – not on the charges laid before it, but for failure to respond to the summons to attend – and called for his deposition. As a result of the violent demonstrations which erupted, the order for his banishment was not acted upon for several days. Scarcely had he set out than he was called back, in response to an ominous mishap involving the empress. Not prepared to return until certain conditions were met, John demurred, spending his time in a suburban villa owned by Eudoxia until the violent death of a number of monks and supporters following an encounter between the two groups caused him to relent. In the months between his return in October 403 and Easter 404 John was in effect to resume all of his normal duties. As Easter neared, however, the situation came to a head and, although he was to continue to reside in the *episkopeion*, he was banned by imperial decree from entering the Great Church or officiating at the Easter services. An attempt to conduct the scheduled baptisms at an alternative location resulted in a bloody confrontation between John's sympathisers and the soldiers sent to disrupt the proceedings. Another two months were to pass before the opposition was able to exert enough pressure upon Arcadius to issue the decree that would send John into a second and final exile (Kelly 1995: 211–49).

On 20 June 404 John summoned the forty bishops who had been staying with him in recent months and the four aristocratic widows with whom he had worked closely at Constantinople and, after saying farewell to each group, quietly slipped out of the city. Under military escort he was hastened from Nicomedia, via Nicaea, Ancyra and Caesarea to Cucusus, a small 'city' in Armenia Secunda. After some time there, during which various friends and supporters from Antioch came to visit him and John was able to increase his exchange of letters with allies at Constantinople and to write to other potential supporters soliciting their help, he was obliged to flee abruptly along with the inhabitants of the city to Arabissus, as the result of a series of particularly violent Isaurian bandit raids. According to Delmaire (1991: 174) he was forced to quit Arabissus for the same reason in autumn 406. Whether he resumed his detention at Arabissus or even at Cucusus when the Isaurian activity died down is uncertain. Whichever is the case, in 407 steps were taken to send John to an even more remote location, Pityus, situated on the eastern shores of the Black Sea some 1,100 km distant from Constantinople. Always in a fragile state of health, and with a body further weakened by the deprivations and exertions of his exile, John was unable to endure the difficult and brutally rapid land journey. On 14 September 407 he died while still en route to the departure point on the Black Sea.

THE CITIES OF ANTIOCH AND CONSTANTINOPLE

John was born into a city whose wealth and status rivalled those of the other prominent urban centres of the late Roman world – Rome, Alexandria and Constantinople. Situated at the nexus of the trade route from the far east to the eastern shores of the Mediterranean and the land route from Egypt through to Constantinople and the west, it enjoyed the availability of a broad range of produce, goods and services as well as providing hospitality for a large volume of visitors. That the markets of Antioch were renowned for their abundance of goods is indicated in *On the statues hom. 17*, while in *Concerning blessed Philogonius* some of the range of goods available are described for us. In the same homily John makes it clear that the markets associated with festival days occasioned the influx of a substantial number of people (both traders and buyers) from the surrounding rural areas.

Other factors contributed to the city's social mix and status. As the locus for military operations on the Persian front, as the capital of Syria, and as the administrative centre for the diocese of Oriens, for much of John's life there Antioch periodically played host to emperors, their officials and their retinue, to military units and their commanders, provincial governors and magistrates, and to vast numbers of athletes and entertainers. Due to instability on the Persian front, throughout the 340s, 360s and 370s the emperors Constantius II, Julian, Jovian and Valens spent a considerable amount of time there. An imperial palace was located on the island in the Orontes and probably also in the suburb of Daphne

(Downey 1961: 641–6). Various military units were likewise stationed in and near the city during these same periods. In addition, every four years more than a thousand athletes would flood into the city for the staging of the Olympic Games. The Games lasted for forty-five days, with contests divided between venues within the city itself and others in Daphne (*In princ. Actorum hom. 1*: PG 51,764–7; Downey 1961: 649–50). The *magister militum per Orientem, comes Orientis* and *consularis Syriae* had their residences and bureaux in the city and were more or less permanent fixtures. On the ecclesiastical front, the status of the Antiochene see in the east was comparable with that of Alexandria.[19] In consequence, the city not infrequently hosted synods of various degrees of importance, which demanded the presence of a greater or lesser number of bishops and accompanying clergy. As Frans van de Paverd (1991: 286) speculates, the Syriac-speaking monk-presbyters who receive mention at the beginning of *Baptismal instruction 8* may well have come to Antioch periodically at the same time of year for consultation with their bishop. These factors ensured that Antioch was usually bustling with life and that the dynamics of the population were constantly changing.

That the citizens of Antioch felt that they had good reason to be proud of their city and its ordinarily elevated and pleasurable lifestyle is reflected in the devastation felt by them at the removal of its status as a metropolis following the riots in 387 (*On the statues hom. 17*; cf. *On Col. hom. 7*). In other homilies of this same series the closure of the baths, theatres and hippodrome, and the marked emptiness of the shops and market-place in the aftermath of the riots, are likewise clearly a cause for anguish.[20] In *On the statues hom. 17* John highlights, along with the status of the city and the abundance of the available merchandise, its many fine buildings, the facility with which its inhabitants frequent the streets and market-places until late in the evening, the colonnaded streets and the charms of Daphne with its sacred grove of cypresses and its numerous springs. Indeed Daphne, with its mild climate, its shady groves, its entertainment venues, its abundant water supply, its renowned temples of Apollo and Zeus and the much-frequented Jewish healing shrine (the cave of Matrona), would alone have been sufficient cause for Antioch's fame and status throughout the eastern half of the Mediterranean. Many of Antioch's wealthier inhabitants had villas in the suburb and repaired there for the summer.

Beyond being wealthy, enjoying high status and offering a sophisticated and enviable lifestyle, Antioch was also a city of religious pluralism. Christians, 'pagans' and Jews mingled in relatively large numbers,[21] while Christianity itself, as mentioned, offered a number of alternative versions and factions. One such group, encountered at Constantinople also, is labelled by John as the Anomoeans – that is, those who claim that Christ is 'not like' the Father, in opposition to the Nicene assertion that Christ is 'like' (*homoios*), namely 'of one substance' with, the Father (Kelly 1993: 249). Aetius, one of the two leaders of the movement, was a native of Antioch. It is against the beliefs of this movement in relation to the nature of God that John addressed his sermon on the occasion prior to *Against the Jews or. 1*. With regard to the Jewish community at Antioch itself, the adherents of Judaism and their practices and cultic sites were prominent and unavoidable. Not only did the Jews appropriate the marketplace every year at Yom Kippur, on which occasion they danced barefoot as part of their ritual, but there existed a synagogue within the city in the quarter known as Kerateion. It is most likely to this site that John refers in *Against the Jews or. 1* in relation to the incident of three days earlier. A second synagogue was situated in Daphne, as too was the already mentioned cave of Matrona. The latter most probably contained the bones of the Maccabean martyrs (Vinson 1994: 180–4), which would have added to its reputation and widespread attraction. Again, the prominence and attractiveness of the Jewish festivals which occurred throughout autumn is a factor highlighted by John in the above sermon.

Antioch was in addition a thoroughly Hellenised city. The statues of Tyche, the deified Trajan and various pagan gods and goddesses were distributed throughout its public spaces (Lassus 1977: 67–74). In Daphne, although the burnt-out shell of the once famous temple of Apollo ominously greeted visitors as they approached from Antioch (*De s. Babyla*: PG 50,532 46–9), the temple of Zeus and other long-significant pagan sites remained and continued to be frequented in association with the traditional festivals. The civic calendar was imbued with the festivals of Poseidon, Artemis, Calliope, Adonis, Demeter and Dionysus (Liebeschuetz 1972: 230–1). Every four years, when the Olympic athletes processed up to Daphne after thirty days of competition in Antioch, the traditional rituals continued to be perfomed by the *alytarch* and other officials, although it is possible that the focus of attention had by this time been transferred from Zeus to Heracles (Downey 1961: 440–1). Daphne was also the site at which there was held in summer a seven-day-long festival, possibly associated with Apollo (Theod., HE 3.10). If this is the same festival for which John expects that many of his listeners will depart on the day following the feast day of St Julianus (*In s. Julianum*: PG 50,672–3), then it offered as an attraction banquets, companies of male dancers and erotic songs with the kind of lyrics that had the potential to cause embarrassment.

When John was abducted on the command of the emperor Theodosius and conveyed to Constantinople to become its bishop in late 397, he arrived in a city that was both similar to the one which he had just left and yet substantially different. Whereas Antioch was situated on a river plain located some miles inland from the Mediterranean coast (the city nestled between a range of mountains and the river Orontes), Constantinople was constructed on less level ground and was coastal, being surrounded by water on three of its four sides. Located on the western shore of the Bosphorus opposite Chalcedon, the city was bound to the south by the Sea of Marmara and to the north-east by the substantial inlet known as the Golden Horn. To the west the wall of Constantine divided the city proper from the cemetery, various martyria and suburban estates, and the hinterland. Where Antioch was at the nexus of a number of road systems from Egypt, Asia Minor and the far east, Constantinople was the focus of sea routes from Egypt and the Black Sea, as well as providing a significant staging post for those journeying by land from Asia Minor and the east to Rome and other regions of the west. Two important roads led from the city – the Via Egnatia to the south-west and to the north-west the highway that connected the east with the Balkans, northern Italy, the Rhineland and Britain (Krautheimer 1983: 42).

More significantly, whereas the Antioch with which John was familiar represented the culmination of development which had taken place over centuries of settlement, both in terms of its physical attributes and its long-established aristocracy and curial class (Lassus 1977: 67–74, 79–83), the city at which he arrived had enjoyed its present status for little more than half a century. Consecrated in 324, it had been substantially rebuilt and enhanced by Constantine and his successors (Dagron 1974: 29–47, 388–409; Krautheimer 1983: 42–6). A new aristocracy had been culled from other parts of the empire and drawn to the city by incentives (Dagron 1974: 119–90; Krautheimer 1983: 46). From around 380 it became the permanent domicile of the emperor in the east and his administration. It was thus not through nature, but due largely to the building programmes of Constantine and Constantius, the residency of the imperial household, and Constantine's deliberate relocation of wealthy and influential aristocrats as part of his policy of building up a new

Roman senate that by the time of John's arrival Constantinople had become a comparably large, wealthy and well-serviced city.

A particular peculiarity, due largely to its location and top-ography, was the incorporation of the water surrounding Constan-tinople into the conceptual structure of the city and its function (Mayer 1998c). The theoretically separate municipality of Chalcedon and the suburbs situated on the northern side of the Golden Horn were likewise treated as an integral part of the city. Mango describes the total phenomenon as a conurbation (Mango 1986: 118). This must have caused John some confusion when he first took over the reins of the episcopate since, from an ecclesiastical point of view, Chalcedon operated as a separate see aligned with the churches of Bithynia and Asia Minor. Its prominent role in the machinations which led to the deposition of John and as a refuge for clergy not in sympathy with the bishop of Constantinople (Soc., HE 6.11, 15; Soz., HE 8.10, 16) demonstrates the ambiguity of its status.

Superficially, however, similarities to Antioch abounded. Despite the overt Christianisation of the city, as at Antioch the civic calendar was predominantly 'pagan'.[22] Many of the same festivals were celebrated and, as we observe in *Against the games and theatres* and *On: 'My father's working still'*, the hippodrome and theatre enjoyed a similarly high level of popularity, offering much the same degree of distraction. As intimated in the homily *On Eutropius*, the political events and entertainments which took place in these venues were equally integral to the life of the city. The public spaces of the city itself were filled by Constantine with statues of the gods which he acquired as essential to the decor, as Krautheimer expresses it, of a late antique city (Krautheimer 1983: 61). The rituals asso-ciated with the cult of the emperor, which had been introduced by Constantine and which probably still persisted in Arcadius' time (Krautheimer 1983: 61–3), would have been neither shocking nor unfamiliar.

As at Antioch, religious pluralism was also a feature. Although we know virtually nothing about the size or nature of the Jewish popu-lation at Constantinople, it is undoubtedly the case that one existed. In the hinterland, if not within the city itself, pagan temples still operated (Dagron 1974: 378–9). The Christian population itself was divided into a number of factions. For the majority of its life as the newly fashioned city of Constantine, Constantinople and its churches had been under the control of the Arians. Even after the churches were handed back to the Nicene Christians by Theodosius in 380 Arian and Anomoean communities persisted. Technically forbidden to worship within the city precincts, the Arians in particular found ways to make their presence known and continued to exert influence (Soc., HE 6.8; Soz., HE 8.8). In addition, Anomoean and other semi-Arian forms of Christianity persisted among a proportion of the monastic communities settled within the city (Miller 1985: 74–85). These groups were prominent through their acts of social welfare. The necessity of combating the Anomoean teaching concerning the status of Christ is demonstrated for us in *On: 'My father's working still'*. One sector of the Christian community which may have been less familiar to John was the Nicene rigorist sect known as the Novatians. Throughout this same period the Novatians were consistently treated as a legitimate, independent branch of Nicene Christianity and, while they often shared the same fortune, there was a tendency to treat them more leniently (Soz., HE 4.20, 6.9). When John arrived in 397 he found himself obliged to tolerate a second bishop with his own set of churches and the equal support of the emperor.

2

THE LITURGICAL SETTING

While there were many similarities in liturgical practice between the two cities of Antioch and Constantinople, the history and topography peculiar to each ensured that there were also differences. At Antioch strong competition from numerous prominent and long-established pagan, Jewish and civic sites and ceremonies meant that Christianity was obliged to develop strategies for marking out its own distinctive territory upon the local urban and suburban landscape. Differentiating itself from its competitors was a primary focus. At Constantinople, by contrast, Constantine had taken a formerly small and insignificant settlement and reconstructed and reshaped it into an imperial city – the New Rome (Krautheimer 1983: 41–67). In doing so, he imposed Christianity upon it as the imperially endorsed religion and ensured that certain churches and Christian sites would play a prominent role in the ceremonial life of the city. By the time that John Chrysostom arrived in the city in late 397, this system had developed in complexity (Mayer 1998c; Mayer forthcoming (a)).

In order to situate John and his audiences and to understand how together they formed part of the liturgical life of each city it is important to study in greater detail the liturgical environment which pertained at each location. By the time that John was ordained presbyter at Antioch in 386 the Meletian faction, now under the leadership of bishop Flavian, conducted regular worship services in at least two churches.[1] The Great Church – an octagonal construction of some splendour begun in the time of Constantine – was situated in the new quarter of Antioch on the island in the Orontes. It lay in proximity to the imperial palace and the hippodrome and was almost certainly the episcopal church of the city (Eltester 1937: 254–70; Deichmann 1972). The second construction, the Old Church (Palaia) was so named because it was situated in the old

17

part of the city. It was thought to date back, in one form or another, to the time of the apostles (Eltester 1937: 272–3). We see both churches mentioned in the title to the sermon *On: 'I opposed him to his face'*, where it is indicated that John's normal place of preaching is the Old Church, but that he had been unable to fulfil this duty at the previous synaxis (a eucharistic or non-eucharistic liturgy or service), since on that day he had been summoned by the bishop to attend him in the Great Church. A third church, the Church of the Maccabees, situated to the south in the Jewish quarter of Antioch (Kerateion) between the colonnaded main boulevard and Mt Silpios, was in John's time a recent construction.[2] Probably built as a deliberate means of distinguishing a Christian cult of the Maccabees from the older Jewish cult, with its locus in the Cave of Matrona at Daphne, the precise function and status of this church is difficult to determine. If it served no other purpose, it was the location at which the festival of the Maccabees was celebrated every year on 1 August (*De ss. martyribus*: PG 50,647 1–3).

There existed a fourth church, likewise only recently completed (*c.*381), which was situated on the opposite side of the Orontes to the city, facing the island which contained the palace-hippodrome complex and the Great Church.[3] It is unknown whether this church was used for ordinary worship in Chrysostom's day. Its main use appears rather to have been as the locus for the festivals of St Babylas and Meletius (*De s. Babyla*: SC 362,294–312; *De s. Meletio*: PG 50,515–20), both former bishops of Antioch whose remains had been interred in a common sarcophagus in the centre of the cruciform building.[4] In common with other martyrs' and saints' festivals at Antioch at the time, it is possible that on the feast day of each bishop the current bishop of the city led the Christian community in a procession from the Great or Old Church to the Church of St Babylas. On such days it was usual to then hold a non-eucharistic service celebrating the life of the saint at the location most closely associated with that person. The recent date of the building and the fact that it was almost certainly constructed by Meletius with the intention that it would become his mausoleum and not just a monument to the revered Babylas may mean, however, that the church was intended to be used for more than occasional worship. The choice of site, within relative proximity of the Old and Great Churches, and at the edge of the military exercise ground used for assembly by the Meletian faction of the Nicene Christian community at the time of the emperor Valens, suggests that the church was in any case intended to immortalise the triumph of Nicene Christianity at Antioch – particularly since the remains of Babylas, in whose honour it was being constructed, had effected a spectacular victory against the temple of Apollo at Daphne in the time of the emperor Julian.[5]

The location of numerous significant Christian burial sites immediately beyond the walls of Antioch, in the surrounding rural areas and in the suburb of Daphne determined the location of further places of worship known as martyria. The architecture and size of these buildings at the time of John's presbyterate is unknown to us, but several sites which receive mention in his homilies can be identified. The main cemetery, located outside the city walls at the side of the road leading to Daphne, seems to have contained one or more buildings of this kind (Franchi di Cavalieri 1928). It was to one or another of these that the Christians of Antioch walked in procession on the feast days of Sts Julian, Drosis and Ignatius, among others.[6] Another martyrium, constructed in the mid-fourth century to house the translated remains of Babylas and other martyrs, was situated near the now ruined temple of Apollo in the suburb of Daphne.[7] The references to orchards, meadows and gardens and to the availability of pubs on the way home suggest that it may be at this martyrium that John and his audience celebrated the festival at which he preached *A homily on martyrs*.[8] Another martyrium was situated across the river from the city just outside the Romanesian Gate near the road to Alexandretta, the beginning of the land route from Antioch to Constantinople. This is the same martyrium to which John was summoned by Asterius on the day on which he departed Antioch. It too contained numerous burials, many of them a source of embarrassment to the Nicene Christian bishop Meletius and his successor Flavian, because they were individuals who had played a prominent role in the Arian community, having been interred at the site during the years in which the churches of Antioch had been in the hands of the Arian faction. At the time that John preached the homily *In ascensionem* (CPG 4342), Flavian had recently solved the problem by having the coffins of the approved Christian martyrs raised from beneath the floor of the martyrium, where they had formerly mingled indiscriminately with the 'heretics', and displayed prominently and separately (PG 50,443 22–37). What is of particular interest in the case of this martyrium is that it was used not just on the festivals of saints and martyrs, but also for certain liturgical festivals, which clearly involved a procession to and from the site. Good Friday and Ascension are specifically mentioned.[9]

Martyria tended to be used occasionally rather than regularly for public worship, because of their location and the strong association with certain hallowed remains. On days when a festival service was held at one of these locations the liturgical rite will have incorporated several of the following elements: a procession, a night-long vigil, scripture readings, a sermon, the eucharist. The last four are described for us by John in *A homily on martyrs*. The structure of the service outlined in that homily, however, is likely to have been exceptional (van de Paverd 1970: 10–12). That is, it is not at all certain whether lengthy vigils would have been observed or the eucharist celebrated on the feast days of individual saints or martyrs. The martyria did not lie idle, however, on the days when no festivals were held there. In *In ascensionem* John indicates that the laity have for years been in the habit of going to the martyrium to pray (PG 50,443 10–15).[10] In other of his festival sermons John encourages the audience to visit these sites in between times for private devotional purposes. Thus in *A homily on martyrs* he sets out for the audience a regimen of weeping at a particular martyr's tomb, physically embracing the coffin, anointing oneself with holy oil as a mental prompt and using the martyr as an advocate in one's prayers.[11]

Although familiar through his child- and adulthood in Antioch with liturgical processions and the stationing of special services at a particular church or martyrium on certain dates in the liturgical calendar, John was to encounter a more complex and developed set of stational practices when he arrived in Constantinople. This was due partly to his change in status, partly to the status of the city itself and its particular history, and in part to the markedly different local topography. Another contributing factor was the simple fact that by late 397 Constantinople possessed a larger number of churches in which Nicene Christian congregations regularly gathered for worship.[12] The church in which John seems to have preached the most frequently is the Great Church. This is because, together with the *episkopeion*, to which it was adjacent, it formed the administrative centre of the Constantinopolitan episcopate (Mayer forthcoming (a)). He also preached in the Church of the Apostles, St Eirene, St Anastasia and St Paul (Mayer 1997a: 73) – the last named after a former Nicene bishop of the city, whose remains had been translated from Armenia in 381 by Theodosius and deposited somewhat ironically in a church that had been built by his hostile semi-Arian successor (Soz., HE 7.10; Soc., HE 5.9). At the time that John preached there it was in the possession of a congregation of Nicene Goths.[13] The congregation had its own complement of clergy and worshipped in its native language. Of the other churches, St Eirene, situated close to the Great Church and imperial palace, had operated as the episcopal church from the time of Constantine until the Great Church had superseded it on its completion in c.360. It shared the complement of clergy attached to the Great Church and appears to have continued to operate even after the Great Church took over its original function. Originally the reception hall of an aristocrat's mansion in which Gregory of Nazianzus had resumed Nicene worship within the city in 379 (Bernardi 1995: 184), St Anastasia continued to be used for worship after the churches of the city were handed back to the Nicene Christian community by Theodosius in November 380. It appears to have been located about halfway between the Great Church and the Church of the Apostles.

The Church of the Apostles itself had a peculiar status within the city. Originally a mausoleum constructed by Constantine within the city limits on a prominent rise at the end of the northern axis of the two ceremonial routes that Constantine developed within the city, it was augmented by a cruciform church, completed in 370. By the time that John arrived in 397, it contained the remains not only of Constantine and Theodosius, but also of the apostles Luke, Andrew and Timothy. By Roman law and tradition, because of their location inside the city limits neither building should have been permitted to contain human remains. Furthermore, on analogy with what was occurring at Antioch and in other cities at this time, even with the remains the church and mausoleum ought to have been treated as a martyrium. By 381, however, we not only see remains translated to another urban church – that of St Paul – but we also find services being held on a regular or semi-regular basis within both locations (Mayer forthcoming (a)). This was one distinction which must have struck John forcibly on his arrival. In addition, it seems that he also inherited a tradition of the bishop periodically celebrating the eucharist or preaching in each of the urban churches under his jurisdiction (Mayer forthcoming (a)), a custom for which there is no evidence at Antioch. It had perhaps developed during the decades in which the churches had been under the possession of a succession of Arians, semi-Arians and Novatians as a means by which the bishop of the dominant Christian faction might periodically reinforce his claim over his territory within the city.

In addition to the urban churches there existed a substantial number of suburban churches and martyria – St Thomas in Drypia (Janin 1969: 251–2); St Mocius and St Acacius, both beyond the

Constantinian wall (Dagron 1974: 393–5); St John the Baptist at Hebdomon (Janin 1969: 413–15); St Euphemia at Chalcedon;[14] Sts Peter and Paul in neighbouring Rufinianae (Pargoire 1899–1900: 156); a church of the Maccabees across the Golden Horn in Galata (Janin 1969: 313–14); and a church to which the city processed on Ascension likewise across the Golden Horn in the suburb of Elaia.[15] With respect to the homilies translated in this volume, it is to the church of St Thomas that the empress and city walked in solemn procession during the night prior to John's delivery of *Homily delivered after the remains of martyrs etc.* The destination which John and his parishioners eventually reached by boat on the Wednesday of the storm in the homily *Against the games and theatres* is the church of Sts Peter and Paul at Rufinianae. There may have existed other suburban martyria – for instance, there is mention in the *Life of Isaac* of a martyrium of St Stephen financed by John's enemy Aurelianus (*Vita s. Isaacii* 4.18; see Liebeschuetz 1990: 141) – but those listed above are the ones which can be identified as playing a role in the liturgical life of the city from the record of John's life and from his sermons.

Unlike the situation at Antioch, which had been a partially Christianised city for several centuries and therefore possessed an abundance of native burials, few of the buildings at Constantinople had been erected over the remains of local saints and martyrs.[16] Instead, the dearth of local material had caused remains to be imported and deposited in purpose-built churches or already existing martyria in the suburban regions. Thus in 360 the remains of the apostles Andrew, Luke and Timothy were brought to Constantinople and interred in the foundations of the Church of the Apostles both as a means of satisfying part of Constantine's original plan and of giving rise to the name to which John refers in *Against the games and theatres* – 'City of the apostle' (Woods 1991). Most of the translations were of more recent occurrence. Several took place during the years of John's episcopate. The casket which the empress and people escort in *Hom. delivered after the remains of martyrs etc.* contains relics which have only recently been imported into the city and which are being conveyed in solemn procession from the Great Church to their final resting-place.[17] From the homily delivered on the following day (*Hom. dicta praesente imperatore* (CPG 4441.2)) we learn that the celebrations lasted two days. Two days are also set aside for the celebrations that occurred when the remains of St Phocas were conveyed to the city from Pontus (*De s. Phoca*: PG 50,699–706). Again the emperor and empress are present and there are various processions and special services. On this occasion a flotilla of boats and brightly lit pyres escort the remains over the waters surrounding the city as part of the solemnities (Mayer 1998c). In the case of the church of Sts Peter and Paul at Rufinianae, the remains had been secured by Rufinus, the owner of the palace which housed the shrine, no earlier than 389 (Vanderspoel 1986: 247). The custom of processing across the Bosphorus in boats and holding a service at that site on the feast day of Sts Peter and Paul (29 June) can thus only have been established a few years before John's arrival. This further suggests that the service held in the Church of the Apostles on the Wednesday morning in *Against the games and theatres* may not be opportunistic so much as a reflection of former practice.

The liturgical calendar which John encountered at Constantinople was likewise both largely familiar to the newly installed bishop and yet subtly different. At Antioch the feast of Christmas (25 December), to which he refers in *Concerning blessed Philogonius*, had been introduced a few years prior to John's ordination as presbyter (*In diem natalem*: PG 49,351 24–9). In the same homily he mentions Epiphany, Easter, Ascension and Pentecost. It is possible, however, that the separate feast of Christmas had not yet been introduced to Constantinople and that the birth and baptism of Christ were still celebrated together there on Epiphany (6 January).[18] The other festivals, however, were already an established part of the Constantinopolitan calendar.[19] At Easter, as we are informed in *On his return*, a large number of baptisms usually took place.[20] People expected that these would be performed by the local bishop. At Antioch he was familiar with the conducting of baptisms at Pentecost also (*De s. pentecoste hom. 1*: PG 50,457 58–61). In what is probably a Constantinopolitan sermon John declares, however, that in this city it is the custom of the fathers not to baptise at Pentecost (*In Acta apost. hom. 1*: PG 60,22 16–27). At both locations baptism at Easter was preceded by a period of intense instruction, during part of Lent, which then continued for a further week following the ceremony (the paschal octave). It is within this latter period of catechesis that *Baptismal instruction 8* falls, although the homily is inaccurately titled, since it is addressed to a full congregation, including visitors. Lent provided another new experience for John, since it lasted for eight weeks at Antioch, whereas its duration was only seven weeks at Constantinople (van de Paverd 1991: 250–4). During this period shorter than usual services were held early every evening from Monday to Friday (van de Paverd 1991: 161–201), although local events, such as those outlined in *On the statues homily 17*, could disrupt their sequence. The large number of local saints' and martyrs' festivals which were observed in each city, as distinct from the small number which were most probably common,[21] provided another aspect of the liturgical calendar that was noticeably different. The festival of Philogonius, a former bishop of Antioch, which would have been of little interest to anyone beyond that location, is one such example.

There was a further domain in which John's experience of the liturgy between and within each city varied. This domain encompasses the spaces within which he and his various audiences worshipped. Between each of the different churches in Antioch or Constantinople in which services were regularly held and between those churches and the local martyria there existed noticeable differences (Mayer 1997b). The greatest variation lay in the shape of each building and in the way in which the audience and preacher were disposed within it. At Antioch the Great Church was octagonal in shape, with upper-storey galleries surrounding a central atrium, covered by a lofty dome (van de Paverd 1970: 3–8). The ambo, or location from which the scriptures were read and the presbyter delivered his homily, was most probably situated beneath the dome in the centre of the atrium. At Constantinople, on the other hand, the Great Church was a basilica or rectangular in form, with two to four aisles flanking the nave (Mathews 1977: 11–19; Krautheimer 1983: 52–5). Like the Great Church at Antioch, it too seems to have had galleries. In a building of this shape the ambo was once again in the centre of the nave, while the bishop's throne, from which he was expected also to preach, was situated in the centre of the top level of a synthronon in the apse – that is, a semicircular tiered dais set into a niche at the rear of the building behind the sanctuary. In a building of this shape the line of sight of the preacher in relation to the displacement of the audience was somewhat different. A similar arrangement most probably existed in the Old Church at Antioch, which is thought to have been a basilica also (Eltester 1937: 272; van de Paverd 1970: 9). The audience here seems to have been distributed in an entirely different way, however, since a wooden barrier had been constructed during the course of the fourth century, which bisected the nave cross-wise and distributed the men and women between the front and rear of the church, rather than between the left and right side of the nave, or between the ground floor and the galleries (*In Matt. hom.* 73/74: PG 58,677 4–24; Mayer 1997b: 108–9).

There existed other variations. The church of St Babylas at Antioch was neither octagonal nor basilical in shape but cruciform, with each arm of the cross of even length (Lassus 1938). This is likely to have been the case with the Church of the Apostles in Constantinople too, which was also cross-shaped (Greg. Naz., *Somnium de Anastas. eccl.*: PG 37,1258 60). In both locations the line of sight of the audience would have been slightly more focused and the potential for distraction to some degree restricted. Other variations will have related to the liturgical furnishings. There is still argument concerning the liturgical furnishings to be found in martyria as opposed to churches in which worship was held regularly (van de Paverd 1970: 11–12), on the assumption that the eucharist was rarely, if ever, celebrated in such locations. *A homily on martyrs*, however, in which there is clear reference to the eucharist, throws the question open; while it is also the case that Constantine arranged for an altar to be located in the mausoleum which existed prior to the cruciform Church of the Apostles, against all norms for such a location (Eusebius, *Vita Const.*, 4.58–60; Mango 1990). Whether episcopal thrones were to be found in all regularly used churches or only the episcopal church in each of the cities and what kind of seating for the clergy existed in the local martyria are two further questions which have yet to be answered. At Constantinople episcopal thrones were undoubtedly present in the Church of the Apostles, St Anastasia and St Eirene in addition to the Great Church (Mayer forthcoming (a)).

3

JOHN AS PREACHER

Just because an episcopal throne was available in many of the churches in which John preached at Constantinople and because this was the place from which a bishop was expected to deliver his sermon, it did not mean that he always observed the time-honoured custom. Indeed there is clear evidence to the contrary. Socrates tells us that, as bishop, he more often than not preached seated on the ambo out in the middle of the nave, where he could be better heard by the people (HE 6.5). That there existed a tension between such pragmatic behaviour and the occasional necessity to assert his episcopal authority by preaching from the traditional position is demonstrated by events on his return to the city after his first exile. The crowd insisted that he seat himself on the episcopal throne as soon as he entered the city, declare from it his usual benediction and then deliver a homily (Socr., HE 6.16; Soz., HE 8.18). Both actions were clearly considered a public statement that he had resumed his duties as the legitimate bishop of the city. Being seated, however, whether on the ambo or on his throne in the apse, seems usually to have been sufficient affirmation of his elevated status. This can be seen from Antioch, where all of the available evidence indicates that by contrast, as a presbyter, John stood while preaching from the ambo.[1]

Stance is only one of many aspects of John's life as a preacher. His advanced rhetorical training under Libanius and his years of spiritual and scriptural learning under Diodore and Carterius contributed strongly to the content of his preaching and to the characteristics of his style. The influence of his years in the *askētērion* (the place where *askēsis* is practised) of Diodore and Caterius are most clearly seen in his exegetical homilies. The literal interpretation of scripture generally favoured at this time in Antioch (as opposed to the allegorical method preferred in that other influential eastern city,

26

Alexandria) shines through in the matter-of-fact historical comment, pragmatic theological debate and observations on the techniques employed by Paul and the gospel writers. This preference for directness is characteristic of his preaching in general. The traces of John's rhetorical education can be seen in every aspect of his sermons' structure, content and delivery. Nowhere are they more evident than in the homilies delivered on special occasions. In these the freedom from the demands of the liturgical year, the lectionary system or other customary considerations allows him to give his oratorical skills full rein. Some of the most spectacular examples are the homilies *On Eutropius*, *Hom. delivered after the remains of martyrs etc.* and *On his return*. In the latter two cases the genre of the encomium, a literary work commemorating the deeds of a famous person, is exploited to the full. Exaggerated flattery of the empress, on the one hand, and of the audience, on the other, permeates each sermon and it is with the intention of praising his subjects that almost every topic, metaphor or verbal flourish is introduced. Just as in classical rhetoric the design of the encomium is to 'glorify and honor', so the sole aim of the diatribe is to 'vilify and defame' (Wilken 1983: 112). The exploitation of this latter rhetorical set piece is exemplified here in *Against the Jews or. 1*.[2]

The full range of the rhetorical tricks at the disposal of the well-trained orator are to be observed throughout John's sermons.[3] *Against the games and theatres* begins powerfully with an example of *epanaphora* or the repetition of the same word at the beginning of a clause, phrase or sentence ('Is this bearable? Is this to be tolerated?'). The repetition of these same two rhetorical questions throughout the opening section of the homily itself produces the effect of an insistent refrain. *Epanaphora* is used extensively elsewhere (e.g., 'this slavery . . . this slavery . . . this slavery': *On his return*). In *Against the games and theatres* we also see him anticipate the objection of the audience ('"What evil?" someone asks . . . "What, then", you say, "if I don't look at her . . . ?"'), another favourite technique, which allows him to create the effect of a dialogue and enliven the delivery. In *On his return* John employs a third technique, *parison* or the juxtaposition of parallel phrases, to emphasise his point.

> For there, there was a serpent setting snares,
>   here, Christ is instructing us in the mysteries;
> there, Eve was working her deception,
>   here, the church is being crowned;
> there, Adam was being deceived,

here, a people is being publicly acclaimed;
there, there existed trees of different kinds,
here, there are gifts that are diverse and spiritual.

Arsis, an ornament in which an idea is first stated negatively and then positively also appears frequently (e.g., 'not over many days but in a brief critical moment': *Against the statues hom.* 17; 'don't simply applaud but wish to be corrected . . . don't recoil, but take refuge': *On: 'My father's working still'*). *Diaporesis*, or pretended doubt, combined with *epanaphora* creates a strong beginning to *Hom. delivered after the remains of martyrs etc.* ('What can I say? What shall I speak?').

The metaphors and similes that John employs often come straight from the orator's textbook (Ameringer 1921: 56–67). The athletic and wrestling metaphors in *A homily on martyrs* and *Concerning blessed Philogonius*, and the hunting exempla and medical imagery that recur throughout the latter half of *Against the games and theatres* and in *Against the Jews or. 1* and *On: 'My father's working still'* are all part of the standard repertoire. Many are characteristic of his preaching. Debt metaphors (*Concerning blessed Philogonius*), references to hospitality and the furnishing of a lavish table (*Against the Jews or. 1*; *Baptismal instruction 8*; *On: 'I opposed him to his face'*), and calling the audience a theatre (*On Eutropius*; *Baptismal instruction 8*) are all favourite ways of opening a homily. Reference to the ephemeral as 'dust', 'spring flowers', 'smoke', 'bubbles' or 'a spider's web' (*On Col. hom. 7*; *On Eutropius*) or the employment of exempla from the theatre and hippodrome, the military and maritime milieux, agriculture, the animal kingdom, and the world of children, school, parents and household slaves is as commonly to be encountered in John's preaching. In concluding his chapter on John's use of metaphors Ameringer wryly comments on 'the prodigal exuberance' of them (Ameringer 1921: 67).

The topics that occupy John and the scriptural exempla which he adduces also tend to fall into familiar patterns. As we observe in *On Col. hom. 7*, *On Eutropius*, *On Acts hom. 3* and *On 1 Cor. hom. 21*, wealth, pride and power and their negative consequences are issues frequently addressed by him. In association with these topics he is anxious to promote the virtues of humility (*tapeinophrosynē*) and charity (*eleēmosynē*). *On Ephesians hom. 11*, *A homily on martyrs*, *Concerning blessed Philogonius* and *Against the Jews or. 1*, on the other hand, demonstrate how the correct behaviour and belief of his parishioners is also of primary concern to him. On other occasions (*Hom. delivered after the remains of martyrs etc.*; *On his return*; *On: 'I opposed him to his face'*), even when the rhetorical exaggeration is taken into account, he is simply filled with pleasure at the responsiveness of the audience. A sermon such as *On Eutropius* highlights the strong pastoral emphasis in John's preaching, as he is unable to resist the opportunity that has been handed to him for drawing a powerful lesson from the current events and his own part in them. Although they are little represented in the texts presented here, the Old and New Testament *exempla* of Job, the three boys in the furnace, the tax-collector and pharisee and the widow who gave everything she had are firm favourites and appear frequently throughout his homilies. The ministry, life and character of the apostle Paul are much admired by John and likewise receive frequent emphasis. John's command of scripture, developed during his years sampling the ascetic life, is evident from his frequent citation of a diverse range of passages.

Whereas the contents of his sermons were shaped by the different strands of his education, it was the liturgical calendar in operation at each city, in conjunction with the civic calendar and local events, which to a large degree determined the kinds of homilies which John preached. Collectively his sermons range from festival homilies, and panegyrics on saints and martyrs, to primarily exegetical commentaries, polemical or ethical discourses, and catecheses (that is, pre- and post-baptismal instructions). In addition he preached what are termed occasional sermons, that is, homilies which have as their focus a specific and often unique occasion or event – for instance, the riots at Antioch, his ordination, and the deposition of Eutropius. Examples of all of these are found among the homilies translated in this volume. In many instances, however, the labels traditionally used are more convenient than accurate, since the categories have a tendency to overlap. Thus *Concerning blessed Philogonius* starts out as a panegyric on Philogonius and his life, but ends as an ethical discourse on the behaviour of those who receive the eucharist only on the day of a major liturgical festival. *Hom. delivered after the remains of martyrs etc.* exhibits all of the characteristics of a festival sermon, but is in many respects an occasional homily too since the event which it records has elements that are unique. *Against the games and theatres* is both occasional homily and moral discourse since it is preached in response to various recent events, but has as its focus a specific failing which John wishes to correct. *Against the Jews or. 1*, on the other hand, is almost pure polemic, occasioned by the proximity of the prominent autumn festivals celebrated by the local Jewish community.

The exegetical homilies are often more distinctive, since in these John tends to pursue a close verse-by-verse exegesis of the pericope or scriptural lection, which he then follows with an ethical discourse on some issue. This second half of the sermon is not always directly related to the subject-matter of the first. Instead it can be occasioned by some concern which happens to be close to John's mind at the time or he may continue a theme which was initially addressed in other sermons preached before the same audience. The exegetical homilies translated in this volume tend to have closely linked exegetical and ethical parts, but in one instance do provide some indication of the diversity to be observed in this respect. Whereas in *On Ephesians hom. 11*, *On Acts hom. 3* and *On 1 Cor. hom. 21* the ethical subject-matter is recognisably linked to the contents of the scriptural text, in *On Colossians hom. 7* John initially follows his exegesis with a related discussion about baptism but soon diverges on to less relevant topics such as the folly of pride, power and wealth. The precise relationship between the pericopes exegeted in such homilies and the lectionary system in use at each city is difficult to determine.[4]

Having examined the issues of where John delivered his sermons, his stance during delivery and the characteristics of his sermons' contents, structure and genre, it remains to ask how he composed them, how they were published, what control he had over the process, how often he preached and what occurred when other clergy preached at the same synaxis. The first three questions are difficult to answer. There is much debate concerning the issues of composition, publication and editorial control in relation to the homiletic activity of John Chrysostom. Some of the questions that have been raised are whether certain of the homilies were ever preached or were written purely for publication (Baur 1959: 299; disputed by Kelly 1995: 92–3; Hill 1998); and whether the lack of polish in some cases or the degree to which obvious homiletic features have been removed in others is indicative of the degree to which John himself had a hand in the editorial process and the production of material for publication (Goodall 1979: 62–78; discussed by Kelly 1995: 93–4). The reality is likely to be more complex than simple. In relation to the homilies preached in Constantinople Socrates (HE 6.4) states that some were published by John himself, while others were taken down by stenographers as he delivered them. Sozomen (HE 8.18) refers to a homily that tradition held to have been preached entirely extemporaneously. That the manuscript title to the series on Hebrews states that the collection was published after John's death by an Antiochene presbyter (PG 63,9) serves to add weight to the suspicion that a range of persons and procedures could be involved in the publication process.

Unfortunately this information tells us almost nothing about how John actually prepared his sermons. Goodall does argue that homilies from the exegetical series which demonstrate 'spontaneous' elements and contain stylistic lapses are more likely to refer back to an orally delivered and stenographically recorded (but not subsequently edited) version. This orally delivered version, he supposes, is to some degree also extemporaneous (Goodall 1979: 78).[5] If this is true, then it may also be the case that conversely sermons which are highly polished and structurally sophisticated will prove to demonstrate either a greater degree of preparation by John in the first instance and/or editorial tidying by the homilist after the event and personal involvement in their publication. While further investigation will probably prove that these suppositions need additional refinement, it is an inescapable fact that the versions of the homilies available to us today can vary markedly in quality. Considerations related to the processes involved in editing sermons into series and the transmission history of individual texts further complicate the issue.

The frequency with which John preached at each location is no less difficult to determine. It is widely assumed that by far the greater number of the surviving sermons were preached at Antioch, not simply because of the greater number of years spent there, but because as a presbyter John had greater leisure to compose, preach and publish homilies. It is thought that at Constantinople the weight of his episcopal duties interfered greatly with his ability to perform this task. To what degree these assumptions are true is at present difficult to determine. Certainly it is the case that at Constantinople John was distracted for various periods of time by his involvement in negotations with Gainas and his trip to Ephesus, while he was also prevented from preaching at various points as a result of his first exile and subsequent delay in re-entering the city, his ban from officiating in the city's churches during the months leading up to his second and definitive exile, or factors as simple as the protocol to be observed when a fellow bishop visited. On the other hand, as we observe in *On: 'I opposed him to his face'*, the demands of his presbyteral duties too could temporarily remove him from the homiletic arena.

The above factors are in any case no reason for assuming, as does Pargoire (1899–1900; cf. Kelly 1995: 130), that at Constantinople John was therefore preaching only once a week on a Sunday. At both cities synaxes were regularly held on Saturdays and Sundays during ordinary times of the year, while liturgical festivals and saints' days sporadically increased the number of opportunities available. As we see in *Baptismal instruction 8*, at Antioch the month of April was filled with a number of martyrs' festivals which followed each other in quick succession. During the eight weeks of Lent at Antioch or seven at Constantinople there were in addition services in the late afternoon every weekday in the course of which a homily was preached. Yet although the expectation of a sermon each day at such times was normative, as already noted, circumstances could intervene, as in the case of the Antiochene riots, to interrupt this sequence (van de Paverd 1991: 363–4). The demands of instructing the catechumens during the second half of Lent further increased the potential number of sermons that an individual might preach, since these instructions were delivered early on weekday mornings over the course of three or four weeks, in addition to the late afternoon synaxis (*De diabolo tentatore hom. 2*: PG 49,258 8–10). As we can see, the number of opportunities to preach during a year were considerable, while any number of circumstances could intervene at any point in an individual year to prevent John from participating. In sum, the most likely scenario is that the frequency with which John preached varied from week to week at each location.

The final aspect of preaching that requires mention is alluded to in *Concerning blessed Philogonius*. There John informs us that the local Antiochene bishop, Flavian, will be preaching a sermon at this same festival immediately after him. He anticipates that in it Flavian will cover the topic of Philogonius' life more thoroughly. This habit of having more than one homilist preach on special occasions is recorded by the late fourth-century pilgrim Egeria in relation to the practice at Jerusalem. There, she says, on such occasions as many presbyters as wish preach, while it is the bishop who always preaches last (*Itin.* 25.1). That this situation pertained at Antioch is demonstrated by the homily *De s. Babyla*, where John says that he will leave such details to the more senior of the 'teachers' and 'the common father' (SC 362,296 5–7), implying that a number of presbyters as well as Flavian are to preach after him on that particular occasion. Such circumstances will have affected the length of the homily as well as perhaps introducing a note of competitiveness in terms of holding the audience's attention. Similar challenges faced John when he was bishop. As we discover in *On: 'My father's working still'* visiting bishops were supposed by custom to be given the opportunity to preach, perhaps even precedence. Certainly there is

at least one homily in addition to the latter which suggests that those
who preached at the same synaxes as John at Constantinople could
suffer by comparison (*In illud: Filius ex se nihil facit* (CPG
4441.12): PG 56,247 1–10), while on another occasion the presbyter
who preached before him did so in the native language of the audience, altering the dynamics and producing a different set of expectations (*Hom. habita cum presbyter gothus* (CPG 4441.9)). The problems
that could arise from the competition posed for a bishop by his peers
are alluded to at length in *On Ephesians hom. 11*.

4

JOHN'S AUDIENCE

If Antioch was a city of great wealth and elevated status, which offered a high standard of living to those who could afford it, it was also a city of great poverty. As John indicates in *On 1 Cor. hom. 21* there existed a highly visible class of beggars and homeless people who solicited the rest of the citizens of Antioch as they went about their business in the market-place and streets. This same class of people is discussed at length in another Antiochene sermon (*De eleemosyna*: PG 51,261–72). Constantinople, with its economic and political attractions as the seat of the emperor in the east, is likely to have been host to a similar proportion of the economically and socially disenfranchised. Recognition of their existence is important not just from the point of view of pastoral care but also in relation to the question of precisely who attended church and constituted John's audience.

That the wealthy members of Antiochene and Constantinopolitan society attended church and, when they did so, constituted a high-profile sector among John's audience is readily evident, since he often addresses them directly (*On Col. hom. 7*; *On 1 Cor. hom. 21*; Leyerle 1994; 1997). Contrary to previous opinion on the subject (MacMullen 1989), it has recently been asserted that women also attended in reasonable numbers on ordinary occasions in a number of the churches in both cities (Mayer forthcoming (b)). We see the wealthy among them being addressed by John in *On Col. hom. 7*, while in *Hom. delivered after the remains of martyrs etc.* we observe that on the day of a spectacular festival at Constantinople a diverse range of women are present, including the empress, the elderly and ascetics. The presence of men in the audience on every occasion is self-evident and requires no more than a simple statement. The questions that are more difficult to answer are whether the audience was comprised only of the élite or more broadly represented secular

34

society, whether the truly poor were ever present, and whether children and slaves were included.

With regard to the presence of slaves it is likely that they were usually to be encountered in the company of their mistresses or masters. In *In 2 Thess. hom. 3* John tells us that if a rich man attends he is typically accompanied by a flock of young slaves with the intention of emphasising to the rest of those present his elevated status (PG 62,484 11–14), while in his account of a miracle which occurred during John's episcopate Sozomen (HE 8.5) assumes that it was normal for a female slave (*therapaina*) to accompany and stay close to her mistress. In a rare instance John actually addresses the slaves in the audience directly (*In Titum hom. 4*: PG 62,686 14–22). Whether slaves ever attended of their own volition and without their owners is difficult to determine. The numbers in which slaves were to be found and whether attendance was uniform across all of the churches in each city are likewise open to question since, despite his comments in *In 2 Thess. hom. 3*, in another sermon John accuses the audience of providing little opportunity for their slaves to learn Christian ethics, since, contrary to the audience's habit when attending the theatre or baths, they tend not to set out for church with a flock of slaves in attendance (*In Eph. hom. 22*: PG 62,158 2–4). In the case of children their presence is much more difficult to establish. If it were not for the rare allusion (*In Acta apost. hom. 29*: PG 60,218 4–5 – 'I'm not addressing those who've been here a year, but those who've been attending since they were very young'; cf. *In Acta apost. hom. 44*: PG 60,313 23–4), we would be tempted to conclude that they did not form a part of the regular audience. While such allusions suggest that the admonition at the conclusion of *Against the Jews or. 1* may perhaps be more than a simple topos, the presence of children cannot be considered normative since in other homilies John exhorts members of the audience to bring them with them to synaxis (*Contra Anomoeos hom. 11*: SC 396,314 315–18) or admonishes them for failing to do so (*In illud: Si esurierit inimicus*: PG 51,176 15–20).

On the question of the truly poor and socially disenfranchised, Peter Brown (1992: 91–103) refers to their exclusion from participation in the activities and benefits of the *dēmos* (the people, populace or citizenry) and argues that it was the bishops' championship of this class which empowered and increased the status of both the local bishop and the 'poor' of the city. Within this scenario one might expect that the poor who physically surrounded the churches and were the focus of the welfare programmes of the church and the recipients of its largesse were also to be found within the church buildings at the time of synaxis and were among those who listened to the preacher's message. Yet in this respect it seems more likely that the audience within the church mirrored external society. While it is impossible to state definitively that the exclusion of this class from synaxis was in fact the case, the evidence is suggestive of this conclusion. In the *Sermo 5 in Genesim* (PG 54,602 57–603 1) John says that when the audience departs from the church they see the poor standing on both sides of the entrance, an impression reinforced by information supplied in other homilies (*Hom. in illud: Habentes eumdem spiritum* 3: PG 51,300 18–42; *In 1 Thess. hom.* 11: PG 62,466 19–29). It is almost certainly with this scenario in mind that John makes his final comments in *On Col. hom.* 7. Further, in *De eleemosyna* (PG 51,261 3–9) the poor, disabled and beggars who so inspire his sermon are to be found elsewhere in the market-place and streets and not within his audience. Rather, when John directly addresses the poor in his sermons it is usually not the genuinely poor to whom he directs his remarks, but those who think themselves poor when they compare their own lifestyle with that of their friends and neighbours (Mayer 1998b: 123). In this light, John's comments that at baptism or during the eucharist the disabled and poorest of the poor stand next to the rich and powerful should be treated with a degree of scepticism (*Cat. 2*: SC 50[bis],140 13.1–8; *De resurrectione*: PG 50,437 17–29).

If the truly poor are unlikely to have been among John's audience as he preached, the next issue to be resolved is whether the audience was in fact predominantly wealthy. Ramsay MacMullen proposes that this was indeed the case and that it was in the main the élite members of society who attended (MacMullen 1989). While there is no denying that the foibles of the rich are a constant focus of John's homilies, the question remains whether this overwhelming focus reflects a genuine preponderance of members of this class within the audience or whether, just as in the case of women John's address is predominantly directed toward the males in the audience regardless of the real numbers of both genders present (possibly because men are socially and culturally more significant),[1] so the attention paid to the élite within the audience reflects the social and cultural status of these persons in society rather than their actual numerical dominance. This latter possibility cannot be dismissed. Certainly there was a more diverse range of people within the audience than is evident at first impression. As both *Baptismal instruction* 8 and *On: 'My father's working still'* remind us, most of the churches in each city had a large number of clergy and liturgical and administrative assistants attached to them – a number augmented not infrequently by the presence of non-local clergy visiting for synodical and other reasons.[2] Although various members of the clergy and support staff can be presumed to have been present on most occasions when John preached, rarely do they receive explicit mention.[3] Moreover, the background of these individuals is likely to have varied considerably. However, as we shall see in Chapter 6, Flavian came from a wealthy family, as did other members of the Antiochene clergy,[4] at least one of John's presbyters at Constantinople had formerly been a slave (Soz., HE 8.24). The visiting monk-priests who swell the congregation in *Baptismal Instruction 8* are likewise neither of elevated background nor wealthy.

A close examination of John's homilies also reveals some degree of variety of economic and social status in relation to the more general audience. This variation is seen mainly in homilies of Antiochene provenance. In a number of them John clearly expects that a sector of the audience is comprised of tradespeople.[5] In another homily he says that the 'poor' who were in attendance recently are excused from being present today because they have to work for their living (*In princ. Actorum hom. 1*: PG 51,69 51–61). On the other hand, he expects that others who are absent are at this moment being harassed by their accountants, managers and slaves (PG 51,69 36–43). In yet another Antiochene homily he suggests that married men who work every day can only attend once a week (*De mutatione nom. hom. 3*: PG 51,136 21–7). On another occasion he says that some of the men in the audience are soldiers, others artisans (*De poen. hom. 3*: PG 49,291 31–3 *a.i.*). This evidence that the congregation attached to at least one church in Antioch included artisans, tradespeople, wealthy estate owners and perhaps also soldiers accords well with John's description of his audience in *Baptismal instruction 8*. He expects that when they leave the synaxis some will be working with their hands, others at military duties, and that yet others will be involved all day in political or civil affairs. That the native language and ethnicity of individuals contributed to the diversity of the audience is suggested by *Hom. delivered after the remains of martyrs etc.*, *Baptismal instruction 8* and the homily delivered by John at Constantinople in the church of St Paul, the worship centre of the Nicene Goths.

The size of the audience and the frequency with which individuals attended varied markedly according to the time of year and the nature of the occasion. As is already evident external commitments in some cases dictated when men were able to attend. It is also the case that the major liturgical festivals and spectacular occasions, such as the translation of martyrs' remains, drew larger than usual crowds, while the heat of summer could as readily deter them (*In illud: Si esurierit inimicus*: PG 51,174 49–175 3). On the former occasions the diversity as well as the size of the audience increased (Mayer forthcoming (b)). Accidental occurrences, such as the coincidence of Eutropius' flight to the Great Church on the day before a regular synaxis, could also prove a major attraction. In *On Eutropius* John remarks that he has not seen such a large crowd since Easter. That the audience dwindled in between times and that the attendance habits of individuals varied considerably is evident from John's comments in *On Ephesians hom. 11* and in homilies such as *De mutatione nom. hom. 1* (PG 51,113 1–5) and *Sermo 9 in Genesim* (PG 54,620 4–6 *a.i.*). Not only does the size decrease with each successive synaxis following Easter, but John is often obliged to repeat himself because many of those who were there at the previous synaxis are not present today and vice versa. Furthermore, as we learn in *On Ephesians hom. 11*, the loyalty of even the most faithful members of the audience could be diverted away from John and towards another preacher.

Regardless of the mix of people in attendance on any one occasion external social dynamics often entered with the individual members of the audience and influenced their stance and behaviour. Thus, although at this time in the churches of Antioch and Constantinople it was normal for the audience to stand throughout the course of the liturgy and sermon, while the clergy and bishop had seating available to them, there is evidence that certain (probably very wealthy) members of the audience sat also.[6] While it may be the case that some of these individuals were incapable of standing for any length of time due to lifestyle-related diseases, it is as likely that the action of being seated in the midst of a standing majority served to isolate and emphasise their wealth and social status.[7] The physical separation of the men from the women by various means, another reflection of external cultural norms, has already been remarked upon. The audience's behaviour in some ways differed little from when they were in each other's homes or at the hippodrome or theatre. A display of oratorical brilliance elicited much applause, as we learn from the opening comments of *Against the Jews or. 1*. People gossiped, chatted and laughed during the liturgy and sermon (*In Heb. hom. 15*: PG 63,121 50–7). Others crowded around John, pushing and shoving so that they could get closer to this star performer (Soz., HE 8.5;

De proph. obscur. hom. 1: PG 56,176 23–7). In other respects the audience simply responded as human beings to the subject-matter of the sermon as their emotions were manipulated by the power of John's rhetoric. So in *Against the games and theatres* he says that he sees some beating their heads and subsequently looking gloomy as he threatens to ban the offenders from the premises. In *On Eutropius* a portion of the audience is moved to tears. In *On Colossians hom. 7* he evokes a response from the women in the audience as he speculates that they would wish to have golden hair. Other all too human behaviours are documented in *Concerning blessed Philogonius*.

A glimpse of the audience's attachment to John as a preacher and pastoral carer, their expectations of him and the interaction that took place between John and individual members beyond the realm of the sermon serves to round out the picture. John was an extremely popular preacher. The not infrequent references to applause, the testimony of the church historians (Palladius, *Dial.* 5; Soc., HE 6.4, 6.16; Soz., HE 8.2, 8.5) and the massive numbers in which John's sermons survive to the present day all bear witness to this. In *On his return* John openly revels in the attachment of the people of Constantinople to him, just as the fact that many among the audience came just to hear him is evident in their rejection of the bishop of Galatia as replacement homilist on the Sunday prior to *On: 'My father's working still'*. However, not everyone was enamoured with his philosophy of care. At Constantinople direct censure both from the ambo and during personal encounters in the home or on the street alienated a significant minority. We see a possible allusion to members of this group in *On Ephesians hom. 11*.

Glimpses of the interaction between John and members of his audience beyond the confines of the church are supplied in two Antiochene homilies. In *On: 'I opposed him to his face'* it is evident that members of the congregation that he serves have recounted a summary of the locum's sermon to him shortly after the event. This information implies either that his daily routine was such that he encountered parishioners casually outside of synaxes or that some of them were in the habit of meeting with him in between. In *Against the Jews or. 1*, John relates an encounter with two Christians on the street, in which he took it upon himself to upbraid the offender and explain to him the error of his ways. Here we see not a pre-arranged counselling session with a parishioner but the opportunistic administration of pastoral care to a member of the wider local Christian community. In *On his return* at Constantinople he addresses the complaints that have come to his ears about his absence during the baptisms at Easter. Combined with his comments about receiving regular reports of the situation at Constantinople from travellers during his absence, this information hints at some of the effective communication networks which existed between John and his parishioners.

5

JOHN AS SOUL-CARER

These brief snaphots of his audience lead us to ask several related questions, which are significant to understanding the relationship between both John and his audience as a preacher and John and his parishioners as a carer of souls. As both presbyter and bishop did John minister to a single congregation for lengthy periods or did he rotate between different churches in the course of his duties? If he was attached to a single church, which duties and what percentage of them did John perform? How often were these same duties performed by other clergy? If he did rotate, did the audience follow him? The different options predicate different degrees of intimacy. The more detail we can accumulate about the extent to which John connected with the lives of those around him, the greater our understanding of his own style of pastoral care and the greater the possibility of placing it in the context of the general character of the care available at Antioch and Constantinople in the late fourth and early fifth centuries.

There is sufficient evidence to suggest that in some ways there were distinct differences between John's experiences at each city. From the homily *On: 'I opposed him to his face'* it is evident that at one point during his years at Antioch as a priest he preached regularly before a congregation at the Old Church. This circumstance suggests that, despite Flavian's periodic claims upon his time, John was a member of the complement of clergy attached to that church and therefore had an opportunity to develop a relationship with the particular audience that worshipped there. It may even be that it is this audience that is reflected in the Antiochene homilies which refer to soldiers, artisans and other businesspeople. On the other hand, the fact that Flavian is interfering with John's duties at that church by requiring him to accompany him elsewhere indicates that there were disruptions to that relationship. However, such disruptions

would mean little except in terms of disturbing a planned programme of pastoral education through preaching, if John continued
to perform his duties between synaxes without interruption. At
Constantinople, on the other hand, it appears that the bishop of
the city, while based at the Great Church, preached according to a
developed system in other churches of the city also (Mayer forthcoming (a)). As observed in *On: 'My father's working still'*, moreover,
the flood of visiting bishops could interfere with the frequency with
which John preached before the audience in the Great Church. When
these factors are combined with the weight of episcopal duties in
general it is likely that the opportunity for John to develop a close
rapport with individuals within the different congregations at
Constantinople was more limited.

What, then, were the different forms of pastoral care in which John
personally became involved at each location? As already hinted, the
episcopal role itself inevitably attracted additional duties, while the
weight of these additional duties at times interfered with those that
were more mundane and familiar. Other pastoral activities developed
by virtue of the different circumstances which pertained at each city.
Thus at Constantinople the proximity of the female ascetic and
deacon Olympias' monastery to the *episkopeion* and Great Church
saw the development of a close relationship between John and the
women in this community. Not only is it likely that a proportion
of their number attended the Great Church and constituted part of
his regular audience (Mayer forthcoming (b)), but John himself
was the only outsider permitted to enter the walls of the community.
He did so frequently for the purposes of instructing the women (*Vita
Olymp.* 8). He also ordained several of the inmates to the diaconate so
that the forms of care available within the monastery could be
expanded and assured continuity (*Vita Olymp.* 7). John's care of
these women, instigated initially because of the accident of their
proximity, thus developed on at least three levels – through preaching, through extra-homiletic instruction and indirectly through the
institution of permanent pastoral delegates in the form of deacons.

Another avenue of care which is likely to have been specific to
Constantinople and to John's role as bishop there is mediation
between the emperor and the high-ranking officials in the imperial
bureaucracy in times of dispute. His involvement at this level
could be time-consuming and had a tendency to interrupt his
other more regular duties. Thus in a sermon delivered in 400 John
excuses himself to the audience for his absence from preaching,
due to his involvement in negotiations over hostages with the

dissident Gothic general Gainas (*Cum Saturninus et Aurelianus*: PG 52,413 2 *a.i.*–415 50). In *On Eutropius* likewise we see John in a position of defending the once powerful eunuch-consul from the wrath of the military and using all of his rhetorical skill to turn the audience's natural antipathy towards Eutropius into sympathy, despite his own personal feelings towards the individual. The description of the interaction between John and Eutropius over the status of the church prior to the latter's downfall, if not invented for the occasion, shows John persistently and frankly challenging Eutropius' actions out of care for him when few people, if any, would dare to do so. Boldly reminding the emperor of his obligations towards the Nicene Christians at Constantinople and advising Arcadius to resist the demands of Gainas that he assign a church to the Arian Gothic community (Soz., HE 8.4) demonstrates John's own perceived broader duty of care as bishop towards the souls of all Christians at Constantinople. It requires him to ensure that orthodox Nicene Christianity persists within the walls of the city unchallenged.[1] The journey to Asia Minor to which he refers in *On his return* is one further example of John's expanded perception of the boundaries of pastoral care appropriate to the bishop of Constantinople. The reality is that by undertaking to travel to Ephesus personally to sort out matters regarding his peers in a see not his own John is technically in breach of his jurisdiction.

So far we have observed that as bishop John considered that a broad range of activities came within his purview. He mediated between the emperor and his officials, especially in matters of life or death; he took direct action whenever necessary to ensure the preservation of Nicene Christianity within the city precinct; he intervened at least once in disciplinary matters in neighbouring sees, convening synods, deposing bishops, closing non-Nicene churches and supervising the appointment of replacement clergy; he regularly admonished a high-level official for his behaviour and encouraged him to modify it; he frequently visited a neighbouring all-female monastery to instruct members of the community and ordained three of them to ensure the continuity of pastoral ministry within the community. There were also other forms of care which were more common to his experiences as a priest at Antioch.

Preaching is a major avenue for pastoral care and one at which John excelled throughout his career. The down-to-earth, yet cleverly manipulated language of his sermons, the genuine concern for the souls of his listeners that permeates and prompts virtually every word, the willingness to seize opportunities to teach that others might well avoid, are all aspects that serve to highlight John's desire to move his audience and effect genuine change in their lives. His constant frustration with the audience's lack of progress and his praise of those who do achieve are also indicative of his desire that those who listen to his sermons learn and not just enjoy being entertained. If he moves the audience to applause or tears it is in the hope that they will thereby more effectively remember his point. When he threatens the audience in *On Col. hom.* 7 and *Against the games and theatres* it is in the manner of a parent who understands that discipline is necessary, if a child is to learn how to behave appropriately. His constant citation from the scriptures is as much a ploy to hammer some of it into the memory of his listeners as to justify a particular point. These are the words of a preacher who understands that the homily is a powerful educative tool and medium of persuasion, as well as an effective means of forging a bond with those who actively listen to what he has to say.

Letter-writing is another major avenue for pastoral care. Although only a selection of the letters which he wrote in exile survives, from the collections of letters attributed to other bishops in this and later centuries it is clear that as bishop, if not also as presbyter, John would have been constantly engaged in writing to colleagues, former parishioners, contacts and friends. Some of the letters that he does write from exile can be considered typical of those that would have been included among such correspondence. Among these are several letters of consolation to grieving friends and acquaintances – for instance, *Letter* 197 to Studius the Urban Prefect, in which John commends and counsels the recipient on the appropriate way to grieve a virtuous Christian's death; and *Ep.* 71 to Malchus on the death of his daughter, in which he not only counsels the grieving father, but also asks him to convey the same advice to his wife (PG 52,647–8). In a different, but no less pastoral, way, John writes to Theodora, a woman of considerable status, on hearing that she has fallen out with a certain member of her household. Without knowledge of the specific circumstances, he nonetheless feels it his duty to counsel forgiveness and to urge her to let go her anger (*Letter* 117). An even stronger tone is taken in a letter to another person, Adolia, a noblewoman of Antioch (Delmaire 1991: 103), with whom he enjoys frequent correspondence. He has advised her time and again to get her priorities straight and to ignore worldly concerns and tells her that the treachery of which she complains is in essence her own fault. He further expects that, if she wanted to, she could come to visit him and receive his advice on the current situation in person –

an allusion to the possibility of private counselling (*Ep.* 133: PG 52,691–2). In two rare letters he upbraids presbyters of the church of Constantinople for failing in their duties at a time of particular need (*Letters* 203, 212). There his concern is both for the souls of the priests themselves and for those of the parishioners whose care is being neglected.

The letters reflect other pastoral avenues and concerns that are less personal and more complex than the ones that have been mentioned. A number are addressed variously to clergy of different ranks, lay people of high status and monks urging them to deal with issues related to a mission which John supports amongst the pagans in Phoenicia. The well-being of Nicene Goths in their own homeland also comes under discussion (*Ep.* 9 (14) *Ad Olymp.*: SC 13bis,236–8 5.b), as does the welfare of the Nicene Gothic community in John's now former see, Constantinople (*Epp.* 206–7: PG 52,726–7). In none of these instances does John expect to be involved directly, but he clearly has a network of people which he either administers or supports who are involved at different levels. Thus in *Epp.* 221 and 225 John addresses a presbyter, Constantius, in the first instance telling him that he has found an eremitic monk in Nicaea, whom he has persuaded to join Constantius in his mission work; in the second, making it clear that Constantius, whom he describes as a manager (*oikonomos*) of the project, has responsibility for the destruction of paganism, the building of churches and the care of souls in Phoenicia, Arabia and throughout the east (PG 52,732–3 and 735). In Phoenicia Constantius is also involved with the care of the traditional clients of welfare – the orphans, widows and poor. John himself tells the monks and presbyters who are doing the hands-on work in Phoenicia that he has ensured the line of supply of essentials for their work by securing funding and that Constantius will be able to supply shoes, clothing and food to their brothers as freely as before (*Ep.* 123: PG 52,676–8). In other letters John urges wealthy laypersons to support missionary and local welfare projects financially, indicating that the élite as well as clergy are an important part of the system (*Letters* 51, 217). Such letters demonstrate that throughout his episcopate John was involved in the complex organisation and administration of missionary activities in a number of locations at some distance from Constantinople, and that he continued to work hard behind the scenes to ensure the continuity of these projects in exile. They also raise the slight possibility that he had already become involved in these same or similar networks during his years at Antioch.[2]

Locally the networks for the provision of certain types of pastoral care were no less complex. Even though John was undoubtedly involved personally in the private counselling of individuals,[3] including perhaps the hearing of private confession (Soz., HE 8.5), and although at Constantinople he presided in person over informal synods (Palladius, *Dial.* 13–14) and perhaps also a form of episcopal court and therefore dealt with the broader issues of care through these media, it is doubtful whether he had any direct involvement in the hands-on provision of care to the needy (i.e., widows, orphans, sick transients, beggars and other persons lacking family or adequate means of support). As we shall see in Chapter 6, at both locations there were already well-established institutions and structures in place for the provision of such care. At Constantinople John's contribution to these enterprises seems to have consisted of an overhaul of the registers and the number, administration and financing of various institutions, in addition to the planning of new hospitals and institutions for the care of the sick (Palladius, *Dial.* 5; ACW 45: 39). In exile we find him continuing to drum up finance for the presbyters involved in the administration of various projects (*Letter* 217). Through his preaching he constantly tries to persuade the wealthy to become benefactors of the poor and to help relieve the burden of care that is placed upon the church (*On 1 Cor. hom. 21*).

Indeed it may be that there exists in John's case a direct relationship between his care for individuals and the means by which he provides care for the broader Christian community. There is some evidence in both his correspondence and the external sources that not just at Constantinople but even during the period of his presbyterate at Antioch John's personal ministry of care is directed particularly toward individuals who function at the élite level of society and that it is through these same individuals and their associates that he elicits the financial and physical assistance necessary to ensure the provision of a wide range of pastoral care.[4] If Sozomen can be relied upon, these relationships and networks continued into the period of John's exile, where the financial support of Olympias and others provided the means by which he was able to effect the release of captives of the Isaurians, restoring such individuals to their families, and to assist those who were in material or spiritual need (Soz., HE 8.27).

6

PASTORAL CARE AND DAILY LIFE

If the provision of pastoral care by John as priest and as bishop could cover a relatively broad range of avenues, there were yet other ways in which such care could be administered and in which its provision impinged upon the lives of Antioch's and Constantinople's inhabitants. One of the more obvious avenues was the permanent philanthropic institution. Both cities, by virtue of their status and resources, attracted a large number of visitors. Not all of these were in good health or capable of supporting themselves after their arrival. In addition, among those who dwelt permanently in the cities children, women and the elderly who became deprived of the · support of immediate or extended family were vulnerable to poverty and disease. By the time that John was ordained priest at Antioch church-administered orphanages, hostels, hospitals and perhaps even old people's homes were becoming a familiar part of the urban landscape.[1]

At Antioch, a city plagued by the economic effects of seasonal work (*De eleemosyna*: PG 51,261 21–47; 269 65–270 9), periodic drought (Downey 1961: 383–4, 419–20; Libanius, *Or.* I.205–11), and the economic strain caused by periodic military activity (Downey 1961: 382–3), the evidence suggests that institutions for the care of indigent visitors were felt to be necessary from at least the mid-fourth century onwards. The *Chronicon paschale* asserts that bishop Leontius (344–58) founded a number of hostels (*xenodocheia* and *xenōnes*) for the poor and the strangers in the city (PG 92,30–3). Devreesse (1945: 111 n. 11) notes that the Yakto mosaic, a fifth-century artifact recovered in archaeological excavations at Daphne, depicts a building labelled *to Leontiou*, which he identifies with the hostel mentioned in that document. Writing in the sixth century John Malalas, who was himself from Antioch, states that a *xenōn* was founded in the city in the time of Constantine under

47

the Christian governor Plutarch (*Chron.* 13.3; *ByzAus* 4: 172–3). Whether it is the case that this hospice, said to be situated in proximity to the Great Church, genuinely dates back to that time, local tradition clearly held it to be of some antiquity. John himself confirms the existence of at least one *xenōn* associated with the care of the sick, when he tells Stagirius to go to its administrator and ask to see the inmates as a cure for the despair the young man is experiencing as a result of his own chronic epilepsy (*Ad Stagirium*: PG 47,490 31–7). That private individuals could use their own property and resources for a similar purpose is suggested by an Antiochene sermon in which John points out to his audience that their bishop, Flavian, has in effect turned his ancestral home into a *xenōn*. The scale on which he provides hospitality for these people is such, John says, that the house could as well be said to belong to the strangers who are its inmates as to its owner (*Sermo 1 in Gen.*: PG 54,585 47–67).

At Constantinople the range of philanthropic institutions for which evidence exists is broader. Timothy Miller argues at length that the Sampson *xenōn*, an institution which was still operational in the tenth century, was established between 350 and 360 by a semi-Arian ascetic of the same name who worked under bishop Macedonius. This foundation, which cared for the sick, was traditionally located between the Great Church and St Eirene. Miller highlights its contemporaneity with the orphanage (*orphanotropheion*) founded by Zotikos (Miller 1990: 104–13). The historian Sozomen makes reference to poorhouses (*ptōcheia*) founded under Macedonius, of which the deacon Marathonius was director or *epitropos* (HE 4.20). Thus by the time that John took up the reins as bishop of Constantinople in early 398 there already existed several church-run institutions for the care of the sick, the poor and the orphaned.[2]

It is possible that when Nicene Christianity was enforced at Constantinople under Theodosius not only the churches of the city but also the associated welfare institutions were transferred from the hands of the Arian Christians.[3] Palladius mentions that Chrysostom himself transferred surplus expenditure from the budget of the bishop's residence (*episkopeion*) to 'the hospital'; and that he constructed further hospitals (*nosokomeia*), each of which he staffed with two presbyters and an unspecified number of doctors, cooks and other persons devoted to the ascetic life.[4] In addition, in *In Acta apost. hom.* 45 John makes it clear that the church at Constantinople administers a *xenōn* or *xenodocheion* to provide care for poor travellers to the city who require accommodation. The imaginary individual with whom he argues in this sermon expects that the church will maintain the institution entirely from its own income, to which John replies that it is as much the duty of individuals to pay for and provide such care (PG 60,319 10–320 29). While the imagined response of this parishioner suggests that the laity were grateful that the church relieved them of all responsibility for such care and were happy to leave it in its hands, their feelings were not always so sanguine. Kelly, on the basis of the as yet unpublished panegyric on the life of Chrysostom by 'Martyrius', describes the reaction of the wealthy of Constantinople to John's plans to build a leper hospital in the suburbs in proximity to their properties. They were decidedly unenthusiastic and unamused (Kelly 1995: 119–20).

The reference by Palladius to celibate individuals assigned as carers to Chrysostom's new hospitals highlights the unique pastoral role that men and women of an ascetic persuasion were able to assume. In the case of Flavian, who was an ascetic as well as bishop, it is in all probability precisely because he had no heirs, anxious to protect their inheritance, that he was able to put his father's house to such a use. Olympias, too, orphaned, childless and left as a young widow with a vast inheritance under her personal control,[5] was able to dispose of sections of her property holdings and quantities of gold and silver as she wished in support of the welfare activities of the local church (*Vita Olymp.* 5, 7). Indeed her generous material support extended even beyond the confines of the church at Constantinople to the churches of many of the bishops who visited there during the episcopates of John and his predecessor Nectarius.[6] In the case of Olympias, independent wealth and a dearth of male relatives made it possible for her to use her property for such purposes without interference from family.[7] Had there been any possibility of objection on the part of her remaining female relatives, she cleverly subverted it by ensuring that they too were enrolled among the ascetics in her private community and that a number of them were ordained by John as female deacons of the Great Church (*Vita Olymp.* 6–7).

The freedom to act which arose from proclaiming oneself celibate and living the life of an ascetic did not just involve supporting the pastoral activities of the church at second hand. The fact that Olympias was present when Optimus, bishop of Antioch in Pisidia, died on one of his visits to Constantinople and was able to close his eyes with her own hands suggests that she had been at his sickbed either to supervise or herself to undertake his physical care.[8] John himself tells us that he has heard reports of young women from wealthy backgrounds who live a harsh ascetic life, neglecting their status and personal comfort to care for the bodies of the sick, wash feet and handle beds. Many, he says, even cook meals.[9] It is possible that the ascetics who worked as carers in John's new hospitals came from similar backgrounds. In any case, in the time of Macedonius the form of asceticism promoted at Constantinople by the deacon Marathonius had as its focus shelter for the poor and care for the sick. This work was carried out by both male and female ascetics living together in loosely organised communities, called *synoikiai*.[10]

Ascetics and wealthy widows were not the only members of the wider community to provide such care. In one of his letters John commends the tribune Marcianus for his philanthropic activities in the midst of the confusion and persecution which occurred at Constantinople in the months immediately following John's exile. Marcianus, he says, has been caring for orphans and widows in every possible way, alleviating their poverty and becoming their protector. He has also been keeping the whole population, as it were, in grain, wine, oil and everything else (*Ep.* 122: PG 52,676). By the whole population John appears to mean his supporters, whom Delmaire expects were excluded from the regular distribution of the dole under John's successor Arsacius (Delmaire 1991: 140). At Antioch in the time of the emperor Julian it is married women who are said to be actively involved in feeding the Christian poor at their husbands' expense (Julian, *Misopogon* 363A). Nor is care for the socially disenfranchised the exclusive province of Christians. Libanius alludes to the fact that at Antioch individual pagan temples were equally the gathering place and shelter of elderly men and women, orphans and the disabled, all of them poor (*Or.* 2.30; 30.20). He hints, moreover, at the active provision of care by the personnel attached to these premises. It is quite possible that the local Jewish community, following Judaism's long history of care for widows, orphans and other unfortunates,[11] also had in place its own welfare systems.

When we examine pastoral care in everyday life from the perspective of the care that laypeople provided not for those less fortunate than themselves but for the clergy, we see that the distinctions between such care and the behaviour required by ordinary client–patron relations become blurred. In exile John is the recipient of a number of gifts, some financial, others material (e.g., *Letters* 51, 75). In the case of Carteria, who sends perhaps both money and medication (*Letter* 34; cf. *Ep.* 232: PG 52,738–9), the intention in the latter instance is to provide John with a salve that he cannot acquire locally and that will help ease his long-standing physical complaints. Other women, situated not at Antioch but at Constantinople, are also instrumental in assisting him in this way (*Ep.* 17 (4) *ad Olymp.*: SC 13[bis], 370 26–40). The Harmatius to whom John addresses *Letter* 75 is likewise concerned for John's comfort and well-being and appears to have lent him a house at Cucusus and given him the use of his servants. Like Carteria, Harmatius is a member of the nobility at Antioch. In another letter we begin to catch a glimpse of the links within the networks that provide such care. Arabius, a member of the élite at Constantinople, has written offering John the use of his property at Sebasteia for his comfort in exile. John expresses his gratitude and asks if, now that he has found out that he is going to Cucusus instead, Arabius could write on his behalf to any friends he has there (*Ep.* 121: PG 52,676 1–11). On further reading, it becomes clear that Arabius is not a disinterested well-wisher but the husband of a close acquaintance of Olympias (*Ep.* 5 (8) *ad Olymp.*: SC 13[bis],120 20–122 23). Care, at a number of levels, is intimately connected to the social networks in operation both within and between each city.

Hospitality is one realm in which the two become almost indivisible, whereby considerable tension can come into play. As bishop, John was obligated to provide food and lodging for visiting clergy at the *episkopeion*. Apart from the strain caused to the episcopal and church budget by the flood of bishops and satellites who came and went, it was for political reasons not always expedient for John to provide such hospitality. When such conflicts occurred he can be seen to resort to his closest networks of care. Thus when the fifty Egyptian monks came to Constantinople to present their case against the Alexandrian bishop Theophilus, it was to the resources of a number of women in his immediate circle that he resorted. Although he allowed the monks the use of some space in St Anastasia as a place to sleep, it was the women who funded and provided their daily food (Palladius, *Dial.* 7; ACW 45: 47). The status of the individual women was apparently such that it placed them outside of the tensions which existed at that time between John and Theophilus and their associates. There is a certain irony in John's actions in this respect, since in the same homily in which he complains that his Constantinopolitan audience expect the church to be the sole provider of hospitality for strangers in its *xenōn*, John also exhorts his audience to permanently set aside a room in their houses for this purpose and to instruct their most trusted slave to supervise its use (*In Acta apost. hom. 45*: PG 60,319 33–53). The impoverished holy men to whom he denies his own hospitality in the above instance are precisely the sort of people who he endeavours to persuade his audience will bestow a blessing upon the household which offers them a bed or meal (cf. *In Eph. hom. 20*: PG 62,447 46–53). In consequence it is doubtful whether any of the audience, other than those ascetically inclined men and women who provided such hospitality in any case,[12] took John seriously.

So far we have looked at the role of permanent philanthropic institutions, ascetics and the wealthier members of the laity in the provision of care on a daily basis. We have also examined the reciprocation of care towards the clergy, the connection between such care and prevailing social networks and their collision in the realm of hospitality. One final area in which ordinary people encountered pastoral care in their everyday lives for which there exists some slight evidence is on the occasion of weddings and funerals. In what is probably an Antiochene homily (Allen and Mayer 1995: 337–9), John mentions that it has become a habit for Christians to summon presbyters and people who chant the psalms as part of the funeral arrangements (*In Heb. hom. 4*: PG 63,44 19–28). While the precise role of the presbyters is not specified, he does suggest that part of their function is to stress for those present the message of the resurrection and to educate them in the appropriate way for a Christian to behave at the death of a loved one. John's distaste at the persistence of originally pagan cultural practices, such as the hiring of professional mourners, alongside the newer Christian ones indicates that the role of the priest in the rituals attached to death is at this point still marginal. Elsewhere he indicates that in the same way at weddings some families bring in Christian clergy on the first day, while on the second they revert to the usual full-blown drunken partying. This latter half of the wedding includes such pagan rituals as the singing of hymns to Aphrodite (*In illud: Propter fornicationes uxorem*: PG 51,211 1–35). Regardless of the marginal status of priests at such family affairs, their presence is indicative of a growing role for the clergy in private rites of passage performed in the streets and home.

Texts

GENERAL INTRODUCTION
TO THE TEXTS

Care has been taken in this volume to present only sermons which can be attributed to Antioch or Constantinople with certainty or something approaching near certainty, so that the information which they contain can be situated carefully in context. Likewise, in our selection we have tried to avoid material which is frequently quoted in other publications, such as the letters to Olympias. Our intention is to present a side of John Chrysostom which is less well known to the reader. We have made an exception in the case of the sermons *On Eutropius* and *Against the Jews oration 1*, because of the wealth of detail which they contain regarding John's preaching and the relationship between John and his audiences, and the balance that they bring to the picture. It is also our policy to present the full text of a sermon wherever possible in order to avoid giving a false impression to the reader, as is often the case when only an extract is supplied. We have relaxed this rule in the instance of *Baptismal instruction 8*, where a careful modern translation in English already exists (Harkins 1963), and in the case of *On the Acts of the apostles hom. 3*, where the available Greek text of the first half of the homily contains certain difficulties. In the latter instance these problems make it preferable to adjourn a full translation of the homily until one of the promised new critical editions of the series appears in press (Gignac 1987; Devine 1989). In the cases of *On: 'I opposed him to his face'*, *On 1 Corinthians hom. 21* and *On: 'My father's working still'* we present a shortened text likewise, for reasons of space and because the style of homily is already well represented.

The letters we have selected are here translated into English for the first time as are a number of the homilies. The majority of those texts which have previously been translated into English appeared in the *Library of the Nicene and Post Nicene Fathers* in the late nineteenth century in language which now fails to convey the immediacy and vitality of John's preaching. In the case of *Against the Jews oration 1*, we present a full text of the homily in a fresh translation because of the significance of the detail which it contains. This has been prepared with the recent translation by Paul Harkins (1979) in mind.

Because of the numerous biblical citations which occur in a majority of the sermons selected, in the case of citations from the Old Testament we refer the reader to the standard modern titles and numbering of the texts unless the book in question is exclusive to the Septuagint, or the Septuagint reading differs substantially from the Hebrew (e.g., Gen. 22:3; Isa. 41:2 LXX). By this same rationale the psalms are cited according to the Hebrew rather than the Greek numbering. This preference for the Hebrew over the Greek reference system is purely for the convenience of the modern reader. John himself used only the Greek versions of both the Old and New Testament which were at the time available to him. It should be noted that in some cases these deviate from the standard text. In two instances apparent scriptural citations are unidentifiable. In these cases the citation is italicised, but no reference appears in parentheses after it. Attention is drawn in the notes to the lack of identification. Italicisation is also used to set apart from the rest of the text formulae which John cites from the liturgy. The translations of scriptural citations are largely our own.

Parentheses are employed in two ways in our translations. Where John makes an aside, the comments are placed within parentheses as is usual in English syntax. Parentheses are also used to indicate to the reader where we have inserted words into the text which do not exist in the Greek original. In these cases, the words have been added to improve the clarity of the translation. Occasionally we also explain in parentheses what should be understood by a particular word or phrase. Such explanations are always prefaced by 'sc.' (*scilicet*).

There are several words which recur throughout the sermons and letters which have a range of meanings and are difficult to translate with consistency. One such term is *philosophia*. This is sometimes translated by us as 'philosophy' (in the general sense), sometimes as 'wisdom'. In a very broad sense it can also mean 'a Christian way of life' or 'the ascetic way of life'. More rarely it is used by Chrysostom in its technical sense (philosophy). Where the word is translated by us as other than 'philosophy', indication is given in the notes. *Parrhēsia* is another word to which there attaches difficulty. Sometimes we translate it as 'frank speech', sometimes as 'confidence' or 'boldness'. In the context of speech with the emperor the meaning becomes something like 'easy access'. Again, where the translation differs from the primary meaning ('frank speech'), indication is given in the notes. *Philanthrōpia* likewise presents difficulties. In relation to God it is most often translated by us as 'love for humankind'. However, in Hellenistic society it can also constitute a technical term which refers to acts of public benefaction.[1] In cases where this sense is stronger we tend to translate it as 'generosity'. One final word which presents particular difficulty is *spoudē*. While in the sermons we have selected it can usually be translated as 'zeal', in the context of the letters it takes on a more complex range of meanings. There it has been translated by us variously as 'enthusiasm' or 'attention'.

The text from which the sermons and letters are translated is most commonly that of Montfaucon, as preserved in volumes 48–63 of the *Patrologia Graeca*. The majority of John's sermons have yet to appear in modern scientific editions. In the case of *On Ephesians hom. 11*, *On Colossians hom. 7* and *On 1 Corinthians hom. 21*, a text based on a more discriminating view of the manuscripts than is provided by Montfaucon was prepared by Frederick Field in the mid-1800s. This text represents the most scientific edition of these homilies to date and is generally more reliable.[2] In these three cases we have based our translation on the Field text.[3] All instances in which we prefer the punctuation or reading of the Montfaucon text as preserved in PG are indicated in the notes to each of the three homilies. An exception to the use of the Montfaucon and Field editions occurs in the case of *On his return* and *Baptismal instruction 8*. In the first instance the only edition of the Greek text was published in the twentieth century in an article by Antoine Wenger in the journal *Revue des Études byzantines*. In the second, an edition of the homily was made available for the first time in 1970 in the series *Sources Chrétiennes*. We regret that the new edition of the letters by Anne-Marie Malingrey and Roland Delmaire, which is scheduled for publication in 1999 in *Sources Chrétiennes*, will appear too late to influence our translation of the nine letters which are presented at the end of this volume.

It has been our policy to adopt inclusive language throughout our translations. It should be borne in mind by the reader, however, that in the sermons John habitually refers to and addresses people in the masculine, distinguishing women by gender only when he wishes to address them directly. Since women were almostly certainly present in the audience on every occasion that he preached (Mayer forthcoming (b)), the use of inclusive language in our translations serves to present a more faithful rendering of the reality, even if it does not reproduce exactly the style of the preacher. We have also adopted a policy of employing contractions (don't, can't, etc.) in our translations of the sermons to convey the more familiar tone which John adopts in them. By contrast, we employ a varied but generally more conservative approach in the letters in order both to preserve their more formal style and to help convey the different levels of familiarity which existed between John and his correspondents. The division of sermons and letters into paragraphs is largely our own. In those homilies which are presented in an abbreviated form, the reference to the number of paragraphs that have been skimmed over is necessarily somewhat arbitrary. Its purpose is simply to give the reader some idea of the proportion of the homily that has been omitted.

For the benefit of the reader who wishes to examine the texts more closely, the corresponding column or page and line numbers of the Greek edition are located in the margin to each translation. The numbers conform to the edition indicated at the end of each introduction.

ON EPHESIANS HOMILY 11

INTRODUCTION

The city in which this homily was preached is almost certainly Constantinople, since in the final paragraph John makes it clear that the so-called 'schism' in the local church is caused by once faithful members of his audience transferring their allegiance to a rival peer, whose activities in the city have the appearance, at least, of legality.[1] The emphatic but inexplicit manner in which John finds himself obliged to press his case makes it clear that the members of his congregation are unaware that by attending worship in another church presided over by another bishop they are doing anything that might be considered questionable. This situation accords well with the circumstances at Constantinople, where from the beginning of his episcopate large numbers of bishops took up residence in the city for short to lengthy periods in order to curry favour with the bishop, the élites of the city and the imperial household. To have twenty or more bishops enjoying the hospitality of the *episkopeion* at any one time was not unusual (Palladius, *Dial.* 14; ACW 45: 89).[2] As we shall see in the homily *On: 'My father's working still'*, John was obliged to permit his visiting colleagues to preach, if they so wished, in the churches of the capital.[3]

The situation to which John alludes in this homily, then, is most likely one in which one of the more permanent visiting bishops is preaching regularly in a church other than the Great Church and is beginning to draw to himself a loyal crowd of adherents. The emphasis on 'adultery' ('you are consorting with him, when you are married to me') and the fact that John feels unable to do more than allude to the person and situation in question support this conclusion. It is even possible that the bishop is Severian of Gabala, who had ample opportunity to build up a devoted crowd of followers

59

while he acted as locum preacher during the months of John's journey to Ephesus. If this is the case, it would locate the homily somewhere between mid-402 and early 403.[4]

A solution which cannot be discounted, however, is that the bishop to whom John alludes is Sisinnius, head of the Novatian community at Constantinople. Socrates alludes to a dispute between John and Sisinnius over the existence of two bishops in the capital (HE 6.22), as well as attesting to Sisinnius' eloquence as a wit and preacher. His talent as a preacher was clearly sufficient to have set him up in competition with John from the point of view of their respective audiences, while the failure of the laity to distinguish between the legitimacy of the two bishops in this instance is readily explained by the status of the Novatian church in Constantinople at this time. If this scenario is the correct one, then the homily is perhaps more likely to date to the earlier years of John's episcopate.

Regardless of which solution is correct, this homily illustrates the competition that a preacher inevitably faced from both visiting or local peers and his own clergy. It provides an insight into the attendance habits of the audience. It also demonstrates the pastoral emphasis of John's exhortation. His concern is not for his own immediate welfare but for the long-term well-being of the church and of his parishioners' souls.

Translated from Field (1852: 214–27).

TEXT

214B *There is one body and one spirit, just as, when you were called, you were called in one hope. There is one Lord, one faith, one baptism; one God, Father of all, who is over all and through all and in us all. Grace was given to each one of us according to the measure of Christ's gift* (Eph. 4:4–7).

c Paul seeks from us no ordinary love, but one which binds us together and makes us inseparable from one another – a love which supplies as great and as precise a union as if we were limb (joined) to limb. It's this love which produces great blessings. That's why he says *'one body'*, meaning both feeling the same things and not being put out at others' blessings and rejoicing together, and he has demonstrated all of these qualities

D together in this expression. He speaks well when he says *'one spirit'*, showing that the one body will result in one spirit.

Either it's possible for the body to be unified, but not the spirit (for instance, if someone were an associate of heretics); or, through this statement, Paul is shaming us – that is, he means that you who've received one spirit and have drunk from one spring ought not to have differences of opinion; or by 'spirit' he means in this instance 'willingness'.[5]

Then he says: *'Just as, when you were called, you were called in one hope'*. 'God has called you', he says, 'for the same purpose.' He
E allots no more to one person than to another. He has given everyone the gift of immortality, everyone eternal life, everyone undying glory, everyone brother- or sisterhood; he has made everyone his heir. He is the head of everyone, he has aroused everyone equally and has seated them equally in the one place. Seeing that you possess so much equality in spiritual matters, on what grounds, then, do you feel proud? Is it because the one person is rich, and another is powerful? In what respect wouldn't that be ridiculous? Tell me, if the emperor happened to
215 take ten individuals and dress them all in purple and sit them on
F the imperial throne and give all of them the same honour, which of the ten would dare disdain the other, on the grounds that they
(81) were richer or held greater prestige? None. I haven't yet stated the whole case, for the distinction in heaven is not as great as we experience here below.

One Lord, one faith, one baptism. Indeed, the hope in which you were called. *One God and Father of all, who is over all and through all and in us all.* Is it the case that yours is the greater, that person's the lesser calling? Is it the case that you are saved by faith, while that person is saved by works? Is it the case that your sins are remitted through baptism, while that person's are not? *One God and Father of all, who is over all and through*
B *all and in us all. Who is over all*, namely who is Lord and above all things. *And through all*, namely the one who plans and administers. *And in us all*, namely who dwells (in all). And yet people claim that this refers to the Son, such that, if it were a matter of diminution, it couldn't have been said about the Father.

Grace was given to each one of us. 'Why?', someone asks. 'On what basis are there different gifts of the Spirit?' This question continually reduced the Ephesians, the Corinthians and many others to desperation, on the one hand, and to despondency
C and envy, on the other. That's why Paul adduces the example of the body everywhere. That's why he has employed it also at this

point, because he was about to mention different spiritual gifts. While he addresses the issue more precisely in the Letter to the Corinthians, since this sickness held sway there in particular, he only hints at it here. See what he says. He doesn't say: 'Each according to their faith', so that he doesn't cast into despondency those who haven't received much. What does he say? *'According*
D *to the measure of Christ's gift.'* The most important gifts of all –
216 baptism, salvation through faith, that we have God as Father, that we all share the same Spirit – Paul says, are shared by all. Don't grieve, however, if someone does possess something more by way of a spiritual gift, since their burden is greater also. The servant who received the five talents extracted five more. The one who received the two talents, on the other hand, added only another two and yet he possessed no less than the first (Matt. 25:14–17). In this situation Paul therefore
E comforts the listener on the same basis. *'For the preparation of the saints'*, he says, *'for the task of serving, for the building up of the body of Christ'* (Eph. 4:12). That's why he said too: *'Woe is me, if I don't preach the good news'* (1 Cor. 9:16). For instance, should someone receive the gift of being an apostle, there is woe to them, because they received it. You, on the other hand, have had that risk removed. *According to the measure.* What does *according to the measure* mean? It means this: not for our own merit, since (had that been the case), no-one would have received what they have received. Rather, we have all received what we have as a gift.
F Why, then, has one received more, another less? This is of no moment, Paul says. Rather, it's a matter of indifference. This is because each contributes to the building process. In this way he shows that it isn't as a result of individual merit that one has received more, another less, but for the sake of others, to the degree of God's measure. Since in another place Paul says:
(82) *'God positioned each one of the body's members precisely as he wished'* (1 Cor. 12:18). He doesn't mention the reason, in order to avoid confusing the thoughts of his listeners.

That is why it says: *'He ascended on high and made captive captivity and gave gifts to humankind'* (Eph. 4:8). This means: 'Why are you full of yourselves? Everything has come from God.' While the Prophet says in the psalm: *'You received gifts among humankind'*, Paul says: *'He gave gifts among humankind.'* It's the same thing. Similar too is the reflection: *What does the fact that he ascended*
B *mean, if not that he also first descended into the deeper regions of the earth? The one who descended is the very same person who ascended*

above all the heavens, in order that he might fulfil everything (Eph. 4:9–10). When you hear this, don't think of an exchange. For Paul supplies the information which he provides in the Letter to the Philippians in this instance too. Just as, when he is speaking persuasively about humility in that instance (Phil. 2:3–8), Paul adduces Christ, so is it his practice at this point too, since

217 *he descended into the deeper regions of the earth*. For if that circumstance were not the case, this statement which he makes would be without point: *'He became obedient unto death'* (Eph. 4:8). The

C descent is suggested by the fact that Christ ascended. According to the opinion of people, 'the depths of the earth' means 'death', as Jacob said too: *'You will lead my old age with sorrow down into Hades'* (Gen. 44:29). Again it is expressed in the psalm: *'I shall become like those who descend into the pit'* (Ps. 143:7), namely those who die.

Why does Paul adduce this region at this point? What kind of captivity is he talking about? The capture of the devil. For Christ took the tyrant as his prisoner, namely the devil, as well as death and the curse and sin. Do you see booty and spoils? *What does the*

D *fact that he ascended mean, if not that he also descended?* This speaks against those who follow Paul of Samosata.[6] *The one who descended is the very same person who ascended above all the heavens, in order that he might fulfil everything.* 'He descended', Paul says, 'into the deeper regions of the earth*, beyond which there are no others; and he ascended above* everything, beyond which nothing else exists.' This achievement is a mark of his absolute power and creative energy, since, in fact, everything has long since been fulfilled.

And he gave some the gift of being apostles, others prophets, others evangelists, others shepherds and teachers, for the preparation of the

E *saints, for the task of serving, for the building up of the body of Christ* (Eph. 4:11–12). The remark which Paul makes in another place: *'That's why God exalted him'* (Phil. 2:9), he makes in this instance too: *'The one who descended is the very same person who ascended.'* It did Christ no harm at all to *descend into the deeper regions of the earth*, nor did it prevent him from becoming higher than the heavens. That's because the more one is humbled, the more

F one is exalted. Just as, in the case of water, the more a person pushes it down, the more the water rises in height; and the greater the distance from which one shoots, the more it hits the mark, so is it the case with humility. Whenever we talk

(83) about the occasions on which God ascended, it's necessary to

63

218 think first of a descent; but it isn't the case when we talk about a human being.

Next Paul shows God's forethought and wisdom, in that the being who performed such feats and displayed such strength and for our sake didn't refuse to *descend to the deeper regions* wouldn't have distributed the spiritual gifts at random. In another place he says that the Spirit performed this task, expressing it in this way: '*In which the Holy Spirit has placed you as*
B *supervisors to tend the church of the Lord*' (Acts 20:28). And yet in this situation he says that it was the Son, in another place, that it was God. *He gave the church apostles, on the one hand, on the other, prophets* (1 Cor. 12:28). On the other hand, in the Letter to the Corinthians, he says: '*I did the planting, Apollo did the watering, but it's God who has induced growth*' (1 Cor. 3:6); and again: '*The one who plants and the one who waters are equal. Each shall receive the wage appropriate to the particular labour*' (1 Cor. 3:8). It's the same case in this instance. What does it matter if your contribution is less? It's as much as you have received. *First,*
C *apostles*, because they had every gift. *Second, prophets*, for there were some who were not apostles, but prophets, like Agabus (cf. Acts 18:28; 21:10). *Third, evangelists*, namely those who didn't travel around all over the place, but preached the good news alone, like Priscilla and Aquila (cf. Acts 18:26). *Shepherds and teachers*, namely those entrusted with the care of an entire race. So what? Does this mean that the shepherds and teachers were worth less? Certainly, those who sat (in one place) and were concerned with a single location, such as Timothy and Titus, were less valuable than those who travelled around and preached the good news. To put it another way, it wouldn't
D be possible to work out who was subordinate and who was elevated in honour other than from another epistle. '*He gave*', it says, so that you might have no grounds for objection. Perhaps by 'evangelists' Paul means those who wrote the gospel.

For the preparation of the saints, for the task of serving, for the building up of the body of Christ. Do you see the authority? Each one builds, each one prepares, each one serves. '*Until such time*',
E he says, '*as we all arrive at the unity of the faith and of the knowledge of the Son of God, at full manhood, at a measure of maturity of the fullness of Christ*' (Eph. 4:13). By '*maturity*' Paul means in this case 'perfect knowledge'. For, just as an adult male is firmly focused, while children are carried all over the place by their
219 thoughts, so too it is with those who believe. '*The unity of the*

faith', he says; namely until it can be seen that we all hold one faith. I mean that unity of faith exists when we are all one, when we all similarly recognise that we're bound together. If that's why you've received a spiritual gift, so that you might build up others, see that you don't destroy yourself, through envying another. God has honoured you and positioned you so that you might prepare another. Indeed, it was towards this end that the apostle existed, and it was towards this end that the prophet prophesied and persuaded, and the evangelist preached the gospel, and that the shepherd and the teacher too existed. They were all bound up in one task. Don't talk to me about the disparity among the spiritual gifts, but that they all had one task. Unity exists at the moment when we all believe alike. It's evident that this is what Paul means by *full manhood*. What's more, in another place he says that we're infants, even when we're mature. However, he's looking at a separate issue. For in that instance he calls us infants in respect of the knowledge that is to come. For after he says: *'We know in part'*, he adds: *'through enigmas'* and other such expressions (1 Cor. 13:9–12). In this case he addresses another issue, that of the ease with which our status can be changed, just as Paul says in another place: *'Solid food is for the mature'* (Heb. 5:14). Do you see how he speaks of maturity in that case too? Observe how he calls them mature in this case also, when he continues, saying: *'That we may no longer be infants'* (Eph. 4:14). He states that the measure we've received is minimal, so that we might make every effort to preserve it, with firmness and security. *That we may no longer.* With the expression *'no longer'* Paul indicates that they had been in this state for a long time. He both places himself in a position to correct the situation and does so.[7] 'The reason there are so many builders', he says, 'is so that the building won't be unstable, so that it won't be moved around, so that the stones will be firmly fixed in place.' He means it's in the nature of infants to be *tossed about*, to be carried all over the place, to be unstable.

'That we may no longer be infants', Paul says, *'tossed about and carried around by every puff of doctrine, by the throw of people's dice, by trickery cunningly intended to promote error'* (Eph. 4:14). *'And carried around'*, he says, *'by every puff of air.'* He adduces the metaphor as a means of demonstrating the degree of danger that doubting minds are in. *'By every puff of air'*, he says, *'by the throw of people's dice, by trickery cunningly intended to promote error.'*

Kubeutai is the name given to those who play games with coun-
ters. That's what scoundrels are like when they seize on persons
more simple than themselves. They transpose the position of
everything and change everything around.

At this point Paul touches upon life too. *'Rather, when we speak
the truth in love, we shall grow in every way in Christ, who is the head.
Since it's from him'*, that is, from Christ, he says, *'that the entire body
is joined and fitted together through every connection that's supplied, in
accord with the function apportioned to each and every part the body*
E *effects its growth and builds itself up in love'* (Eph. 4:15–16). His
explanation is extremely unclear, because he wants to say everything at once. What he in fact means is this: just as the signal
that descends from the brain doesn't send sensations through
the nervous system everywhere at random, but instead does so
to the degree appropriate to each body part – to that which is
capable of receiving more, it sends more, to that which requires
F less, it sends less (for the brain signal is the root) – so too is it the
case with Christ. Since people are appended to him like parts of a
body, his forethought and the spiritual gifts he has supplied in
appropriate measure effect the growth of each and every part.
What, then, does *through every connection that's supplied* mean? It
means this: through sensation. My point is that the signal
(85) that's supplied to the parts of the body from the head activates
each part by touching it. One could express it in this way: the
body, by taking over in turn the activity of supply, proportionate
to the parts within it, effects its growth. Or, to say it another
way: the parts of the body grow through receiving that which
is supplied in the degree appropriate to their own measure.
Or, in other words: when the signal flows down copiously
from the brain and makes contact with all parts of the body,
each receives the supplied signal according to its capacity and
B in that way grows. Why, then, did Paul add *in love*? He added it
because there's no other means by which that signal can descend.
Just as, if it happens that a hand has been amputated from the
body, when the signal from the brain looks for continuity and
doesn't find it, it doesn't leap out of the body after making a
221 hole in it, and go off looking for the hand – rather, if it doesn't
find the hand lying there, it doesn't make contact – so it is the
case in this situation, if we haven't been bound together by love.

In fact, all of these points have been made by Paul with a view
C to humility. What does it matter, he asks, if someone has
received more? They have received the same spiritual signal,

that's been sent forth from the same head, that activates in the same manner, that takes hold in the same way. *Joined and fitted together*, namely benefiting from considerable care. Paul says this because the body should not be set up haphazardly, but should be set up in a very skilful way. For instance, if it leaves its place, it's no longer in order. As a result, not only should you be united with the body, but you should also occupy your own place, since, if you overstep it, you are not in unity, nor

D do you receive the Spirit. Rather, don't you see how the entire body is harmed and death often results when bones are transposed as the result of some accident, when the one moves beyond its proper location and occupies another's space? In some cases it is later found to be undeservedly occupying that place. I use this example because it's a common practice to cut the bone out and render the space vacant. This is because redundancy is harmful in every respect. In the case of the physical elements too, everything is harmed when they abandon their appropriate symmetry and become overabundant. That is what

E Paul means by *joined and fitted together*. Think how important it is for each thing to remain in its own place and not approach territory that belongs to another and isn't appropriate to it. You fit the parts of the body together, Christ does the supplying from above – just as there exist in the body organs that are receptive in this manner, so also do they exist in the case of the spirit, where the entire root extends from above. For example, the heart is the root of the life force; the liver is the root of the blood, the spleen is the root of the bile and others are the root of other

F things; yet they all take their cue from the brain. That is what God does too. Since he holds humankind in very high esteem and doesn't want to keep away from them, on the one hand he has made humankind dependent upon him for his cue, while on the other hand he has set humans up as his assistants. He has positioned the one person for this task, the other for that.

(86) For instance, an apostle is one of the most vital arteries of the body, since they receive everything from God. As a result, they make eternal life circulate to everybody as through veins

222 and arteries, namely through the Word. The prophet foretells the future and provides the same benefit. And, while the one puts the bones together, the other supplies them with life, *for the preparation of the saints, for the task of serving.* Love builds the body up

B and does the gluing and fastening and fitting of the parts to one another.

Therefore, if we wish to enjoy the spirit that proceeds from the head, we must hold onto one another. I say this because there are two ways of splitting away from the body of the church. The first is when we let our love grow cold. The second is when we dare to commit acts whereby we don't deserve to mature in that body. By either means we separate ourselves from the whole. What's more, if we've been put in office to build up others, what would those experience who don't work at building, but in fact create division first? There's nothing that is as capable of

C dividing a church as a love of wielding power. Nothing stirs up God as much as seeing the church being divided. Even if we have done innumerable good works, if we slice up the fullness of the church we shall pay as severe a penalty as if we had cut God's own body in two. While the latter at least occurred for the benefit of the world, even if that wasn't the intent, the former has nothing at all useful about it; rather, it inflicts a great deal of damage.

I address these words not only to those who govern, but also to those who are subject to their rule. A certain holy man made a

D comment which seems to be rash, yet he uttered it nonetheless. What was the comment? He said that not even the blood of martyrdom was capable of wiping out this sin. Tell me, for what reason do you become a martyr? Isn't it for the glory of Christ? How, then, can you, who are giving up your life for Christ, work at destroying the church for which Christ gave his life? Hear the words of Paul, when he says: '*I don't deserve to be called an apostle, because I persecuted the church of God*, and destroyed it' (1 Cor. 15:9). The damage this causes is no less than that inflicted by enemies; rather, it's much greater. I say

E this because, while that damage renders the church even more
223 noteworthy, when war is declared against it by its own children the resultant damage dishonours it in particular among its enemies. For it is considered among them a major indication of deceit when those who were born and raised in the church and who have learnt its mysteries in detail suddenly turn around and treat it like enemies.

My comments are addressed to those who give themselves

F indiscriminately to those who are splitting the church. I do this because, on the one hand, if the latter in fact hold contrary teachings, it is on that account inappropriate to mix with them; yet, on the other hand, if they hold the same beliefs, it is much more the case. Why? Because the sickness stems from a love of power.

Don't you know what those associated with Korah and Dathan and Abiram experienced (cf. Num. 16)? Surely it wasn't the (87) three alone (who suffered), but also those who were with them? What do you claim? 'It's the same faith. They're orthodox too.' If that's so, why then aren't they with us? *One Lord, one faith, one baptism.* If they're in the right, then we're in the wrong; but if we're in the right, it is they who are in the wrong. *'Infants'*, Paul says, *'tossed about and carried around by every puff of air.'* Tell me, do you really think that it's enough to say: 'They're orthodox', when the process of ordination has disappeared and perished? Of what use is everything else, when this process has not been followed precisely? I mean, just as one should fight B for the faith, so should one fight for this point also. Since, if it's possible for anybody and everybody to fill their hands and become priests (cf. Exod. 29:9 LXX), like those of old, then let everyone come forward. It will be in vain that this altar was built; it will be in vain that the fullness of the church exists; it will be in vain that the number of priests exists. Let's take these things and destroy them.

'Heaven forbid!' someone says. You do the things that you do and you exclaim: 'Heaven forbid!'? How can you say: 'Heaven forbid!' while these very things are happening? I speak and I give testimony, not with a view to my own position, but with a C view to your salvation. If a person didn't care either way, they would know. Yet if a person cares nothing about these events, it's at least a matter of concern to me. Paul says: *'I planted, Apollo watered, but God induced growth'* (1 Cor. 3:6). How shall we endure the laughter of the pagans? I mean, if they criticise us over the heresies, what won't they say about these events? 'If the teachings are the same, if the mysteries are the same, what reason could the one authority have to attack the other's church? You can see', they will say, 'that everything to do 224 with the Christians is full of conceit and that there exists among them a love of power and deceit. Strip them of their numbers and D they're nothing. Cut out the disease – the corrupt part of the crowd.' Would you like me to recount what they are saying about our city, how they accuse us of being complacent? 'Anyone who likes can find people who believe them and there would never be any doubt about it.' How ludicrous! Yet how much shame attends these claims. Rather, laughter is one thing, shame is another. 'If some among us are caught committing utterly shameful deeds and are about to pay some penalty, there is much trembling, much fear in every quarter lest they leap away',

E someone says, 'and align themselves with the others.' All right! Let such a person leap away any number of times and be with them. I don't mean with those who've sinned. Rather, if a person happens to be blameless and wishes to change sides, let them change. I say this because I suffer pain and grieve and mourn and my insides are torn apart as if I were being deprived of a part of my own body. No, I should say, I don't feel pain as strongly as I am compelled, through this fear, to do something that is ill-suited to my position.

Beloved, we don't exercise control over your faith nor are we
F issuing these instructions in a despotic way. It's to the teaching of the word that we've been appointed, not to leadership or authority. We hold the position of a person offering advice, giving encouragement. The person who advises speaks from their own point of view, not forcing the listener, but allowing
(88) them control over their choice of what's said. In this respect alone is the person accountable, if they don't speak what's on their mind. That's why we're making these statements, why we're expressing these thoughts, so that on that day[8] it will be impossible for you to say: 'No-one told us. No-one explained it. We didn't know. We really didn't think it was a sin.' That's why I state and protest that to divide the church is no less an evil than to fall into heresy. Tell me, would a person who was subject to a particular emperor, and who didn't ally themselves to a second emperor nor yield themselves to another, be punished any the less than those who did ally themselves to a second emperor, if, after they had received the purple robe of that
B very emperor, they kept it and released all of it from its fastening
225 and ripped it up into numerous shreds? And what if, after that, they grabbed the emperor himself by the throat and killed him, and tore apart his body limb from limb? What penalty could they possibly pay that would compensate? If, then, the person who has done this to an emperor, who is their fellow servant, has committed a crime greater than any penalty, of what hell[9] wouldn't that person be worthy who's killed Christ and has torn him limb from limb?

Is this the punishment that's threatening us? I certainly don't
C think so, but rather others that are far worse. All of you women who are present (after all, this failing is for the most part exhibited by women) speak, convey this exemplum to those women

70

who aren't here, instil them with fear. If certain people think that they can grieve us and avenge themselves in this way, let them know for certain that what they're doing is without point. I mean that if you want to avenge yourself against us, I'll give you a method by which you'll be able to get revenge without doing yourself harm. I should say, it isn't possible to take revenge without causing oneself harm, although it's possible to lessen the damage. Beat me, spit upon me when you meet me in public, and get in some good blows!

D   Do you shudder when you hear these words?[10] If I say: 'Beat me!', you shudder with horror; and yet you don't shudder when you rip apart your Master? You tear apart the components of your Master's body and you don't tremble? The church is our Father's house. It's *one body and one spirit*. Yet, is it against me that you want to be avenged? Then confine your attentions to me. Why do you take revenge on Christ instead of me? Rather, why do you kick at your own corns? After all, there's no circumstance in which vengeance is good. Yet, to do violence

E   to one person, when it's another who's committing the wrong, is far worse. Have you been wronged by us? Why do you hurt the person who's done no wrong? It's completely insane. I'm not trying to be ironic when I say what I'm about to say, nor do I speak in generalities, but as I really think and feel. I would prefer that each person who's aggrieved along with you against us, and who's harming themselves as a result of that hurt and taking themselves off elsewhere, punch us right in the face and strip us naked and scourge us with whips, regardless of whether

F   their accusations are just or unjust, and rather release their anger against us than do the things that they're now doing.

   If this happened, it would be nothing for a worthless human being of no account to suffer such abuse. In any case I, who've
226   been wronged and abused, would call upon God and he would
(89)   forgive you your sins. (I would do this) not because I have the licence to address him so freely but because, when the person who's been wronged pleads on behalf of the wrongdoer, they acquire much licence of speech. *'If someone sins against a person'*, it says, *'they will pray for him'* (1 Sam. 2:25). Had I been unable to do it myself, I would have sought out and requested it of other holy men and they would have done this. But as it is, to whom shall we address our request, seeing that God has been abused by us? Look at the anomaly. For, when they have

attained maturity in this church, some never attend church again or do so only once a year (and then, at random and
B when they feel like it); others, while they attend more frequently, do so in a random and frivolous fashion too, talking and making witty comments about nothing. Others again make a good show of being zealous, yet they're the very ones who are the agents of this disaster. If, then, it's for these reasons that you're zealous, it would be better for you too to be ranked with those who don't care. Rather, it would be better if neither they were indifferent nor you such as you are. I'm not talking about you who are present, but about those who have leapt away.

The matter is one of adultery. If you won't put up with hearing these comments about them, then you shouldn't (put up with hearing them) about ourselves. I say this because, of the two
C situations, one of them must have come about illegally. Consequently, if you entertain these suspicions about us, I'm prepared to give up my office to whomever you wish. Just let the church be one. But if it's we who've come about by legal process, convince those who've ascended the throne illegally to put it aside. I've said these things, not as a person giving orders, but as one who's securing your position and protecting you. Seeing that each is of age and will pay the price for what they've done, I ask that you don't throw the lot at us and think that you yourselves are free from liability, lest you deceive yourselves for
D nothing and come to grief. For, although we'll have to give an account for your souls, it will be for the moments when we were deficient in our duties, when we didn't exhort, when we didn't admonish, when we didn't protest. After these points, grant that I too may say: '*I am clean of the blood of everyone*'
227 (Acts 20:26), and: '*God will rescue my soul*' (2 Tim. 4:18). Say what you want, in particular give just cause as to why you stopped attending, and I'll respond. But you can't. For that reason, I exhort you, strive earnestly both to stand firmly yourselves from this point on and to bring back those who've changed
E sides, so that with one mind we may render thanks to God, because his is the glory for ever and ever. Amen.

ON COLOSSIANS HOMILY 7

INTRODUCTION

Preaching in Antioch (Allen and Mayer 1994: 30–5) some years after
the riot which occurred in 387, in this homily John provides useful
information about the composition and status of his audience at a
particular ordinary synaxis. Women as well as men are present and
certain of the women, at least, are wealthy. In addition we have an
opportunity to observe the preacher at his exegetical best – crisp,
direct speech; an abundant use of exempla; challenges to the values
most cherished by the audience (in this case power, fame and
wealth); threats to exclude persistent offenders from the church;
strong and unflinching exhortation. What the style and contents of
this homily tell us is that, whether he was a bishop or a presbyter,
John did not resile from tackling awkward subjects with his audience
or from using whatever means were available to him to encourage the
audience to change behaviour which he considered harmful to their
salvation.

Translated from Field (1855: 241–52).

TEXT

241 (371)   *Therefore let no-one pass judgement on you in the matter of food or*
drink, or in the case of a festival or a new moon or sabbaths – these
are a shadow of what is to come – but the body of Christ. Let no-one
disqualify you, insisting on humility and worship of angels, taking a
B   *stand on visions, puffed up without reason by their sensuous mind, and*
not holding fast to the head, from whom the whole body, nourished and
knit together through its joints and ligaments, will grow with a growth
that is from God (Col. 2:16–19).

73

First he speaks elliptically, saying: *'See to it that no-one makes a prey of you according to human tradition'* (Col. 2:8), and again further back: *'I say this in order that no-one may deceive you with* C *beguiling speech'* (Col. 2:4). Having preoccupied their mind and made it concerned, he subsequently inserted the benefits (brought by Christ) and amplified his subject. Then he added the final charge with the words: *'Therefore let no-one pass judgement on you in the matter of food or drink, or in the case of a festival or a new moon or sabbaths.'*

Do you see how he compresses his points? 'If you've attained benefits of this kind', he says, 'why do you make yourselves guilty on small counts?' And he disparages them with the words *'or in the case of a festival'*, because they weren't observing all the previous injunctions. *Or a new moon or sabbaths.* He didn't say: 'Therefore don't observe them', but *'let no-one pass judgement* D *on you'*. He showed them up as having transgressed and relaxed (the law), but he transferred the accusation onto others. 'Don't put up with those who pass judgement', he says. But it's not even that – he reasons with them, all but silencing them by saying: 'You shouldn't enquire into it.' He wouldn't have fixed on these points. He didn't say: 'On pure and impure occasions'; nor did he say: 'At the feasts of tabernacles and unleavened bread and Pentecost', but *'in the case of a festival'*, because they didn't dare to observe everything. And if they did observe (a feast), it wasn't in order to celebrate it. *'In the case of'*, he says, showing that more of it was relaxed. For even if they observed the E sabbath, it wasn't according to the letter of the law. *These are a shadow of what is to come*, meaning the New Testament. *But the body of Christ.* Now some punctuate in this way: 'But the body belongs to Christ'. But the truth is in Christ. Others interpret: 'Let no-one disqualify you from the body of Christ', that is, 242 (cause you to) make abusive comments. Disqualification occurs when victory is won by one person, but the prize goes to another F when the victor makes abusive comments.[1] You stand above the devil and sin. Why do you subject yourself to sin again? It's on this account that he says: *'Because he is bound to fulfil the whole law'* (Gal. 5:3), and again: *'Is Christ bound to be an agent of sin?'* (Gal. 2:17), which he said in his letter to the Galatians. When he filled (372) them with anger by saying *'disqualify'*, he began at that point to say: *'insisting on humility and worship of angels, taking a stand on visions, puffed up without reason by their sensuous mind'*. What does

74

he mean by *on humility*, or by *puffed up*? He shows that every-thing is vainglory.

But what does he mean in the whole verse? There are some who say: 'We shouldn't be attracted by Christ, but by the angels, because he is above our station.' It's on this account that he turns over and again what has been done by Christ:

B *Through the blood of his cross* (Col. 1:20); it's on this account that he says: *'he suffered for us'* (1 Pet. 2:21), *'he loved us'* (Eph. 2:4). And on this very point their attention is fixed again. And he doesn't mean 'attachment' but 'religious observance'. *Taking a stand on visions.* He didn't see angels, but is affected as if he had. On this account Paul says: *'puffed up without reason by their sensuous mind'*, not about any true fact. The person is puffed up because of what they believe, and uses the pretext of humility. This is the result of fleshly ideas, not spiritual ones. The reason-ing is human. *'And not holding fast to the head'*, he says, *'from whom the whole body'*. It is to (the head) that the whole body owes its

C being and proper existence. Why, when you've dispensed with the head, do you hold on to the limbs? If you're deprived of the head, you're lost. *From whom the whole body.* Whoever it is derives not their life but even their construction from that. The entire church, as long as it has its head, will grow, because

243 it's no longer a question of the experience of arrogance and vain-glory, but of finding human intention. Look at the words *'From whom'*, applied to the Son. *'Nourished and knit together'*, he says, *'through its joints and ligaments, it will grow with a growth that is from God.'* It's a growth from God, he says, and from leading a life of virtue.

D *If you died with Christ.* He puts this in the middle, and more forceful comments on either side of it. *'If you died with Christ to the elemental spirits of the universe'*, he says, *'why do you consider that you still live in the world?'* (Col. 2:20). He doesn't spell out the consequences, for he should say: 'How is it that you're still living in subjection to the elements?' But having left this aside, what does he say? *'Don't handle, don't taste, don't touch – these all perish as they are used, according to human precepts and doctrines'* (Col. 2:21–2). 'You're not of this world', he says, 'and how is it that you're subject to its elements? How is it that

E you're subject to the surveillance of the world?' And see how he makes fun of them: *Don't touch, don't handle, don't taste*, as if they were cowards and keeping clear of some great (taboos). *These all perish as they are used.* He punctures the puffed-up state of many,

and adds: *According to human precepts and doctrines.* What do you
say to that? Do you talk about the law? Therefore it's human
teaching according to the time; or it's the case that they were
perverting it, or that he was alluding to pagan (taboos). 'The pre-
F cept is totally human', he says. *These things have a semblance of
wisdom in terms of superstition and humility and severity to the
(373) body, (but) they have no value against the indulgence of the flesh* (Col.
2:23). '*Semblance*', he says, not 'power', not 'truth'. The upshot is
that, even if you have the *semblance of wisdom*, we'll be opposed.
For someone may seem to be reverent and moderate and to
despise the body. *They have no value against the indulgence of the
flesh.* I mean that God gives honour, but they don't use it with
honour. Thus when there is a precept he can call it honour.
They dishonour the body, he says, depriving it and removing
244 its power, not permitting it to rule of its own accord, but God
has honoured the flesh.

 If, then, you've been raised with Christ. He includes them (in
what he says) because he had already established above that
B Christ had died. This is why he says: '*If, then, you've been raised
with Christ, seek the things that are above*' (Col. 3:1). This observation does not take place here. *Seek the things that are above, where
Christ is, seated at the right hand of God.* Goodness! Where has he
conveyed our mind? How has he filled them with great purpose?
It wasn't enough for him to say *the things above* or *where Christ is*,
but what? *Seated at the right hand of God.* With that he prepared
them so that they would no longer see the earth.[2] *Set your mind on
C things that are above, not on things that are on earth. For you have died
and your life is hidden with Christ in God. When Christ who is our
life appears, then you also will appear with him in glory* (Col. 3:2–4).

 Your life, he means, isn't this one; your life is a different one.
He's already forcing them to change places, and is keen to show
that they are seated above, and even dead, as he prepares them
from both sides not to seek the things of this world. For if
you're dead, you don't have to seek; if you're above, you don't
have to seek. Christ isn't appearing? Then nor is your life
D either. It's above with God. Well, then? When shall we live?
When Christ who is your life appears, then seek glory, then seek
your life, then seek your delight. Such is the preliminary training
for leading them away from delight and repose. Such is Paul's
custom – by preparing one aspect to jump to another. For
example, just while speaking about those who are anticipating a

feast, he suddenly falls into the observation about the mysteries. For the argument is weighty when it happens unexpectedly.

It *'is hidden'*, he says, from you. *Then you also will appear with*
E *him.* So that now you don't appear. See how he transfers them to heaven itself. For, as I said, he's always keen to show that they have the same things as Christ. And throughout all his letters (there is) this same reasoning: to show that they have everything in common with Christ. Therefore he speaks of the head, and the body, and he does everything to describe this.

245 If, then, we shall appear on that occasion, let's not grieve when
F we don't attain honour. If this life is not life, but is hidden, we should live this life as corpses. *'Then you also'*, he says, *'will appear with him in glory'.* It's not for nothing that he says *'in glory'*, since the pearl too is hidden while it's in the oyster. If, then, we're
(374) insulted, let's not grieve, whatever we suffer, for this life isn't ours. We're strangers and pilgrims. *'For you have died'*, it says. Who is so stupid as to buy servants for a dead and buried body, or to build houses for it, or to prepare expensive clothing for it? No-one. Therefore let us not either. Rather, just as we have but a single objective – not to be naked – so too let us have a single objective here. The first human being in us was buried, buried not in earth but in water; it wasn't death that destroyed it but the one who destroyed death by burying it, not according to the law of nature, but according to the com-
B mand of the Master, which is stronger than nature. For even if somebody can destroy the things that are the products of nature, they can't at all (destroy) the things that are subject to (the Master's) command. Nothing is more blessed than that grave over which all rejoice, both angels and human beings and the Master of angels. For that grave there is no need of clothing, of a coffin or of anything else of that kind. Do you want to see the sign of this? I'll show you the baptismal font in which one person was buried, but another rose up. In the Red Sea the Egyptians were drowned, but the Israelites rose up. The same event buries the one and gives birth to the other.

C Don't be surprised if birth and destruction occur in baptism, because – tell me – isn't to melt the opposite of to make adhere? It's clear to everyone that it is. This is what fire does, in that it melts and destroys wax, but makes metallic earth adhere and produces gold. So it is too in the case of baptism: the power of the fire destroys the wax statue, and produces gold in its stead. For we're indeed muddy before the bath, but golden

after it. How is this evident? Listen to Paul saying: *'The first*
246D *human being was from earth, dusty; the second human being is from*
heaven, heavenly' (1 Cor. 15:47). While I've spoken of how far
mud is from gold, I've found a greater difference between the
heavenly and the earthly: it's not so much how far mud is
from gold, as much as earthly things are from heavenly things.
We were made of wax and muddy; indeed the flame of passion
melted us much more than fire does wax, and whatever temptation arrived broke us much more than stone does mud. And, if
you like, let's describe our former life (to see) if everything
E wasn't earth and water, and easily blown about, and dust both
unstable and readily dispersed.[3]

And, if you like, let's examine not past events but present
events (to see) if we won't find that everything that exists is
dust and water. What do you want to say? Public offices and
positions of power? For nothing seems to be more worthy of
emulation in the present life than that.[4] But a person would
find the dust standing in the air more (worthy of emulation)
F than these, particularly nowadays. For to whom aren't they subjected? To their lovers, to eunuchs, to those who do everything
for the sake of money, to the whim of the people, to the rages of
the more powerful. The man who yesterday was lofty on the tribunal, who had heralds calling out at the top of their voices and
(375) many people running before him and clearing the way through
the market-place, is today shabby and lowly and bereft and
denuded of all that, scattered like dust, like a wave that has
passed on. Just as dust is raised by our feet, so too are public
offices born of those who are concerned with money, who play
the role of feet in every aspect of life. And just as dust, when
it's raised, takes on a large part of air but is itself insignificant,
B so too is it with public office. And just as dust blinds the eyes, so
too does the humbug of public office disable the eyes of the
mind.

Well, do you want us to examine the more desirable object –
wealth? Come on, let's examine it in its parts. It contains
delight, it contains honours, it contains power. First, if you
247 like, let's examine delight – isn't it dust? Rather, it passes over
quicker than dust. For the pleasure of (tasting) delights goes no
further than the tongue, but when the belly has been filled, it
doesn't go even as far as the tongue. 'But', someone says, 'honours themselves are a sweet affair.' And what is less sweet than
that honour when it comes about through using money? When
C

it doesn't come about through free choice, nor from some eager-
ness, it's not you who enjoys the honour, but wealth. The result
is that this very fact makes the wealthy person the most dishonourable of all. For, tell me – if everyone honours you as a
friend, but they admit that you are of no worth, but that they're
compelled to honour you because of your wealth, how could they
dishonour you (more) in another way? The result is that wealth
causes us dishonour, being more worth honour than those themselves who possess it, and a sign of weakness rather than power.

D How, then, isn't it absurd that we don't consider ourselves
worthy of earth and ash (that's what gold is), but are honoured
on account of gold? We deserve it, but the person who despises
wealth doesn't. For it's better not to be paid honour than to be
paid honour in this way.

Tell me – if someone says to you: 'I don't think you're worth
any honour at all, but I hold you in honour because of your
servants', what could be worse than this dishonour? If it's a
cause of shame to be honoured because of one's servants, who
share the same soul and nature as ourselves, it's much worse to
be honoured because of objects of a lower order – I mean walls

E of houses and courtyards and golden vessels and clothing. These
are truly ridiculous and shameful – better to die than to be paid
honour in this way. Tell me, if you were in danger from this
delusion and someone who was shabby and despicable wished
to get you out of the danger, what could be worse than that?

But what you say to each other about the city I want to say to

F you. Once our city offended the ruler and he ordered it to be
totally destroyed, with men and children and homes.[5] (Such
are the whims of royalty. They indulge in power to the extent

(376) that they wish; power is such a great evil.) The city was thus in
the direst peril. The neighbouring city, the one on the coast,[6]
interceded with the emperor on our behalf, but those living in
our city said that this was worse than the destruction of the
city. Being paid honour in this way was thus worse than being
brought into dishonour. See where honour has its root. Chefs'
hands cause us to be honoured, such that we have to be grateful

248 to them, and swineherds who supply a rich table, and weavers

B and woollen-workers and metal-workers and pastry-cooks and
table-setters.

Isn't it better, then, not to be honoured than to owe gratitude
to these people for the honour (they bring us)? And apart from
that fact, I'll try to demonstrate clearly that being wealthy is

full of dishonour. It produces a shameful soul – what's more dishonourable than that? For, tell me, if the body were in the prime of life, and surpassed all in beauty, but the advent of wealth promised to make it shameful, and sick instead of well, and inflamed instead of working properly, and filling all its limbs with dropsy

C caused the face to swell up and made everything swollen, and caused the feet to swell up and made them heavier than beams, and caused the stomach to swell up and made it larger than any wine-jar, and after that ordered that not even those who were willing to cure it should be permitted to do so (for this is power), but that so much freedom should be given that if anyone came forward to release it from its sufferings he should be punished. Tell me, how could being rich be beautiful, when it does that to the soul?

But power is more serious than that disease, for when a sick

D person doesn't obey even the rules of doctors, it's more serious than being sick. What wealth has makes the soul inflamed everywhere, and forbids doctors to come. The result is that we don't call these people blessed on account of their power, but we pity them. Nor would I call someone blessed on account of power if I saw them afflicted with dropsy, and nobody stopping them being filled with as many drinks as they wished and harmful meats. For

E power is not always a good thing, just as honours aren't either, for they fill one with great arrogance. If you don't want your body to get this illness along with wealth, how will you keep watch on your soul to prevent it receiving[7] not only this but also other punishment? Indeed it's inflamed all over with fevers and inflammations, and nobody is capable of extinguishing that fever – wealth doesn't allow it, in that it persuades us that disadvantages are advantages, for example, putting up with nobody and acting in all things through power. A person

249F wouldn't find another soul full of such great, absurd desires as the souls of those who want to be wealthy. How many trifles don't they design for themselves? More than those who dream

(377) up the hippocentaurs and the Chimaeras and the snake-footed, and the Scyllas, and monsters, you will see them dreaming up (monsters). And if a person wishes to dream up one of their desires, nothing will materialise for that prodigy – neither Scylla nor Chimaera nor hippocentaur, but you will find that (their desire) contains all beasts at once.

Perhaps someone will think that I've been very wealthy since I'm substantiating the course of events in this way. There's a

B story about someone – first I'll confirm the story by means of the pagan bards.[8] There's a story that one of their kings abused luxury to such an extent that he made a golden plane tree, and heaven above, and so sat there, making war on human beings who had learned to fight. Isn't this the desire of the hippocentaurs? Of Scylla? Again, another one threw human beings into a wooden bull. Isn't this Scylla? During former times (wealth) made the one who was formerly king from a man into a woman. What shall I say about (it making) a soldier from a woman? It's an irrational animal, and even worse than this. I mean that if wild animals are under a tree they are content

C with their nature and seek nothing more. But that king went beyond even the nature of wild animals.

What, then, could be sillier than the rich? This happens through the excess of their desires. But isn't it the case that many admire him (sc. that king)? That's why they're as ridiculous as he is. This didn't indicate wealth, but madness. How much better is the plane tree on earth than that golden one? This is so because what's in accord with nature is more pleasing than what goes beyond nature. What did you want with a golden heaven, you silly man? Do you see how great wealth makes

D people mad? how it inflames them? I think that wealth doesn't even recognise the sea, and perhaps wishes to walk on it. Isn't this a Chimaera? Isn't it a hippocentaur? But even today there are people who don't distance themselves from it, but are

250 much sillier. How, tell me, do those who make silver pots and vessels and flasks differ in silliness from the golden plane tree? How do the women differ (I am embarrassed, but have to say

E it) who make silver chamber-pots? Those of you who make them should be ashamed. Christ is starving and you're indulging like that? I should say, are you being silly? What kind of punishment won't these women pay? Then do you persist in asking why there are robbers, why there are murderers, why there are evils, when the devil sweeps you off your feet in this way? Possessing silver plates is not even in accord with a philosophical spirit, but is total wantonness. Making unclean vessels from silver too, is

F that wantonness? I wouldn't say wantonness, but silliness. And not that either, but madness or worse than madness.

I know that many people will make fun of me on this point, but I won't pay any attention – just let there be a further com-

(378) ment. In truth wealth makes people silly and mad. If they had such abundance, they would wish for the earth to be gold, and

walls to be of gold, perhaps even heaven and air to be of gold. What madness is this, what transgression of decency, what fever? Another person, made in the image of God, is dying of cold, while you're equipping yourself with such things? What arrogance! What more would a mad person do? Do you so revere excrement that you would receive it in silver? I know that you're stunned as you listen to this, but it's the women who act like this who should be stunned and the husbands
B who pander to such illnesses. This is intemperance and cruelty and inhumanity and brutality and insolence. What kind of Scylla would do this, what kind of Chimaera, what kind of dragon – or I should say, what kind of demon, what kind of devil? What's the use of Christ? What's the use of the faith when one has to put up with people being pagans, or rather, not pagans but demons? If you shouldn't adorn your head with gold and pearls (cf. 1 Tim. 2:9), what kind of pardon will the person encounter who uses silver for such an impure service? Other objects won't suffice, although they aren't to be put up with
C either – solid silver chairs and footstools? These too are silly.

Everywhere there is excessive wantonness, everywhere vain-glory. Nowhere is there use (for such objects) but everywhere there are excesses. I'm afraid that proceeding from such madness the female sex will take on the aspect of monsters, in that it's likely that they'll desire and acquire gold hair. (In truth, you
251 must confess that you felt something at what I said and came to attention, and were seized with longing, and if it weren't that
D shame at least prevailed, you wouldn't have made excuses.) For if people dare to perform acts more absurd than even these, I think that they'll desire much more to have golden hair and lips and eyebrows and thus to anoint themselves all over with liquid gold.

But if you don't believe me and you think that I'm speaking in fun, I'll tell you what I heard – rather, it's so today as well. The Persian king has a gold beard; those who are skilled in these matters, as with a thread, so braid the hairs with gold leaf, and he lies there like a monster. Glory to you, Christ! How many good things have you filled us with? How have you prepared us to be healthy? How many monstrosities, how many absurdities have you freed us from? Look, I'm making a public statement, I'm no longer advising, but commanding and
E giving orders. Let the one who wants to, hear; let the one who doesn't, disobey. If you continue to do this, I won't put up with you, nor shall I accept you or allow you to cross this

threshold. What use do I have for a crowd of sick people? What use if in educating you I don't stand in the way of excesses? Indeed, Paul stood in the way of both gold and pearls. Let's become the laughing-stock of the pagans: our beliefs seem to be myths. And to the men I give the following advice: if you come for teaching to be instructed in spiritual knowledge, do away with that excess.

F   The following advice I give both to men and women, and even if someone does otherwise, I won't put up with (that excess) any more. There were twelve disciples, and hear what Christ said to
(379) them: '*Do you too wish to go away?*' (John 6:67). If we flatter all the time, when shall we revive? When shall we make progress? '*But if*', it says, '*there are other heresies, they too will be changed.*'[9] This saying is chilling: '*One person doing the will of the Lord is better than a thousand transgressors*' (Sir. 16:3 LXX). And you, what do you want, tell me? Do you want to have thousands of runaway slaves and thieving servants, or one well-disposed one? Look, I'm advising and enjoining you to smash facial adorn-
252 ments and containers such as these and to give to the poor and no longer suffer this madness. Whoever wants may shy away, who-ever wants may bring an accusation; I won't put up with anyone.
B   When I'm about to be judged before the tribunal of Christ you will stand at a distance, and so will your charm[10] as I render my account. The following words destroy everything: '*lest you go*', it says, '*and change to another heresy*'.[11] (Your case) is weak – submit. For how long (will you carry on)? Until when? Once, and twice, and a third time, not forever. Look, I enjoin you again, and testify with blessed Paul: '*that if I come again, I won't spare them*' (2 Cor. 13:2). When you behave properly, you'll know the extent of the gain, the extent of the usefulness. Yes, and I ask and I beg
C   you, and I wouldn't refuse to clasp your knees and to make petition on this point.

What's this softness? What's this indulgence? What's this insolence? (This isn't indulgence, but insolence.) What's this silliness? What's this madness? There are so many beggars stand-ing around the church, and the church has so many children so rich, it can't come to the aid of a single beggar. One is hungry, the other is drunk; one relieves herself in silver, the other doesn't even have bread. What's this madness? What's this great savagery? Let's not enter into the temptation of proceeding against those who disobey or enter into the indignation of not encouraging them in these matters, but let's readily and patiently

D avoid all these defects, so that we may live for the glory of God, and be freed from punishment in the hereafter, and may attain the blessings promised to those who love him, through the grace and love for humankind of our Lord Jesus Christ, with whom to the Father, together with the Holy Spirit, be glory, power, honour for ever and ever. Amen.

HOMILY DELIVERED AFTER THE REMAINS OF MARTYRS ETC. (NEW HOMILY NO. 1)

INTRODUCTION

That this homily was delivered in a suburban martyrium in the vicinity of the city of Constantinople is clear not just from the title, but also from the presence of the empress and the expected attendance of the emperor at the synaxis to be held on the morrow. From the opening to the homily we learn that such spectacular occasions draw a large crowd, presenting the preacher with a diverse audience. In this particular instance a variety of language groups are also represented. The piety displayed by the empress throughout the lengthy procession and accompanying ceremonies occasions an opportunity for John to launch into an example of imperial panegyric, such that the majority of the homily is taken up by exaggerated praise of the young woman and her virtues.

The destination of the procession and location of the martyrium at which the homily was delivered, Drypia, has yet to be securely identified, but is thought to have lain to the south-west of the city along the Via Egnatia (Janin 1969: 252). This identification has been made on the basis of John's comment that the procession at night resembled a 'sea' that 'stretched from the city right up to the present location'. However, John uses the sea and associated images frequently as a topos in his preaching and his subsequent assertion that the procession could likewise be called a 'river of fire' discourages one from placing too great a weight upon the statement. Regarding the date of the homily, as Kenneth Holum argues the imperial regalia that Eudoxia sets aside for the duration of the festivities indicate that she had been elevated to the status of Augusta (Holum 1982: 56). Since that ceremony took place on 9 January 400 the homily can only have been delivered after that date. Holum further argues that it must date before 10 January 402, since there is no mention of the imperial heir Theodosius II, who must otherwise have been somehow involved in the proceedings (Holum 1982: 56 n. 35). Whether this latter supposition is correct or not, the overblown praise of the empress may indicate that relations between John and Eudoxia were at this point relatively cordial, which would suggest an only slightly later *terminus ante quem*. Regarding the status of the trade in martyrs' remains in the late fourth century with special reference to Constantinople and this homily see the Introduction, Chapter 2.

Translated from PG 63,467–72.

TEXT

467 *The address delivered in the martyrium in the presence of the empress and the entire city and the magistrates, after the empress had gone to the Great Church in the middle of the night and taken from there the remains of the martyrs and escorted them through the extent of the market-place as far as Drypia. The martyrium there is nine miles outside the city.*

8 *a.i.* What can I say? What shall I speak? I'm jumping with excitement and aflame with a frenzy that is better than common sense. I'm flying and dancing and floating on air and, for the rest, drunk under the influence of this spiritual pleasure. What can I say? What shall I speak? (Shall I speak) about the power of the martyrs? the enthusiasm of the city? the zeal of the empress? the assembly of the magistrates? the disgrace of the devil? the defeat of the demons? the noble lineage of the church? the power
468 of the cross? the miracles of the Crucified? the glory of the Father? the grace of the Spirit? the pleasure of all the people? the excited jumping of the city? the groups of monks? the bands[1] of virgins?
10 *a.i.* the ranks of priests? the effort of the laymen, the slaves, the free, those in authority, those subject to it, the poor, the wealthy, the strangers, the citizens? It would be fitting to say of it all: '*Who will speak of your powers, Lord? Who will make heard all your praises?*' (Ps. 106:2).

Women, who keep to their chambers and are softer than wax, left their covered dwellings and rivalled in enthusiasm the strongest of the men by completing the lengthy journey on foot –
469 not only young women, but old ones too. Neither the weakness of their nature nor the delicacy of their lifestyle nor vanity over their

public image impeded their enthusiasm. Again, even magistrates left behind their carriages and staff-bearers and body-guards and rubbed shoulders with the common people. Yet why should I speak of women or magistrates, when she who wears the imperial crown[2] and is dressed in purple could bear to be separated not even a little from the remains for the entire extent of the journey? Rather, like a maidservant she walked one step behind the holy
10 relics, touching the casket and the veil which covered it. Suppressing all human vanity, she allowed herself to be seen by the crowd at the midst of the vast spectacle – she upon whom it's forbidden for even all the eunuchs who serve in the imperial palace to gaze. Instead, her desire for the martyrs, the tyranny and flame of love persuaded her to cast off all her masks and to display with naked enthusiasm her zeal for the holy martyrs.

Indeed, I'm reminded of blessed David who was likewise clad in a purple robe and wore a royal crown,[3] and held the sceptre of
20 the Hebrew people. When he brought back the ark, he put aside all those props and jumped with excitement and danced and leapt about, playing the complete idiot and prancing around (cf. 1 Chron. 15: 27–9). Through his leaps, he indicated the pleasure which he felt at the celebrations. If he was obliged to display such great warmth in the shadow and the type, it should be much more the case in respect of the grace and the truth, since she (sc. the empress) has led back a casket of much greater value than that of David. For it doesn't contain stone tablets, but spiritual ones – a blossoming grace, a radiant gift, bones
30 that reflect the very rays of the sun. No, rather they release flashes of light that are more brilliant. After all, demons experience no adverse effects when they look at the rays of the sun. But, unable to bear the brilliance that bursts forth from here, they're blinded and flee and take refuge at a considerable distance. So great even is the power of the ashes of the saints that it doesn't just sit inside the remains, but extends beyond them and repels the unclean powers and abundantly sanctifies those who approach with faith.

That's precisely why this woman who loves Christ kept
40 following along beside, constantly reaching out and touching the remains, absorbing their blessing and teaching everyone else about this beautiful and spiritual merchandise;[4] instructing everyone to draw from this fount that's constantly drained but is never emptied. After all, just as the waters that bubble forth from the springs aren't contained within their own hollows

but well over and flow beyond, so too the grace of the Spirit that accompanies these bones and dwells with the saints both extends
50 towards others who follow it with faith and flows from mind into body, and from body into clothing, and from clothing into shoes, and from shoes into a person's shadow. That's precisely why it infused not just the bodies of the holy apostles, but also their kerchiefs and aprons (cf. Acts 19:12). Indeed, it wasn't only their kerchiefs and aprons but Peter's shadows also that performed deeds more powerful than those of any living things (cf. Acts 5:15). Even before then, it seems, a sheepskin placed over Elisha's body brought upon him a twofold blessing. It wasn't just Elisha's body, but the piece of clothing too that became filled with grace (cf. 1 Kgs 19:19; 2 Kgs 2:13–14).
60 Precisely the same phenomenon occurred with the three boys. It wasn't only their bodies that the character of the flame respected,
470 but even their shoes (cf. Dan. 3:27). And in the case of Elisha (the grace) didn't even (diminish) when he was dead. Death was released when another corpse was thrown into the prophet's grave (cf. 2 Kgs 13:21). So too has it turned out to be the case today: while the remains were being conveyed, demons were bursting into flame. Cries of grief and shrieks went up everywhere, as the ray of light leapt forth from the bones and proceeded to burn to a crisp the opposing powers in their phalanx.

That's why I'm jumping with excitement and flying under the
10 influence of pleasure – because by emptying the city you've made the wilderness a city; because today you have demonstrated to us the wealth of the church. See how many sheep are here and not a wolf in sight; how many grape vines, and no thistles anywhere; how many ears of grain and no weeds about! A sea stretched from the city right up to the present location – a sea devoid of waves, that brings no shipwreck, and is free from rocks; a sea sweeter than any honey, more pleasurable to drink than pure drinking water. One wouldn't be wrong in calling this sea also a river
20 of fire. So throughout the night the lamps packed tightly together in a continuous line stretching as far as this martyrium supplied a vision of a fiery river to those watching.

And that was in the night! When the day appeared other lamps were in turn revealed. For as the sun rose, on the one hand it obscured those lamps and rendered them fainter, while on the other it showed up more brightly those in the mind of each participant. I mean that the flame of your enthusiasm was

hotter than that flame which could be seen. Each carried a double
lamp – the lamp of flame in the night; the lamp of
30 enthusiasm in both the night and the day. Rather, I would no
longer even call it night. For it rivalled the day as it wheeled
you, the *sons of light*,[5] around and revealed you brighter than
the countless stars and Bringer of Morn.[6] Just as those who are
drunk make the day night, so too those who stay awake and
observe night-long vigils render the night day. It's for exactly
that reason that all night long they chanted that prophetic
song: *'In my wantonness let light be as night. Darkness won't be
made dark by you, and night will become as bright as day. Its darkness
40 will be like its light'* (Ps. 139:11–12). Didn't this night become
brighter than any day with everyone jumping around in so
great an excess of joy – in possession of a spiritual joy – as the
result of so large a crowd of people pouring out and flooding
both the street and the market-place? I mean that there wasn't
a bare piece of pavement to be seen. Rather, the entire street
was covered by human bodies. For the entire journey you displayed a single golden and continuous chain, a single river carried along with considerable impetus.

When we gazed up at the heavens, we saw the moon and stars
in its midst. When we looked down, (we saw) the crowd of the
50 faithful and, carried along in the middle, more radiant than the
moon, the empress. I mean that, just as the stars below are better
than those above, so too is this moon brighter than that one.
Why? Is the moon as great as a person in so elevated a position
of authority who is adorned with so profound a faith? What
quality of hers would one marvel at first? Her zeal, hotter than
a flame? Her faith, stronger than adamant?[7] Her contrite mind
and her humility, which caused her to hide all her (insignia)?
On the one hand, she cast off imperium[8] and crowns and all of
the vanity that arises from these in considerable abundance; on
60 the other, instead of the stole of purple she donned the stole of
humility and, because of it, became all the more radiant. For,
although there have been many, many empresses who have just
471 shared the stole itself and the crowns and the imperial glory, the
adornment of this woman alone has stood out as exceptional and
this trophy belongs to her alone. I mean that she alone among
empresses has escorted martyrs with such great honour, with
such great zeal and piety, mingling with the crowd, dispensing
with her entire retinue, and banishing virtually the entire
inequality of her lifestyle to a high degree. That's precisely

why she has benefited the populace no less than the martyrs. Just
as everyone was looking in the direction of the remains, so
10 too did they gape at this woman's attentiveness – both rich and
poor – as they watched her hold tightly onto the bones for so
long a journey, neither growing weary nor moving back, but
hanging onto the chest. Because of these actions we won't
cease calling you blessed – not just we, but all the future generations also.

I say this because the ends of the earth and all the land which
the sun covers will hear about what took place here. The people
of our time will hear, as will those who come after them and no
age will consign the event to forgetfulness, since God is spread-
20 ing its fame with much publicity everywhere throughout the
world and throughout all future generations. If he caused the
action of a female prostitute to reach the ends of the earth and
rendered her immortal in people's memory (cf. Matt. 26:13),
even more so won't he allow to be forgotten the work of a
decorous, grave and prudent woman who has displayed such
great piety in imperium. Rather, everyone will call you blessed –
as the woman who showed hospitality to the saints, the patron[9]
of the churches, the woman equal to the apostles in zeal. For, if
you did receive a feminine nature, nonetheless it's possible for
30 you to rival the apostles in good works too. After all, that
Phoebe, who at that time welcomed into her house the teacher
of the world and became his patron, was a woman and shared
the same nature as yourself. Yet, even so, her status became
such that the holy apostle who was worthy of the heavens and
greater than all the rest acclaimed her and said: '*She has become
patron of many and of myself*' (Rom. 16:2). Priscilla too had
received a feminine nature. Yet it was no impediment to her
when it came to being acclaimed and her memory becoming
40 immortal (cf. Acts 18; Rom. 16:3). And there was another large
band of women at that time who shared in the apostolic life.

We wouldn't be wrong therefore if we now numbered you
with them, seeing that you're a harbour for all the churches
and have used to the full the present kingdom for the purpose
of possessing the kingdom that is to come. You've corrected
churches, honoured priests and put an end to heretical error.
You've showed hospitality to martyrs, not with your table but
with your heart, not with your tent but with your character.[10]
472 Rather, it was with both tent and character. Miriam too once led
forth the people, while following the bones of Joseph (cf. Exod.

90

15:20), and sang a song. She did this after the Egyptians had been drowned; you've done it while demons were being throttled. She did this after Pharaoh had been drowned; you've done it following the humiliation of the devil. She did this wielding cymbals; you've done it with your mind and soul resounding louder than a trumpet. She did this because the Jews had been set free; you've done it because the church is being crowned. She did this leading forth a single nation of like tongue; you've done it leading forth countless nations of
10 different tongues. I say this because you've led forth for us countless choruses, who struck up the psalms of David, some in the Roman language, some in Syriac, some in the language of the barbarian,[11] some in Greek. One could see diverse ethnic groups and diverse choruses all holding a single lyre – that of David – and crowning you with their prayers.

Missing from the exuberance of this festival was the emperor, who is very much loved by God and who pulls the plough of piety at your side. But this too stems from your good sense, that you have kept him at home today and promised that he'll be
20 present tomorrow. For, acting in a manner indicative of your intelligence, you divided up the celebration, so that the mass of horses and the din of armed soldiers wouldn't cause grief to virgins, elderly women and older men and throw the festival into chaos. Had they both been present today, the events of the festival would have come to an end today. But, so that she might effect peace and quiet on the present day and cause exuberance to abound through the addition of tomorrow, she has divided the obligation with him and, while she herself is present today,
30 has promised us that he'll be present tomorrow. Just as she shares the imperium with him, so too does she share her piety and doesn't allow him to be without a role in her good works, but in every instance takes him on as a partner.

So, since this spiritual celebration is going to be extended for us into tomorrow, let's again demonstrate the same zeal so that, just as today we saw this woman who loves Christ with the city, so tomorrow we may behold the emperor who is beloved of God present with the army, offering to God the same sacrifice, namely
40 that which stems from piety, from zeal, from faith. Taking the holy martyrs as partners in our prayers, let's pray that they may have a long life, a ripe old age, children and grandchildren. And (let's pray that), beyond all these blessings, this zeal is added to, their piety increased, and that in this way they end

91

the present life, so that throughout the incorruptible ages too they reign together with the only-begotten Son of God. *'For if we endure'*, it says, *'we shall reign together with him also'* (2 Tim. 2:12). May we attain too (may we all deserve them!) the eternal blessings through the grace and love for humankind of our Lord

50 Jesus Christ, with whom to the Father, together with the Holy Spirit, be glory now and always, for ever and ever. Amen.

A HOMILY ON MARTYRS

INTRODUCTION

This festival homily, delivered most probably in a suburban martyrium in the vicinity of Antioch (Mayer 1996: 335–6), is one of the few in this category to appear without a title in the edition of Montfaucon. The circumstances of the procession to the site at which the sermon is preached differ little from those of the preceding homily. In place of the empress is the local governor; in diversity and size the crowds are not dissimilar. The participation of the governor suggests that, in the same way that at Constantinople the imperial couple would involve themselves in the processions associated with major liturgical occasions, so at Antioch one of the resident magistrates (the *comes Orientis* or the *consularis Syriae*), if a Christian, might seek to participate in such processions for political or other purposes.

Just as the previous homily highlighted the attractiveness of such occasions, in this homily John makes it clear that those festivals which had settled into the local calendar suffered from an accretion of behaviours associated with annual non-Christian festivals, such as the Kalends.[1] The habit of calling in at the pub on the way home in order to celebrate, coupled with a few rounds of dice and some socialising, was evidently well entrenched in the lives of John's audience.

It should be noted that, contrary to the practice of employing inclusive language which we follow elsewhere in our translations, we here refer to the generic martyr in the masculine in order to remain faithful to the character of the text, and in order to allow the moment later in the homily when John refers to the martyrs involved as both male and female to be reflected clearly in the translation. The date of the homily is at present unknown.

Translated from PG 50,661–6.

TEXT

661 *2 a.i.* The festivals of the martyrs are assessed not just by the cycle of
662 *2 a.i.* days, but also by the disposition of those who celebrate them. For
example: have you imitated a martyr? have you emulated his
663 virtue? have you run in the steps of his philosophy? Even when
it hasn't been a martyr's day, have you celebrated a martyr's
festival?[2] I mean that to honour a martyr is to imitate a
martyr. For as those who commit worthless acts don't participate
in the festivities on actual festivals, similarly too those who
pursue virtue celebrate a festival even when no feast day exists.
For the festival is characterised in the purity of the conscience.
Paul too made this clear when he said: 'As a result *let's feast
not on the old yeast of evil and wickedness, but on the unleavened*
10 *bread of sincerity and truth*' (1 Cor. 5:8). Mind you, unleavened
bread exists among the Jews, as it does too among us. But in
their case the unleavened bread is made of flour, in ours it is
purity of life and a way of life free of all evil. Thus the person
who keeps their life free of filth and blemish celebrates a festival
every day, is constantly observing a holy day, even if it isn't on
the day or they aren't at the shrines of martyrs, but are actually
sitting at home. I mean that it's possible to celebrate the festival
of martyrs by oneself too. I also say these things not so that we
20 avoid being present at the tombs of the martyrs, but so that,
when we are present, we approach with the appropriate zeal
and show the same reverence not just on their days, but also
apart from these.

For who wouldn't wonder today at our assembly, at the magnificent spectacle, the fervent love, the warm disposition, the
unrestrained desire? Virtually the entire city has transferred
itself here, and neither has fear of one's master kept away a
slave, nor the necessity of begging a poor person, nor the
infirmity of age an elderly male, nor the softness of nature a
30 woman, nor the vanity of wealth a rich person, nor the madness
of power the governor.[3] Rather, the yearning for the martyrs has
disposed of all of this inequality and physical infirmity and
poverty-driven need and dragged this large crowd here with a
single chain. It has given wings too to the yearning for the
martyrs, as if they were dallying as citizens in heaven. I say
this because you have trodden on any partiality for excess and
licentiousness and are consumed with longing for the martyrs.
40 For just as wild animals flee with the sun's first rays and sink into

94

their holes, when the light of the martyrs irradiates your minds
every sickly thought is buried and the bright flame of philosophy
is lit. But, in order that we may preserve this flame not just at
this moment, but always, let's go home with the same reverence
when this spiritual spectacle is finished, and not discharge ourselves into pubs and brothels and drinking and revels. You
50 made the night day through the holy vigils. Don't make the day
in turn night through drinking and drunken debauchery and
dirty ditties. You honoured the martyrs with your presence,
your attention, your zeal. Honour them too with your orderly
departure, lest someone see you behaving shamelessly in a pub
and say that you didn't come because of the martyrs, but in
order to increase your passion, to gratify your wicked desire. I
say this not to prevent you from indulging, but to prevent
you from falling into sin; not to prevent you from drinking,
but to prevent you from getting drunk. It's not the wine
60 that's disgusting, but the lack of restraint that's wicked. For
wine is a gift of God, but lack of restraint is an invention of
664 the devil. *Therefore serve the Lord in fear and exult in him in trembling*
(Ps. 2:11).

Do you want to enjoy indulgence? Enjoy it at home where there
are many people to care for you, should you become drunk. Don't
do it in a pub, so that you avoid being a public spectacle for those
present and an offence to others. And in saying this I'm not order-
ing you to get drunk at home, but not to spend time in a bar.
Think how ridiculous it is for a man or woman after a gathering
10 of this kind, after vigils, after hearing the holy scriptures, after
sharing in the divine mysteries and after spiritual fortification
to be seen to spend the whole day in a pub! Don't you know
what kind of punishment awaits those who get drunk? For
they're thrown out of the kingdom of God and fall away from
the inexpressible blessings and are sent off into the eternal fire.
Who says this? Blessed Paul. *'The greedy'*, he says, *'drunkards,
the verbally abusive, robbers – not one will inherit the kingdom of
God'* (1 Cor. 6:10).

What could be more wretched than the individual who's
20 drunk, when for the sake of a little pleasure they lose the enjoy-
ment of such a kingdom? Rather, the person who's drunk can't
even enjoy pleasure. For pleasure is an outcome of moderation;
(the outcome) of immoderation (is) insensibility. How can a
person perceive the pleasure of the beverage, when they can't tell
where they're sitting or lying? How could they enjoy festivity,

when they can't see the sun itself because of the thick cloud of alcohol? For such is the extent of the darkness they encounter that the sun's rays are insufficient to dissolve that gloom. Beloved, heavy drinking is always bad, but especially on a day
30 that belongs to martyrs. For along with the sin there's also considerable violence and delirium and contempt for divine utterances – which is why the punishment too would be doubled. If, then, you're going to attend martyrs and drink after your departure from here, it's better that you remain at home and neither act shamefully, nor do violence to the martyrs' festival, nor cause offence to your neighbour, nor besiege your mind,
40 nor add to your sins. You've come to see people lacerated, covered in blood, decorated with a row of wounds; people who have shed the present life and are clinging to life in the future. Be worthy of the competitors. They despised life. Despise indulgence! They shed the present life. Shed the desire for heavy drinking!

Do you still want to indulge? Stay beside the tomb of the martyr; there pour out fountains of tears. Have a contrite mind; raise a blessing from the tomb. Take her as an advocate in your prayers and immerse yourself perpetually in the stories
50 of his struggles. Embrace the coffin, nail yourself to the chest. Not just the martyrs' bones, but even their tombs and chests brim with a great deal of blessing. Take holy oil and anoint your whole body – your tongue, your lips, your neck, your eyes – and you'll never fall into the shipwreck of drunkenness. For through its pleasant smell the oil reminds you of the martyrs' contests, and bridles and restrains all wantonness in considerable
665 patience, and overcomes the diseases of the soul.

Do you wish rather to spend time in orchards and meadows and gardens? Don't do it now, while there's so large a crowd, but on another day. For today is a time for struggles; today is for the viewing of clashes, not for indulgence or leisure. You didn't come today to give yourself up to recreation, but to learn how to compete, how to excel as an all-rounder[4] and, though human, how to thrash the power of the invisible demons. No-one indulges themselves when they enter the
10 wrestling ring, nor worries about their appearance when the time for the wrestling bout arrives. Neither do they ask for lunch at the moment when battle-lines are drawn. So, then, seeing that you've come to view courage of soul, and strength of mind, and a new and wonderful trophy, and an unusual fight, and

wounds and battles, and an all-round contest involving a human being, don't introduce demonic actions and give yourself up to drinking and indulgence after this strange and terrifying spectacle. Rather, gather together the rewards of the soul and in this way go home, indicating to all by the way you look that you are returning from viewing martyrs.

20 My point is that in the same way that those who descend from
666 the theatres reveal to all that they've been thrown into turmoil, confused, enervated through the images they bear of everything that took place there, the person returning from viewing martyrs should be recognisable to all – through their gaze, their appearance, their gait, their compunction, their composed thoughts. (They should be) breathing fire, restrained, contrite, sober, vigilant – announcing the spiritual life[5] within through the movements of their body. In this way, then, let's return to the
10 city – with the appropriate discipline, with orderly walking, with intelligence and common sense, with a mild and calm gaze. *For a man's clothing, and the laughter of his teeth, and the step of his foot give out information about him* (Sir. 19:27 **LXX**). Let's always return from martyrs, from spiritual incense, from heavenly meadows, from new and wonderful spectacles in this way, so that we ourselves may enjoy much contentedness and become envoys of freedom for others, and attain the blessings that are to come, through the grace and love for humankind of
20 our Lord Jesus Christ, with whom to the Father, together with the Holy Spirit, be glory, power, honour now and always, for ever and ever. Amen.

ON HIS RETURN

INTRODUCTION

Delivered in Constantinople shortly after Easter 402, if we accept the chronology of Kelly (1995: 165–73), this homily demonstrates the tension between episcopal duties and their demands and the desires of John's regular audience. Many in the audience expected that, as bishop, John personally would perform the baptisms that took place at Easter every year and considered that without his participation the rite was somehow less efficacious. Despite his lengthy absence in Asia Minor, however, the goodwill of the general Christian population of Constantinople towards him was at this point still apparently intact. The heights of rhetorical exaggeration, the flattery of the audience and the expressions of false humility uttered in the opening paragraphs and throughout the homily show that John recognises that on this occasion he has his listeners in the palm of his hand.

When Wenger published the Greek text of the homily in 1961, the sermon had previously been known only from the Latin versions available in a number of manuscripts. The Latin texts probably derive from a fifth-century translation from the Greek (Wenger 1961: 110). Important as the Greek text is, it differs in some respects from the Latin and on occasion makes sense only if a phrase or word is imported from the latter. In order to present as clear a translation as possible our translation is based on the Greek text with insertions from the Latin supplied in square brackets as necessary. In addition, divergences in the Latin text from the style and contents of the Greek are noted and the alternate reading in the Latin is provided in the accompanying footnote.

Translated from Wenger (1961: 114–23). Wenger supplies the Greek text found in *cod. Mosquensis 159* and the most ancient of the Latin texts, *Vaticanus lat. 3836.*

TEXT

114 *The same, {John Chrysostom}. When he returned from Asia.*[1]

1. Moses was a great man. He was the servant of God, the chief of the prophets, the one who crossed the sea, the charioteer of the air, the one who set manna on the table. He was thrown away by the woman who bore him and saved by her enemy (his mother put him out to die, but the Egyptian princess picked him up and raised him). He was raised in Egypt and was a citizen of heaven; he set an outstanding[2] trophy[3] over the Egyptians; he froze a sea and split a rock in two and talked with God as a friend.

2. When that outstanding[4] man left his people for just forty days, he found them in a state of rebellion and lawlessness.[5] Yet I, after not forty days, but fifty or a hundred or more, have found you disciplined and displaying both wisdom[6] and piety to a greater degree. [Not because I'm greater than Moses – far from it! (to say that is the height of madness)][7] – but because the people here are more sensible than those.

3. That's exactly why, when he descended the mountain, (Moses) twisted accusations against Aaron;[8] but in your presence I weave hymns of praise[9] and plait victor's crowns.[10] For where there's transgression accusations (follow), but, where there's righteous living, (there follow) praises and crowns. That's why, even if I did spend a great deal of time out of town, nonetheless I was confident of your good intent, your love, your trustworthiness, your goodwill, because I knew that my wife is a woman who strives to be sensible.

4. That's the way it happens too in worldly affairs. I mean that when a man has an incorrigible wife, he doesn't let her set even a foot outside the house. And if ever he's forced to make a trip away, he works hard at getting back quickly, goaded on by suspicion as if by some spur. But the man who has a sensible wife takes his time while he's out of town, leaving his wife's character as an adequate guardian of her safety.

5. It's this situation that I and Moses experienced. For in his case, since he left behind an incorrigible wife – the synagogue – God
116 urged him, saying: *'Get up, go down, for your people have transgressed the law!'* (Exod. 32:7). I, on the other hand, received no such command but kept on tending the sick[11] without concern.[12] *For it's not the healthy who have need of a doctor, but those who are in a bad way* (Matt. 9:12).

6. But, if I deserted you, it wasn't out of contempt for you, but to enhance your wealth. For the faults which have been corrected through me – rather, through grace[13] – are your crown. And that's why I'm filled with joy and jumping with excitement and I'm flying under the influence of pleasure. I'm filled with joy. Yet, when it comes to explaining the extent of my joy, I cannot. What, then, (can I do) to make it happen? How (can I help) you to learn the extent of my joy? I call your consciences as a witness, for, from your own experience on catching sight of me, you know how it was with us, convinced through seeing the sight (for yourselves).[14]

7. If, in my case, the arrival of just one man filled so many people with so much pleasure, how much pleasure wouldn't the sight of so many men, whom I've missed dearly, work up in my heart? When he saw just one son, Joseph, Jacob too was filled with joy and the old fellow was rekindled with life (cf. Gen. 46:29–30). But for my part, it has been on seeing not one son, but tens of thousands one after the other – indeed, the people in their entirety.[15]

8. That's why I'm filled with joy, because I've received my own garden,[16] a garden better than that garden (of old). For there, there was a serpent setting snares, here, Christ is instructing us in the mysteries; there, Eve was working her deception, here, the church is being crowned; there, Adam was being deceived, here, a people is being publicly acclaimed; there, there existed trees of different kinds, here, there are gifts that are diverse and spiritual. In the garden there were trees that withered, in the church there are trees that never shed their fruit; and, what's astonishing, this garden doesn't just protect its plants, but also transforms them.[17] If I find a thistle, I work it into a grapevine; if I find a fruitless olive, I turn it back into one that bears fruit. Such is the nature of this soil.

9. That's why I'm filled with joy and jumping with excitement. Not, mind you, that, because I'm filled with joy, I pass over my justification. For, beloved, seeing that it was so great an interval of time that kept us away, receive my justification. If you'd sent a slave off somewhere, wouldn't you demand an account on his return? 'Where did you drag your heels? Where did you waste so much time?' I too am a slave – of your love for me. You purchased me, not by throwing down silver, but by demonstrating your love. I rejoice in this slavery and would wish that I never be released. For this slavery is better than an (emperor's) crown;[18]

118 this slavery procures the kingdom of heaven;[19] this slavery is better than freedom; this slavery prepares a throne for me on that tribunal;[20] this slavery isn't one of compulsion, but is a matter of free choice.

10. Since you're such crazy lovers, who wouldn't gladly serve you as a slave? Even if I had a heart of stone, you would have made it softer than wax. What can I say about the burning desire which you displayed, the mania of yesterday, the frenzy, the shouting in the market-place.[21] You sanctified the air. You made the city a church. I was held in honour and it was God who was welcomed. Heretics were put to shame, the church was crowned, you were publicly acclaimed. For it's plain sailing for a church when the root is bound firmly to the branches, when the shepherd sleeps in the fold with the sheep.[22]

11. I arrived and I received good news. What sort? That you had run riot over heretics; you had argued into receiving baptism those who were acting lawlessly. It wasn't without point that I said that, while her husband was away, the sensible wife confounded her would-be adulterers; that, in the shepherd's absence, (the flock) chased away the wolves; that, without their captain, the sailors got the ship home safe; that, without their general, the soldiers raised the trophy; that, without their teacher, the students [advanced]; that, without their father, the children [grew up big and strong]. Rather, it wasn't without [their father].[23] For your virtuous actions are my crown, my proud boast.[24]

12. 'But', you say, 'we had out hearts set on observing Easter with you.' If it was the bulk of your anger that you released on catching sight (of me), I offer that as my justification. For, if a father on welcoming his worthless son became reconciled and didn't demand of him an account, but at once enfolded him in his embrace (cf. Luke 15:20), it's far more the case with children when they welcome their father.

13. 'But', you say, 'we wanted to observe Easter with you.'[25] Well, all right, I'll justify myself on that account too. You wanted to observe Easter with me? There's nothing stopping you. Observe Easter with me today.[26] 'Are we then to observe two Easters?' No, rather the one and the same Easter over and over. My point is that just as the sun is constantly rising and we don't see numerous suns – just the one rising day after day – so the Paschal feast too is constantly being celebrated, and yet all the time it's the one Pasch that's being observed.

14.   The Jews' observances and ours are not alike. I'm not a slave to location. I'm not subject to the necessity of particular moments in time. *For as often as you eat this bread and drink of this cup, you proclaim the death of the Lord* (1 Cor. 11:26). On this day too let's proclaim the death of Christ. While then it was a feast day,[27] today too is a festival. For where there's love there's a festival. Where you've lost your father in death, children, there is a festival. For even that occasion is a festival of love. *For God so loved the world that he gave his only-begotten son for us* (John 3:16).

15.   'But a large number were in fact baptised without your being present.' And so what? The grace is no less effective. The gift is not defective. They weren't baptised in *my* presence, but they *were* baptised in the presence of Christ. Surely it's not a human being who does the baptising? A human being lends their right hand; it's God who moves it. Beloved, don't be hesitant about the grace. On what grounds? Let me tell you. Baptism is a gift.[28]

16.   Pay careful attention to what I say! Just as, if you submit a petitition and get it back with the emperor's signature, you don't trouble yourself over with what sort of pen the emperor wrote, nor on what sort of paper, nor in what sort of ink, but look for just one thing – whether the emperor put his signature at the bottom – so too in the case of baptism is a piece of paper the conscience, a pen the priest's[29] tongue, a hand the grace of the Spirit. Whether, then, it's (conferred) through *me*, whether through *that* priest, it's the same hand that writes.

17.   We're public servants, not the people in power. Even Paul is a public servant. *'Thus'*, he says, *'let a person consider us as public servants of Christ and as managers of God's mysteries'* (1 Cor. 4:1). *'For what do you have that you didn't receive?'* (1 Cor. 4:7). If I have something, I've received it. Indeed if I've received it, it isn't mine, but the gift of the person who gave it. Beloved, don't then be in any doubt. When grace was perfected, the location wasn't a hindrance, not even if they were on a ship. Philip baptised on the road, Paul in a prison; Christ led the thief into paradise.[30]

18.   That's why I'm filled with joy and delight and I ask for your prayers – with which I set out, with which I also returned. I took part in a sea voyage; yet at sea your love made the waters calm. I didn't board a boat without you, I didn't disembark for overnight lodgings without you, I didn't enter a city or a church

without you. Instead, even though I was separated from you in body, I was bound close to you in love.

19.   Even at sea I would view the church as tranquil. For our love is of a kind that knows no restrictions. I would enter a church, I would stand beside the altar and all the while I would be thinking of your church and, lifting up my prayers, I would say too: 'Lord, hold in trust the church you entrusted to me. I'm not present, but you are present – you who led me there and by God's grace have brought to pass more than I asked.'[31] I asked that he might keep an eye on you, and he fulfilled it. The

122   large crowd that's here is a witness – so many luxuriant vines and nowhere any thistles, so many sheep and not a wolf in sight. Should there somehow be a wolf, it's transformed and becomes a sheep.[32] God himself kept an eye on you, God himself brought me back home. Your prayers cured my ill-health. This I keep on saying every day.

20.   My travels crowned your city. That you loved me was clear even before this point, but not obvious to everyone. Only the person in love had knowledge of it, but the separation provided proof of that love. Constantly people arriving in Asia would report to me:[33] 'You've set the city on fire!' And yet love withers with time, while your love increased. It didn't succumb to forgetfulness, but was inflamed all the more. But I ask that you love me in the same way now that I'm actually here. This is my treasure. This is my wealth. That's why I seek your prayers. Your prayers (build) a wall around me and (provide) security.

21.   Don't say to me: 'I'm a lay person. How am I to pray for a priest?' Listen to scripture, when it says: *'There was unceasing prayer offered up by the church'* (Acts 12:5) and Peter's chains were released. It was prayer that freed Paul from silence (cf. Acts 13:1–3),[34] prayer that tamed the lions (cf. Dan. 6:19– 22), prayer that muzzled the whale (Jonah 2), prayer which opened up paradise. Prayer opened wide the vaults of heaven.[35] The prayer of Cornelius penetrated to the depths of heaven (cf. Acts 10:1–8). Prayer turned the tax collector into a righteous man (cf. Luke 18:10–14).

22.   I ask for this security from you on my own behalf. There's a further favour that I ask: that God on receiving your prayers bestow upon you an abundance of blessings, both now and in the time to come, in Christ Jesus, to whom be the glory for ever.[36] Amen.

ON THE STATUES HOMILY 17

INTRODUCTION

Delivered at Antioch on Saturday, 27 March 387 (van de Paverd 1991: 352–7), the homily is one in a series preached by John in the course of the Lent that followed the riots during which the statues of the emperor were overturned. In it he details the events that occurred at Antioch on the day of the second trial, at which there presided the imperial delegates Caesarius and Ellebichus. Caesarius was the brother of Aurelianus, whom John was to antagonise as a result of his participation in the negotations with Gainas which took place in the vicinity of Constantinople in 400. In 387 Caesarius held the office of *magister officiorum* at Constantinople. Ellebichus, his fellow judge, was at that time *magister militum per Orientem* and therefore resided at Antioch, where his headquarters were situated. As the title states, they had been authorised by the emperor to convene a second trial in order to assess the guilt of the decurions of Antioch. Despite the focus on the events associated with this trial, the homily was not delivered until nine days later. On the evening of the trial itself it was reported by Ellebichus that, despite the heavy penalties involved in the sentence that was passed, none of the arrested would be executed and that the city would not be razed to the ground, as had been feared.

What is of particular interest in this homily is the picture that John supplies of the monks that lived in the mountains surrounding Antioch. Despite their proximity to the city John suggests that they have little or no participation in its worship life. Yet they exhibit a profound pastoral concern for the well-being of Antioch's inhabitants. They are prepared to take action in a time of crisis and place their own lives at risk by speaking with boldness to the emperor's representatives, rather than rely solely upon their more usual supplication of God in prayer. To a large extent this emphasis on their *parrhēsia* is a rhetorical fiction designed to highlight the contrast between the actions of the pagan philosophers and these true philosophers.[1] Even so, the appearance of virtuoso ascetic individuals in the city of Antioch at a time of crisis is not unprecedented (Theod., HR 8.7–8) and in this respect John's account undoubtedly reflects some degree of truth, even if it is difficult after the event to separate fact from fiction.[2]

Two other aspects of the homily are worthy of note. The equally bold and equally pastoral actions of presbyters from the local Antiochene church at the time of the trial are alluded to, but largely overshadowed by the emphasis on the monks' novel presence and behaviour. In the opening to the homily the allusion to the antiphon for the day provides some insight into the status of the liturgical calendar at Antioch, as well as providing a convenient jumping off point for the topic on which John wishes to embark. If the text as transmitted to us faithfully reflects what John preached, then his opening remark may represent a case of ad-libbing, before he moves onto his preprepared sermon.

Translated from PG 49,171–80.

TEXT

171 *On the officers,[3] the general Ellebichus and Caesarius the magistrate, who were sent by the Emperor Theodosius to examine the offenders on acount of the overturning of the statues.*

It's opportune that we've all sung together today (the antiphon): 'Blessed be the Lord God of Israel who alone works wonders' (Ps. 72:18), because indeed wonderful and surprising events have 30 *a.i.* taken place. An entire city and a great many people who were about to sink and become submerged and be suddenly destroyed completely, he rescued from total shipwreck in one critical moment. Let's give thanks, therefore, not only becase he's put an end to the storm, but because he also permitted it to happen; not only because he's saved us from shipwreck, but because he also allowed us to fall into such great anguish and allowed the extreme danger to hang over us. So Paul too orders us to give thanks in all things. When he says: '*In all things give thanks*' (1 Thess. 5:18), this means not only at delivery from 20 *a.i.* adversities but also at the actual time of adversities. *For those who*

105

love God all things work together for good (Rom. 8:28). Let's give thanks to him for the delivery from trials, and never forget them. Let's be intent on prayer, frequent petitions, great reverence.

When at the outset the grievous fire of these ills was kindled, I said that it wasn't a time for instruction but a time for prayers. I say that now, too, when the fire has been extinguished, because it's now especially a time for prayers, more than before; now it's especially a time for tears and compunction, and for a prepared soul and much zeal and much firmness of purpose.[4] I say this 10 *a.i.* because on the previous occasion the very nature of the afflictions restricted us, however unwillingly, and prepared us to be sensible and induced us to greater reverence. Now, on the other hand, when the bridle has been removed and the cloud has passed on, I'm afraid in case we're inclined to take things easily, in case we become relaxed again because of the remission, in case someone says about us as well: *'When he slew them, they began to look for him, and they repented and rose early to pray to God'* (Ps. 78:34). That's why Moses exhorted the Jews with the words: *'When you have eaten and drunk and are full, remember* 172 *the Lord your God'* (Deut. 6:11–12). Now your rightmindedness will be obvious if you persevere in the same reverence. On the previous occasion many attributed your zeal to fear and the onslaught of adversities. Now, on the other hand, your achievement will be pure, if you persevere in maintaining the same zeal. A boy, too, as long as he's guided by a pedagogue he fears, and 30 *a.i.* lives with common sense and forebearance, is nothing wonderful, but everyone attributes the young fellow's common sense to his fear of the pedagogue. But when he perseveres in the same propriety after he's divested himself of the necessity (of obeying the pedagogue), then too everyone attributes to him the common sense he showed when he was younger. Let's do this too. Let's persevere with the same reverence so that for our former zeal too we may enjoy great praise from God.

We were expecting innumerable adversities: that everyone's property would be plundered, that dwellings would be set 20 *a.i.* alight with their inhabitants, that the city would be plucked from the middle of the world, and all that remained of it would be destroyed, that its foundation would receive the plough. But all of a sudden all of this existed only in our expectation and didn't become reality. And the amazing thing is that God not only did put an end to such great danger, but that he granted us the greatest benefits, and adorned our city, and through that tribulation and disaster made us more esteemed. I'll tell you how this happened.

10 *a.i.* When the representatives were sent from the emperor to examine what had happened, and organised that frightening law-court, and summoned everyone to account for what had been perpetrated, and everyone expected that various people would die, the monks who inhabit the mountain tops demonstrated their particular kind of philosophy. Although they had been shut up for so many years in their own cells, when they saw such a great cloud encompassing the city, at nobody's behest and on nobody's advice, they left their tents and their caves and flowed together from every direction, just like angels

173 arriving from heaven. Then it was possible to look on the city as similar to heaven, when those holy people appeared everywhere, their mere appearance consoling those in grief and leading them to disregard the disaster completely. On seeing them who wouldn't have laughed at death? Who wouldn't have disdained life? This wasn't the only amazing thing, but also the fact that, on approaching the magistrates, they frankly engaged in discussion on behalf of the accused and were all prepared to

10 shed their blood, and lay down their lives[5] so that they might snatch the captured from the expected adversities. They stated that they wouldn't leave until either the judges spared the people of the city or sent themselves together with the accused to the emperor. 'The one who rules over our part of the world', they said, 'is a friend of God, a believer who lives a pious life. We shall therefore win him over completely. We won't permit you, or agree, to bloody the sword, or to cut off a head. But if you don't stop, we'll certainly go to our death

20 with them. We too confess that the deeds that were perpetrated were heinous, but the illegality of what's happened doesn't sur-pass the generosity[6] of the emperor.'

One of them is said to have made another statement, full of wisdom:[7] 'The statues which were thrown down have been erected again, and have resumed their proper appearance, and the crime has been rectified with the utmost speed. But if you were to kill the image of God, how would you be able to make good your mistake? How would you raise from the dead those you had killed, and restore their souls to their bodies?'

30 They spoke to them at length, too, on the subject of the Last Judgement.

Who is there who wouldn't be astonished? Who is there who wouldn't admire the men's wisdom? The mother of one of the accused, with bare head and showing her grey hair, took hold by the bridle the judge-designate's horse and, running through the market-place alongside him, entered the lawcourt in this manner. We were all astonished; we all admired her love for her son, her generous spirit. How wouldn't we be more struck with admiration for those men? I say this because even if she'd died for the sake of her son, this would have been nothing
40 wonderful, because the tyranny of nature is great, and the compulsion caused by giving birth is irresistible. But those men hadn't given birth (to the accused) nor even brought them up – I should say they hadn't laid eyes on them, or listened to them, or ever met them. They knew them only from the calamity they were in. But they loved them to the extent that, even if they'd had a thousand lives, they would've chosen to surrender all of them for the safety of the accused. Don't tell me that they weren't killed or even spilled their blood, but that they availed themselves of much frank talk with the judges as is proper only for those who have given up their own lives, and
50 that with this resolve they had run down from the mountains to the lawcourt. If they hadn't previously prepared themselves for every kind of killing, they wouldn't have been able to speak so freely to the judges on that occasion, or to have displayed such generosity of spirit. Indeed, they spent the whole day sitting outside the doors of the courtroom, prepared to snatch from the executioners those who were about to be taken to prison.

Now where are those wearing threadbare cloaks, sporting a long beard and carrying a staff in their right hands – the pagan philosophers, canine outcasts who are more miserable than dogs under the table and do everything for the sake of their
174 stomachs?[8] At that time they all left the city, they all leapt away and hid in caves. It was only the ones who by their actions had truly demonstrated wisdom who appeared so fearlessly in the market-place, as if no adversity had overtaken the city. While the inhabitants of the cities fled to the mountains and the deserts, the citizens of the desert rushed to the city, showing by their actions what on previous days I haven't stopped talking about, namely that not even a furnace will be able to harm in any
10 way the person who lives a virtuous life. Wisdom of soul is a thing of such magnitude, being superior to everything, and to all auspicious and sorrowful events. For neither does it become

puffed up by the former, nor cast down and humiliated by the latter, but retains its equilibrium through all events, demonstrating its peculiar strength and power. Who wasn't put to shame by the difficulty of the present crisis? Those who hold the highest offices in our city, those in power, those invested with untold wealth, those who had easy access[9] to the emperor, all left their houses deserted and took counsel for their own
20 safety. Every friendship and family connection was treated with contempt, and the people whom they had once known in the time of calamity they didn't want to know, and prayed not to be known by them. The monks, on the other hand, were poor people who had nothing more than a shabby cloak and had lived a rough existence,[10] who seemed before that to be nobodies, being used to mountains and gullies like lions. With great and lofty purpose, while everyone was fearful and cowering, they came publicly and put an end to the adversity, not over many
30 days but in a brief critical moment. They were like noble warriors who don't come into close conflict with their opponents, but simply by appearing in the ranks and shouting cause the enemy to rout. So too, in one day, these men came down from the mountains, and made their point, and put an end to the calamity, and returned to their own abodes. So great is the philosophy that was brought by Christ to human beings.

Why do I speak of the rich and of those in power? When those very men who had the authority to act as judges, those who hold
40 the highest offices, were appealed to by these same monks to grant a sentence of pardon, they claimed they had no power over the outcome. They said that it was unsafe and dangerous not only to insult the emperor, but also to release without penalty those who had insulted him and had been arrested. But the monks were more powerful than everyone, and by taking their seat with generosity of spirit and patience petitioned (the judges) to exercise a power which they hadn't received from the emperor.

When the men were clearly convicted, the monks were able to persuade the judges not to pass a sentence of condemnation but
50 to delay the outcome until the emperor had come to a decision. They promised to win him over completely to grant a pardon to those who had offended against him; and they were about to leave to see him. The judges, out of reverence for the monks' wisdom and being struck by their lofty spirit, didn't allow them to undertake this long journey, but (said that) if they

could only have what they said in written form, they would depart and petition the emperor to cease from anger entirely (which, indeed, we are expecting to happen). When the verdict was to be pronounced (the monks) went into the court and
175 made pronouncements of great wisdom, and appealed to the emperor in writing. They reminded him of the judgement and said they would lay down their own lives if their request wasn't granted. When the judges had taken down these words in writing, they left. This will ornament our city more gloriously than any crown. Now what has taken place here the emperor will hear, indeed the great city[11] will hear, and the whole world will hear that the monks who inhabit the city of Antioch have dis-
10 played the boldness of the apostles. When their letters are read out at court[12] everyone will admire their generosity of spirit, everyone will call our city blessed, and we'll get rid of our bad reputation. Everyone will know that what happened wasn't the work of the inhabitants of the city, but of strange and corrupt people, and that the testimony of the monks will be a sufficient indication of the character of the city.

Well, then, beloved, let's not be distraught, but look to the future with high hopes. If the frankness of the monks towards human beings was able to avert such calamity, what will their
20 frankness[13] towards God not achieve? Let's say this to the pagans when they dare to talk to us about philosophers. From present events it's patent that what they claimed in former times is also false. From present events it's clear that what we claimed in former times is also true, namely the reports about John and Paul and Peter and all the rest.

Because of the fact that they've become successors of the apostles as far as their piety is concerned, they have consequently received the apostles' frankness of speech as well. Because of the fact that they were brought up in the same laws, they've conse- quently emulated the apostles' virtue. The result is that we've no need of writings to demonstrate apostolic virtue, when the
30 facts themselves are crying out and the pupils are pointing to their teachers. We've no need of words to demonstrate the non- sense of the pagans, and pusillanimity of their philosophers, while facts present and past are crying out that everything of theirs is a fable, a theatrical trick, and play-acting.

It wasn't only the monks who manifested the same generosity of spirit, but also the priests, and they shared the responsibility

for our safety. One of them went to the court,[14] giving his love
for you precedence over all else, and he was prepared to die him-
40 self if he couldn't win over the emperor. The other priests, who
stayed here, demonstrated the same qualities as the monks: holding back the judges with their own hands, they prevented them
from entering the court before they had made a promise about
the outcome of the trial. And when they saw them making
signs of dissent, they again spoke very frankly. But when they
saw that the judges were making signs of assent, clasping their
feet and knees and kissing their hands, they gave a pre-eminent
demonstration of both virtues, freedom of spirit and gentleness.
That theirs was not the boldness of presumption they showed to
50 the greatest degree by kissing the judges' knees and clasping
their feet. By the same token, that these acts were not flattery,
nor some kind of servility, nor the product of a slavish mind
was attested to by their former acts of boldness. We harvested
not only such advantages from our ordeal, but also great
restraint,[15] great gentleness. Our city suddenly became a monastery. One couldn't have adorned it to such an extent by erecting
golden statues in the market-place, as it's now brilliant and distinguished through having produced beautiful statues of virtue
and having proven its own wealth.

Yes, the decisions of the emperor are painful. Yet these are not
176 intolerable, but have themselves brought great benefit. Tell me,
what's burdensome in what has happened? Is it that the emperor
has shut the theatre?[16] that he's made the hippodrome out of
bounds, that he's closed and buried the springs of iniquity?
May they never again be opened! From them grew the roots of
iniquity in the city. From them came those who give its character a bad name, who sell their voices to dancers and for three
10 cents[17] make a present of their own salvation to them, turning
everything upside down. It's for these reasons you're distressed,
beloved? For these reasons in fact you should be glad and rejoice,
and express your gratitude to the emperor, because his punishment has become a correction, and his penalty training, and
his anger an instruction. Or is it that the baths are closed to
us? But that's not unbearable either, if it brings those who are
living a soft, empty and dissolute life back to wisdom against
their will. Or is it because the emperor has taken away the
city's status and hasn't permitted it to be called a metropolis
any more?[18] But what should he have done? Praised what had
20 happened and expressed his gratitude? Who wouldn't have

blamed him for not making even a show of indignation? Don't you see that fathers do many similar things to their own sons? They turn away from them and keep them away from the table. This is what the emperor did too in inflicting punishments like these, which in themselves contain no harm but bring great correction. Think what we expected and what happened, and then especially we shall know the grace of God.

30 Are you pained because the city's status has been removed? Learn what the status of the city is and then you'll know clearly that if the inhabitants don't betray it, no-one else will be able to remove the status of the city. It's not that it has the rank of metropolis, nor that it contains large and beautiful buildings, nor many columns, and wide porticos and covered walks, nor that it's proclaimed publicly before other cities. Rather it's the virtue and piety of its inhabitants that's both the status and ornament and defence of a city, such that, if these aren't present, it's the most paltry of all, even if it were to enjoy untold honour from emperors. Do you want to know the status of your city?

40 Do you want to know its ancestry? I'll tell you exactly what they are, not only so you may learn, but so that you may emulate too. What, then, is the status of this city of ours? *It was in Antioch that the disciples were first called Christians* (Acts 11:26). None of the cities in the world has this claim, not even the city of Romulus itself. That's why it's able to look the whole world in the face, because of its love for Christ, because of that boldness[19] and courage.

Do you want also to hear of yet another status which the city

50 has, and of a reason to praise it? Once a very severe famine was imminent, and the inhabitants of Antioch decided, as far as each one had the means, to send relief to the holy people who lived in Jerusalem (Acts 11:27–30).[20] See, this was a second (proof of) status, kindness in a time of famine. The circumstances didn't constrain them in their giving nor did the expectation of the calamity make them reluctant. Rather, when everyone was collecting what belonged to others, they gave freely of what

177 was theirs, not only to those close by, but also to those who were at a distance. Have you seen their faith in God and their love towards their neighbour? Do you want to know of another status which this city has? Certain people came from Judaea to Antioch, defiling the Christian proclamation and introducing Jewish observances. Our people couldn't endure this innovation

112

in silence, nor could they refrain from speaking out. Coming together and having an assembly, they sent Paul and Barnabas
10 to Jerusalem, and had the apostles send everywhere in the world pure doctrines, removed from every Jewish sickness (cf. Acts 15). This is the status of the city. This is its privileged position. This made it a metropolis, not on earth but in heaven. All other honours are corruptible and perishable, and dissolve with the present life, and often even come to an end before the present life does, as indeed they have done in the present circumstances. To me, a city that doesn't have citizens who love God is worth less than any village, and less honourable than any cave.

Why do I speak of a city? So that you may learn exactly that
20 it's only virtue that adorns its inhabitants, I'll say nothing to you about the city, but I'll try to demonstrate my point by adducing the temple of God in Jerusalem, which is more hallowed than any city. For this was the temple in which sacrifices and prayers and worship took place, where the Holy of Holies was, and the Cherubim, and the Tabernacle, and the golden urn, the greatest symbols of God's providence towards that people; where oracles were constantly delivered from heaven, where prophets were
30 inspired, where the construction was a work not of human craft but of the wisdom of God, where the walls on every side shone with copious gold, and, in surpassing excellence and the combination of expensive material and precision of craft, showed that there was only one temple like this on earth at that time. Rather it was not only the precision of craft but also the wisdom of God which assisted in its construction. For Solomon had learned everything not from his own intellect or by himself, but from God, and once he had received the plan (of the temple) from heaven, he marked it out and erected it. Still, when those who used it were corrupted, that beautiful, marvellous, holy
40 temple was dishonoured and despised to such a degree, and profaned, that even before the captivity it was called 'a cave of robbers' (Jer. 7:11), 'a cave of hyenas' (Jer. 12:9 LXX), and afterwards it was given into hands that were barbarous, foul and profane.

Do you want to learn the same lesson about cities too? What was more splendid than the cities of Sodom? For the homes and buildings were splendid, and so were their walls, and the land was rich and fertile, and *similar to the paradise of God* (Gen. 13:10). But Abraham's hut was shabby and small, and had no defences. Yet when a war broke out with the barbarians, the
50 barbarians destroyed the walled cities utterly and captured them,

and went away after enslaving their inhabitants, whereas when
Abraham, the citizen of the desert, attacked them, they couldn't
withstand him. And rightly so, because he had a power much
stronger than numbers and the defence of walls, namely piety.
If you're a Christian, you don't have a city on earth. It's God
who's *the builder and maker* (Heb. 11:10) of our city. Even were
we to gain possession of the whole world, we are *strangers and*
178 *pilgrims*[21] in it all. We're enrolled in heaven; it's there that we're
citizens. Let's not, like little children, neglect things that are
great and admire those that are little.

It's not a city's greatness, but a soul's virtue that counts as its
adornment and security. If you suppose that a city has status,
think to yourself how many pimps, how many degenerate and
corrupt people, and people full of countless vices, share in that
dignity, and finally despise that honour. But (the city in
heaven) isn't like that, because it's impossible for anyone to
10 share in it who hasn't displayed every virtue.

Well then, let's not be silly, but grieve when someone
deprives us of the status of our soul, when we commit sin,
when we have offended the common Master of all. Regarding
what's happened recently, not only won't the events harm the
city in any way, but if we're vigilant, they will in fact benefit
us in the greatest degree. Indeed, now our city seems to us
like a graceful, free-born and sensible woman. Fear has made
her gentler and more dignified, and has rescued her from those
foul people who were involved in the shameless deeds which have
20 taken place. So let's not lament like women. I've heard many
people in the market-place say: 'Poor Antioch! What's happened
to you? How is it that you've been dishonoured?' When I heard
this I smiled at the childish mind that could utter such words.
One shouldn't make those comments in the present circumstances. But when you see people dancing, drunk, singing, blaspheming, swearing, perjuring themselves, lying, then you must
say this to them: 'Poor city! What's happened to you?' But if you
see that the market-place contains a few men who are gentle and
sensible and moderate, you must call that city blessed.
30 I mean that the fact that they're few will never be able to harm
it in any way, if virtue is at hand as well, just as numbers will
never be of any avail whatsoever, if iniquity is present. '*If*', it
says, '*the number of the sons of Israel is like sea sand, the remnant
will be saved*' (Isa. 10:22; Rom. 9:27). It means: 'Numbers

114

won't be able to prevail with me at all.' Christ spoke like this too. He called cities wretched not because of their paucity of numbers and not because they weren't of metropolitan status. And, again, he called Jerusalem itself wretched for the same reason when he said: *'Jerusalem, Jerusalem, you have killed your*
40 *prophets and stoned those who were sent to you'* (Matt. 23:37). Tell me, what benefit do numbers bring if their lifestyle is evil? On the contrary, even injury results from it. Indeed, what else has lately caused the evils which have occurred? Wasn't it laziness, and neglect, and the depravity of the inhabitants? Surely its status didn't avail the city in any way? Surely it wasn't the size of its buildings? Surely not the fact that it was a metropolis? If, as far as the emperor on earth was concerned, nothing could protect it when it had erred on this point, but all those privileges were removed, how much more with regard to the Lord of angels
50 will its status fail to protect it at all. On that day it can't avail us at all that we live in a metropolis which has wide porticos and the other status symbols of that kind. Why do I mention that day? As far as present life is concerned, what will it avail you that your city is a metropolis? Indeed, has anyone put right the miseries of a household by this means? Or had any income? Or got rid of depression by means of its rank? Or put an end to bodily infirmity? Or laid aside evil of the soul?
179 Beloved, let's not play games, nor consider the assumptions of the majority, but learn what indeed the status of a city is, what indeed it is that makes it a metropolis.

I say this in the expectation that the city will recover its former dignity and will reappear in its own place of precedence, in that the emperor is both generous[22] and a friend of God. But if it *is* restored, I don't want you to entertain great ideas on this score, or boast of it, or hold the city in reverence because of it. When you wish to praise the city, don't tell me about its
10 suburb, Daphne, nor about the number and height of its cypress trees, nor its springs of water, nor the numerous people who live in the city, nor that its market-place is frequented with great freedom right until very late in the evening, nor of the abundance of market goods. All these things belong to the senses, and last for the duration of this present life. But if you can call on virtue, gentleness, almsgiving, vigils, prayers, common sense and wisdom of spirit – adorn the city with these qualities. To those who live in the desert, the presence of these qualities

makes Antioch more splendid than any city; and, on the other
hand, the shabbiest of any if these qualities aren't present
20 among its citizens.

Let's make this statement not only of cities, but also of people.
If you see a person who's plump, who's in very good condition,
who's tall and towers over others because of body length, don't
admire them until you've thoroughly ascertained the state of
their soul. It's not from external shapeliness but from the
beauty which adorns the mind that we should call anyone
blessed. David was small and short of stature, but nonetheless
a man who was short and small and bereft of any weapons
30 with one blow brought down a large camp and that tower of
flesh. It wasn't by throwing a spear, or shooting an arrow, or
unsheathing a sword, that he achieved all this, but by throwing
a small stone (cf. 1 Sam. 17). It's on this account that someone
exhorts us in these words: *'Don't praise a person for his beauty, do
not loathe a man for his external appearance. The bee is small among
winged creatures, and yet her fruit is the source of sweet things'* (Sir.
11:2, 3 LXX).

180   Let's say this about cities and men too, and make these wise
comments to each other, and be continually thankful to God
both for present and for past events. Let's appeal to him together
with all our fervour, so that both those who are in prison may be
set free, and those who are going to go into exile may come back.
They too are our members; with us they have been tossed by the
waves; with us they have withstood the storm. Let's, then,
10 request our generous[23] God that they may enjoy the calm with
us. Don't let someone say: 'What concern have I with the rest?
I've escaped the danger. Let that person perish, let the other
one be destroyed.' Let's not provoke God by this disdain, but
feel pain as if we ourselves were in such trouble, so that we
may appeal to God with fervour, fulfilling that saying of Paul:
*'Be with those in prison as if you were in prison with them, be with
those who are ill-treated as if you yourselves were also in their bodies'*
(Heb. 13:3), *'and weep with those who weep, associate with the lowly'*
(Rom. 12:15, 16). This will also be of the greatest advantage to
20 ourselves, because nothing usually delights God so much as our
extreme readiness to feel pain on behalf of our members. Let's
appeal together to him, then, both for present and future
events, so that he may snatch us from that punishment. Whatever the nature of present events, they can be tolerated and they

116

come to an end. But the torments in the future life are eternal and inescapable.

With this consolation let's make an effort ourselves not to fall into these kinds of sin any more, since we know that hereafter we shall be able to enjoy pardon. Together, then, let's all fall down
30 before God, and both when we're here and when we're at home let's say: *'You are just, Lord, in all your dealings with us, because whatever you've brought upon us you've brought upon us with a just judgement* (Neh. 9:33). *If our sins rise up against us, deal with us for your name's sake* (Jer. 14:7), and don't allow us to experience such adversities any longer. *Lead us not into temptation, but deliver us from evil* (Matt. 6:13), because yours is the kingdom and the power and the glory for ever and ever. Amen.'

AGAINST THE GAMES AND THEATRES (NEW HOMILY NO. 7)

INTRODUCTION

That this homily was delivered at Constantinople is evident from John's comment that one year has elapsed since he arrived and from the transmarine procession to the Church of Sts Peter and Paul that took place on the preceding Wednesday. The date can also be determined with relative precision. It was delivered in early July 399[1] only a few weeks before the spectacular and abrupt downfall of Eutropius (Kelly 1995: 147). The arguments which support this date are reliable and make it impossible to interpret as Good Friday the day on which the offending horse-races occurred, as might otherwise seem to be indicated by John's comments in the second paragraph of the homily. It seems that, just as in *On his return* he indicated that every Sunday is to be viewed as a celebration of the resurrection (or Pascha), so every Friday is to be considered a commemoration of Christ's crucifixion.

In this homily the effect of the proximity between the palace–hippodrome complex and the Great Church and *episkopeion* upon the audience is highlighted. Competing secular attractions constantly lure away John's male parishioners. Of interest too is the reference to the liturgical activity occasioned by the festival of Sts Peter and Paul on the preceding Wednesday and the procession which takes place by boat to the Church of Sts Peter and Paul at Rufinianae. As at Antioch, too, we see John threatening to ban offenders from church and bar them from the eucharist. Because a large part of the homily addresses a failing that is restricted to men, we retain the masculine wherever it is clear that John is addressing the male members of his audience exclusively.

Translated from PG 56,263–70.

118

TEXT

263-4 *Our holy father John Chrysostom, archbishop of Constantinople. A homily against those who leave the church and desert it for the hippodromes and the theatres.*

263 Is this bearable? Is this to be tolerated? I want to appeal to you against yourselves. This is what God did with the Hebrews. Appealing to them against themselves, he said: '*My people, what have I done to you, and in what have I grieved you, or in what have I annoyed you? Answer me*' (Mic. 6:3). Again: '*What fault did your fathers find in me?*' (Jer. 2:5). I'm going to copy this and ask you again: Is this bearable? Is this to be tolerated? After long courses of sermons and so much teaching, some left us
10 and went off to watch the horse-races, and became so frenzied that they filled the entire city with cries and disorderly shouting, which involved loud laughing rather than lament. When I was sitting at home and heard the sound erupt, I suffered worse than those buffeted by heavy seas: just as they fear the end because of the danger when the waves have broken against the sides of the ship, so too those shouts broke worse on me, and I hung my head in shame and hid my face. Those who were up high disgraced themselves by such actions, while those down in the middle of the general audience clapped the charioteers and shouted worse than they did.[2]

264 What shall we say? How shall we justify ourselves if some stranger or other who is standing by says accusingly: 'Does the city of the apostles allow this? Does the city that received such a prophet[3] allow this? Does the populace who loves Christ, the simple spiritual theatre,[4] allow this? You don't even revere that day on which the symbols of the salvation of our race were being celebrated. On a Friday, when your Master was being crucified on behalf of the world and such a sacrifice was being offered, and paradise was being opened, and the robber was being led back to his old native land, the curse was being
10 undone, and sin was disappearing, and temporal war was being destroyed, and God was being reconciled to human beings, and everything was being changed – on that day you should have been fasting and giving praise and sending up prayers of thanksgiving for all the blessings in the world to the one who made them. Then did you leave the church and the spiritual sacrifice, and the gathering of brothers and sisters

119

and the sobriety of fasting? Were you carried off to that spectacle as the devil's captive?'

Is this bearable? Is this to be tolerated? I won't stop saying
20 that unremittingly, assuaging my own pain with it, nor oppress-
265 ing it by silence but bringing it into the open and putting it in front of your eyes. How shall we be able to make supplication to God in the future? How shall we placate his wrath? Three days ago rain and heavy showers broke, and swept away everything, snatching the table from the very mouth, as it were, of the agricultural labourers, flattening the long ears of corn, making everything else rot because of the excess of humid matter. There were litanies and prayers of intercession, and our entire city went like
10 a torrent to the places of the apostles, and took as their advocates Saint Peter and blessed Andrew, the pair of apostles, Paul and Timothy. After that, when God's anger was placated, crossing the sea, daring the waves, we went to the chief apostles, Peter the fundament of the faith, Paul *the vessel of choice* (Acts 9:15), and celebrated a spiritual festival, proclaiming their struggles, their trophies and their victories over the demons. And you,
20 who are neither struck by fear at what happened nor instructed by the magnitude of the apostles' achievements, suddenly after an interval of one day do you jump with excitement and shout, as you observe your own soul being swept away, a prisoner to passions? If you wanted to see animals race, why didn't you yoke together the animal passions in yourself, anger and lust, and put on them the yoke of philosophy, which is good and light, and set over them correct thinking, and drive them to the prize of a vocation above, not running from defilement to defilement but from earth to heaven? This kind of hippodrome
30 provides benefits with great pleasure. But you thoughtlessly left your own affairs to turn out as luck would have it, and sat in judgement on the victory of others, spending such an important day without purpose, idly and in evil.

Don't you know that, just as when we entrust silver to our household slaves, we demand an account of them to the last cent,[5] so too does God demand reckoning of the days of our life, of how we have spent each day? What, then, shall we say? What excuse shall we make when we're demanded to account
40 for that day? The sun rose on your account, and the moon illuminated the night, and a variegated band of stars shone down. The winds blew on your account, the rivers ran. Seeds grew on your account and plants were yielded, and the course of nature kept its

266 own order, and day appeared and night was gone. All of these phenomena happened on your account. But, while created things are serving you, do you fulfil the devil's desire? Although you have rented such a great house – I mean this world – from God, you don't pay the rent.

And it wasn't enough for you (to behave this way) on the first day, but also on the second, when you should have ceased for a little from the evil in between, you went back again to the theatres, running from smoke into fire, lowering yourself into another more unpleasant pit. Old men brought shame on their
10 grey hair, and young men threw their youth down a precipice, and fathers took their sons there, from the beginning leading youth without experience of evil into the pits of wickedness, such that one wouldn't be wrong in calling such men child-killers instead of fathers, who destroy their offspring's soul by evil. 'What evil?' someone asks. I feel pain at this because, although you're sick, you don't know it, so that you could look for a doctor. You've become filled with adultery, and you ask: 'What evil?' Didn't you hear Christ warning: *'The one who looks*
20 *at a woman to desire her has already committed adultery with her'* (Matt. 5:28)? 'What, then', you say, 'if I don't look at her to desire her?' And how could you convince me? The man who isn't strong enough to stay away from spectacles but makes such an effort in a matter like this – how will he be able to remain spotless after watching? Surely your body isn't stone? Surely it isn't iron? You are encased in flesh, human flesh, which is ignited by desire more quickly than hay is.

And what shall I say about the theatre? For the most part, if we meet a woman in the market-place, we're disturbed. But you,
30 sitting up there where there's such a great demand to behave disgracefully, if you see a woman who's a prostitute coming on stage with bare head and great shamelessness, dressed in golden garments, weak and corrupt, singing dirty ditties, degenerate tunes, mouthing shameful words, conducting herself so disgracefully (sights which, after you have watched, you take into your mind) – do you hang your head in shame? Do you dare to say that you feel no human emotion? Surely your body isn't stone? Surely it isn't iron? I won't be able to avoid saying the same things again. Surely you aren't more of a philosopher
40 than those great and noble men who were brought down by a mere look? Haven't you heard what Solomon said: *'If someone walks on burning coals, won't he burn his feet? If someone puts coals*

121

in his lap, won't he burn his clothes? The same is true of the man who approaches the wife of another' (Prov. 6:28, 27, 29)?

The point is that, even if you aren't intimate with the prosti-
267 tute, you've copulated with her by desire and have committed
the sin in your thoughts. This doesn't happen either on that
one occasion, but when the theatre is finished and she has
gone, the image of her is stored up in your soul – her words,
her appearance, her glances, her walk, her rhythm, her enuncia-
tion, her lewd tunes, and you go away, taking with you countless
wounds. Aren't homes overturned as a result of that? Doesn't loss
of common sense occur as a result of that? Doesn't the break-up
of marriages result from that? Don't wars and battles result fom
10 that? Don't irrational dislikes result from that? I mean that,
when you return home as a captive, full of this woman, both
your wife seems rather distasteful, and your children seem
rather tiresome, and your servants a nuisance, and your house
too much, and the usual cares associated with running the necessary affairs of the household appear troublesome, and everyone
who belongs to it is tiresome and a nuisance.

The cause of this is that you didn't return home alone but had
the prostitute with you, although she didn't return in a clear and
visible way. That would have been easier, because your wife
would have got rid of her straight away. But the prostitute
was lying in wait in your thoughts and in your consciousness,
20 igniting the Babylonian furnace inside you – I should say, a
much worse one. There was namely no hemp and naphtha and
pitch, but the things I've mentioned became fuel for the fire
and everything was turned upside down. It's like those who
have a fever. Even if they have no cause for complaint against
those who are caring for them, because of the consequences of
the illness they become annoyed with everyone, refusing their
food, abusing the doctors, being angry with their relatives and
furious with those caring for them. So too those who are ill
with that severe illness change, are disagreeable, because they
30 see that woman everywhere. O what difficult circumstances these
are! The wolf and the lion and all the other wild animals flee the
hunter when they're shot; but when the completely rational
human being is wounded he pursues the woman who's wounded
him, so that he receives a much more serious barb and rejoices in
the wound. This is the sharpest thing of all, and renders the illness incurable. How would the man who doesn't hate his wound
or wish to be free of it look for the doctor?

It's because of this that I feel pain and am cut in two, because when you've suffered such great corruption you leave the theatre, and for the sake of a small pleasure sustain a pain that's con-
40 tinuous. Moreover, even before hell[6] and punishment, in this situation you're demanding the extreme penalty for yourselves. Tell me, isn't it in the nature of extreme vengeance to nourish such desire and continually to be on fire, and to carry around everywhere a furnace of absurd love and the accusation of your conscience? How will you come in those holy doors? How will you touch the heavenly table? How will you hear the sermon on common sense when you're full of ulcers and so many
268 wounds, and have a mind enslaved to passion? What need is there to say anything else? From those now present with us it's possible to see the pain of the mind. Yes, now I see those beating their foreheads while I'm saying this, and I'm very grate-ful to you because you're such a compassionate people. I think perhaps that many who haven't sinned at all are doing that, because they're pained by their brothers' wounds.

It's because of this that I feel pain and am cut in two, because
10 the devil is ruining a flock like this one. If you were willing, we could block his way immediately. How and in what manner? If we could see the ill restored to health; if we were to go around unfolding the nets of teaching, looking for those who've been caught by wild beasts, and snatch them from the very jaws of the lion. Don't say to me: 'The deserters are few in number.' Even if there were only ten of them, the loss wouldn't be trifling, or even if there were five, or two or one. Since that shepherd left the ninety-nine sheep on that score and went after the one sheep, and didn't return until he'd brought it back again, and by the
20 restoration of that stray he made whole the number one hundred, which was incomplete (cf. Matt. 18:12–13). Don't say: 'It's just one.' Think that it's a soul, on account of which all things visible were made; on account of which there are laws and penalties and punishments, and countless wonders, and the various affairs of God; on account of which he didn't spare even the only-begotten One. Think what a high price was set even for one soul, and don't think little of its salvation: go and bring it back to us and persuade it not to fall into the same evils any more, and we'll have sufficient excuse. But if it doesn't desist, not even
30 when either we're giving advice or you're encouraging it, I'll then use the power which God gave us, not in order to destroy but to build up.

123

This is why I'm telling you in advance and shouting loudly that if anyone deserts to the lawless corruption of the theatres after this exhortation and teaching, I won't receive him within these precincts, I won't administer the mysteries to him, I won't permit him to touch the holy table. Just as shepherds ward off the mangy sheep from the healthy ones so as not to 40 give the disease to the rest, so I'll do too. If in the olden days the leper was ordered to sit outside the camp, and even if he was a king was thrown out with his crown (cf. 2 Chron. 26:20), how much more shall we throw out of this sacred camp the man who has leprosy of the soul. Just as, to begin with, I used exhortation and advice, so too now, after so much exhortation and teaching, it's necessary finally to begin separating. One year has elapsed since I came to your city, and I haven't ceased frequently and unremittingly to exhort you on these matters. 269 Since, therefore, some have remained in this decay, quick, then, let's give them the chop. Even if I don't have a sword, I have a word that's sharper than a sword. Even if I'm not carrying fire, I have a teaching that's hotter than fire, which is able to burn more fiercely.[7]

Don't, then, think little of our sentence. Even if we're lowly and exceedingly pitiful, we have nevertheless been entrusted by the grace of God with an office which is capable of effecting this. Let such people, then, be thrown out, so that both the 10 healthy may become more healthy and the ill may recover from their serious ailment. If you were terrified on hearing this sentence (I see that many are looking gloomy and depressed), let them change their ways and the sentence is undone. Just as we've received the power to bind, so too have we the power of undoing, and of restoring the sentence again. We have no wish to cut off our brothers, but to beat off disgrace from the church. As it is, both the pagans will laugh at us and the Jews will ridicule us when we allow ourselves to sin in this way. In 20 the other case they will commend us exceedingly and reverence the church because its laws are respected by us. Let none of those who remain in this adultery set foot in the church, but let him be censured by you too and become a common enemy. It says: '*If anyone refuses to obey what we say in this letter, note that person, and have nothing to do with them*' (2 Thess. 3:14). Do this: neither speak with him, nor receive him into your house, nor share a meal with him, neither at the entrance, nor at the exit nor in the market-place. And so we'll easily recover them.

124

30 Just as hunters chase wild animals which are difficult to capture
not from one direction but from everywhere, and cast them into
the net, so too together let's chase those who've become wild
animals and cast them immediately into the net of salvation,
we from this side, you from that.

In order, now, for that to happen, you'll also be vexed along
270 with me, rather, you'll grieve on account of God's laws, and keep
those who suffer from such illnesses and act unlawfully away
from the brethren for a little while, so that you may have
them forever. For the charge to which you're subject is not a
trifling one if you neglect such a great loss, but you'll receive
the severest penalty. If in the houses of human beings one of
the household slaves surreptitiously takes silver or gold, and
not only is the thief, when caught, punished but also those
who knew of it and didn't report it, how much more so is it in
10 the case of the church. God will say to you on that occasion:
'When you saw not silver nor a golden vessel being stolen
from my house, but common sense being carried off, and the
one who received the precious body and partook of a sacrifice
like this departing for the devil's spot, and transgressing like
that, how could you keep silent? How could you bear it? How
didn't you report it to the priest? You wouldn't have had
demanded of you accounts that aren't trifling.'

This is precisely why I, too, even if it will cause me pain, will
spare nobody from the most grievous penalties. It's much better
for us to be pained here and snatch (you) away from future
20 judgement, than for me[8] to gratify (you) by my words and be
punished with you at a later date. Nor is it safe and without
danger for us to tolerate such conduct in silence. Each of you
will give account of yourself; but I'm answerable for the salvation
of all. This is exactly why I won't cease from doing and saying
all I can, even if I have to pain you, even if I have to seem a
nuisance, a burden, so that I can stand on that awe-inspiring
tribunal *having no blemish or wrinkle* (Eph. 5:27) or any such
fault. I pray, through the prayers of the saints, both that those
who are corrupted will now swiftly return and that those who
30 remain unharmed will progress to greater decorum and common
sense, so that both you may be saved and we may rejoice, and
God may be glorified now and always, for ever and ever without
end. Amen.

BAPTISMAL INSTRUCTION 8

INTRODUCTION

Despite the title, what follows is not a typical baptismal instruction but more in the character of a homily delivered at a regular synaxis, as suggested by the presence of the rural monk-priests, the general character of the contents and the specific address to the newly baptised only at its conclusion. In this respect it is not dissimilar to *Ad illuminandos cat. 2* (CPG 4464), which van de Paverd convincingly demonstrates is in fact an ordinary homily (van de Paverd 1991: 216–27). While Wenger identifies it as having been delivered at Antioch on the Saturday following Easter (Wenger 1970: 42), van de Paverd further refines the date, arguing that the presence of the visiting clergy and the recent martyrs' festivals locate it on 12 April 391 (van de Paverd 1991: 290–1).

The instruction is of interest for a number of reasons. It highlights the changing character of a preacher's audience as it is swelled temporarily due to the presence of visitors – in this case relatively poor rural Syrian priests who are also monks and who have difficulty communicating with the Antiochenes because of their language. How John resolved the difficulty of preaching to an audience containing non-Greek speakers can only be imagined. Present in the audience too are the newly baptised, probably as readily to be distinguished by their dress from the rest of the audience as the strange-looking visitors. The reference to the numerous martyrs' festivals of the immediately preceding days and to the cessation of such festivals subsequently also provides a glimpse of the changes in rhythm of the local liturgical calendar and the frequency with which the members of the audience might hear a sermon.

Translated from Wenger (1970: 247–60).

TEXT

247 *The same. Welcome and praise for those who have come from the surrounding countryside. On the theme: while all the just who have received perceptible promises set their eyes upon the imaginable instead of what they could perceive, we, on the contrary, who have received a promise of the imaginable, lust after what we can perceive; and: one should hurry to the church both just before dawn and in the evening to offer prayers and make confessions; and on the newly baptised.*

1. Your excellent teachers have feasted you sufficiently in the preceding days and you've constantly enjoyed their spiritual encouragement, sharing richly in the blessing that comes from the remains of the holy martyrs. Come, then, seeing that those who've flowed in to us from the country have rendered our
248 theatre more splendid, let's furnish for them today an even richer spiritual table, one that's brimming with the generous love that they've displayed towards us. After we've provided them with this repayment, then, and have received in turn their good-will[1] towards us, let's make an effort to show them abundant hospitality. For if they didn't hesitate to undertake such a long journey so as to bring us much joy through their presence, it's even more right that today we serve them a more generous helping of this spiritual food, so that they might return home from here having received adequate provisions for their journey.

2. I say this because they're our brothers and members of the body of the church. So, then, let's show genuine love towards them as if embracing our own members. Let's overlook the fact that they have a way of speaking distinct from our own and instead let's learn in detail the wisdom of their life. Let's overlook the fact that they have a barbarous tongue; instead let's get to know their inner thoughts, and (recognise) that these men demonstrate in practice the philosophy that we make
249 an effort to learn through discourse, and fulfil through their physical labours[2] the law of the apostles which bids that our daily food be supplied by the work of our hands.

3. I mean that they've listened to blessed Paul, when he says: '*Let's grow weary from working with our own hands*' (1 Cor. 4:12), and again: 'That *these hands have served my needs and those who are with me*' (Acts 20:34). And, by making an effort to fulfil these precepts through their own labours, they speak a language more splendid than words, and show through their actions that

127

they too are worthy of the blessing proclaimed by Christ. *'For'*, he says, *'blessed is the person who's practised and taught'* (cf. Matt. 5:19). The point is that, when teaching through deeds is given precedence, there's no longer any need for instruction through words. Indeed you could see each one of these men, at one moment standing next to the sacred bema[3] and reading out God's laws and teaching the people under their authority; at another busying themselves with tending the earth; at one time pulling the plough and carving furrows in the earth and sowing the seed and closing it over in the depths of the soil; while at another, with the plough of instruction in their hands, putting the germ of God's lessons into the hearts of their pupils.

4.   So, then, let's not simply look at their outward appearance and their mode of speech and so overlook their virtue, but rather come to know in detail their angelic way of life, their ascetic[4] conduct. For not only has all extravagance and gluttony been banished among them, but so too has every other lazy habit that's rife in the cities. They take only as much food as they need to stay alive and for the rest of the time they exercise
250 their mind in hymns and in constant prayers, and in this way imitate the angels' way of life.

5.   I mean that, just as those incorporeal powers have just one task – to praise constantly the Creator of all – in the very same way these remarkable men too satisfy the needs of their body, because they're wrapped in flesh. They then persist for the rest of the time in hymns and prayers, renouncing worldly appearances, and make an effort through their excellent way of life to draw the people under their authority into imitating them. Therefore who wouldn't rightly call these men blessed, because, although they've no experience of secular education, they've been educated in the true wisdom and demonstrate that they've fulfilled through their labours that saying of the apostle: *'That God's foolishness is wiser than human beings'* (1 Cor. 1:25).

6.   For how won't you receive a clear demonstration of God's power, when you see this common person, who's of a rural background and knows no more than the details of farming and how to care for the land, taking no account of the present, but lifting his thoughts towards the blessings stored up in heaven, and understanding how to be wise about those inexpressible blessings, and knowing precisely those truths which the philosophers

who base their reputation on their beard and staff[5] couldn't ever
251 begin to imagine? Tell me, from what other source could they
obtain such great wisdom about virtue and their ability to pay
no attention to what they see, and to give precedence over
what is manifest and at hand to what isn't clear and can't be
seen and is only to be hoped for? I mean that it's faith when a
person considers the blessings promised by God, even if they're
not visible to the eyes of this body, more reliable than those that
are visible and lie before our very eyes.

. . . (nine paragraphs follow, in which he develops this
theme, adducing examples from scripture) . . .

256
16.   Please, for this reason let's seek those promises which last forever and aren't susceptible to change. Indeed it's to this end that
I deliberately introduced this topic before you, so that I might
make my encouragement relevant to all — both to those who
were initiated some time ago and to those recently deemed
worthy of the gift of baptism. Seeing, therefore, that in the
days that have just passed, we've harvested considerable blessing
through our constant attendance at the tombs of the holy martyrs
and have benefited from the abundant instruction, while from
this point on the constant succession of services is about to be
cut off, I'm constrained to call upon your love in asking that
you keep fresh in your memory such important instruction and
hold the matters of the spirit in greater esteem than those of
this world.

17.   (I ask) too that you come here just before dawn with great zeal
and render your prayers and confessions to the God of all (cf.
Eph. 4:6), and that you give thanks for the blessings already
received and ask to be considered worthy of assistance in keeping
safe what is to come. And so, after you leave here, each of you
(should) take up the appropriate matters with all caution. Let
the one person apply themselves to the work of their hands,
257 let another hasten to their military duties, while another busies
themselves about public affairs. Let each really apply themselves
to their affairs with fear and anguish and let them complete the
course of the day in the knowledge that they're due to attend
here again in the evening to render an account of their entire
day to the Master and to ask pardon for their deficiencies. For,

even if we secure ourselves many times over, it's impossible not to render ourselves accountable for many and disparate failings. I mean that either we've made an inappropriate comment, or listened to a foolish tale, or considered an unseemly idea in our thoughts, or stared too keenly, or spent time pointlessly and idly and to no good purpose.

18.   That's why it's appropriate that each evening we ask forgiveness of the Master for all these failings and flee for refuge to God's generosity[6] and make our request. And so, after spending the whole night in sobriety, we arrive again at the confession just before dawn, so that through managing our own life each of us will be empowered to both traverse the sea of this present life unharmed and merit the Master's generosity. Whenever a time for worship[7] calls, let spiritual affairs and the assembly here be given priority over everything, so that we may manage the matters in hand too with security.

19.   I mean that, if those affairs are given priority by us, then these will cause us no effort, since God who loves humankind will make them very easy for us. But if we're careless about spiritual affairs and are zealous about these alone, and if we take no account of our soul but concern ourselves incessantly with worldly affairs, we should expect the loss of the former, while

258 in regard to the latter we'll have nothing more. Please, therefore let's not turn the established order upside down; rather, knowing the goodness of our Master, let's hand everything over to him and not stress ourselves with the worries of this world. For, the one who brought us from non-existence into existence (cf. 2 Macc. 7:28; Rom. 4:17) through his innate love for humankind will to a greater degree pay every attention in the future to our needs. *'For'*, it says, *'your heavenly Father knows that you need all these things before you ask him'* (cf. Matt. 6:32).

20.   That's precisely why he wants us to be free from all such worry and to spend every spare moment on spiritual affairs. 'If you seek spiritual affairs', he says, 'I'll provide in abundance everything that your body needs.' It's on this too that the reputation of all the just is based. I mention this because it was from (the topic of) their virtue that our sermon developed. For we said that, although they received a promise of what they could perceive, they sought out what they could imagine. We, on the other hand, practise the opposite to them and, although we have a promise of what we can imagine, we lust after what we can perceive.

130

... (there follow four paragraphs, in which he urges the audience to imitate the just and not to worry about their physical needs, but to pay attention to their spiritual ones) ...

260

25.   And, please, above all, you, who've recently put on Christ and received the descent of the Spirit, take care every day that the brightness of your clothing *receive no blemish or wrinkle* (Eph. 5:27) on any part; neither through inappropriate comments nor through listening to frivolity, nor through wicked thoughts, nor through your eyes darting carelessly and at random over whatever they chance upon. Therefore, let's wall ourselves in on every side with the constant memory of that fearful day, so that, through persevering in radiance and preserving the clothing of incorruptibility spotless and unsoiled, we may be rewarded with those inexpressible gifts. May we all obtain them through the grace and love for humankind of our Lord Jesus Christ, with whom to the Father, together with the Holy Spirit, be glory, power, honour, now and always, for ever and ever. Amen.

ON EUTROPIUS

INTRODUCTION

Delivered at Constantinople on a Saturday or Sunday in either late July or early August 399, the homily represents both a rhetorical *tour de force* and an example of opportunistic preaching. With a markedly increased attendance for the time of year due to the presence of the deposed consul-eunuch Eutropius cowering behind the veil which hid the altar, John is unable to let the opportunity to draw a moral example from the fate of this much-despised man pass him by. The irony of the man who sought to weaken the laws governing the right of churches to grant asylum himself fleeing to the Great Church in fear for his life on the preceding day was clearly not lost on either John and his clergy or the audience. John's generosity in providing the asylum that is sought and in turning Eutropius' shocking plight into a lesson in humility and mercy demonstrates the depth of his pastoral concern, both for a former adversary and for his audience.

Translated from PG 52,391–6.

TEXT

391 *A homily on Eutropius – eunuch, patrician and consul.*

It is always opportune – but particularly at this moment – to say: '*Vanity of vanities, and all is vanity*' (Eccl. 1:2). Where now are the splendid trappings of the consulship? Where are the gleaming torches? Where are the outbursts of applause and the choruses and the festivities and the public holidays? Where are the crowns and banners? Where are the uproar of the city and the

132

acclamations during the chariot-races and the flattering comments of the spectators? They've all gone. A blast of wind has
10 blown away the leaves and revealed the tree to us – naked and shaken to its very root at this moment. For such has been the impact of the wind that it's even threatening to pull the tree up by the roots and to shake its fibres violently.

Where now are those who posed as friends? Where are the drinking parties[1] and the dinners? Where's the swarm of hangers-on, and the undiluted wine[2] that filled glasses all day long, and the varied arts of the chefs, and the cultivators of power who would do and say anything to please him? They were all night and a dream and, when day came, they vanished.
20 They were all spring flowers and, when spring passed, they all withered. They were a shadow and melted away. They were smoke[3] and dispersed. They were bubbles and burst. They were a spider's web and have been torn to shreds. That's why we're chanting this spiritual maxim, saying over and over: 'Vanity of vanities, and all is vanity'. For this maxim should be inscribed permanently on walls and on clothing and in the market-place and in the home and in streets and on doors and in foyers and, above all, in each person's conscience; and it should
30 be studied constantly. Since fraudulent matters and masks and acting are thought to be true by the majority, each of you should address this to your neighbour and in turn hear it from your neighbour at dinner, at lunch and in assemblies every day: 'Vanity of vanities; all is vanity'.

392   Haven't I said to you constantly that wealth is a runaway slave? But you wouldn't put up with us. Didn't I say that it's an ungrateful servant? But you didn't want to be convinced. Look! Concrete experience has shown that wealth isn't just a runaway slave or an ingrate, but even a murderer – it's responsible for your current trembling and terror. When you objected every time that I spoke the truth, didn't I say to you: 'I love you more than those who flatter you. When I criticise, I care more for you
10 than those who aim to please'? Didn't I say in addition to these words that 'wounds inflicted by friends are more trustworthy than the willing kisses of enemies' (Prov. 27:6)? If you had put up with my wounds, their kisses wouldn't have spawned for you this death; for my wounds result in good health. Their kisses, on the other hand, laid the foundation for an incurable disease.

Where now are the wine-pourers? Where are the people who cleared a path in the market-place and sang your praises

countless times in front of everybody?[4] Because of your struggle
they've fled; they've denied their friendship; they're contriving
20 safety for themselves. But we're not like them. On the contrary,
while you vented your displeasure we didn't leap away; and now
that you've fallen we're protecting you and taking care of your
needs. Indeed, the church that you made war against has
opened its arms and taken you in, while the theatres on which
you lavished care and on whose behalf you were often angry
with us have betrayed and destroyed you. Yet even so we
didn't stop saying over and over: 'Why do you do these
things? You make frenzied attacks on the church, and yet
you're carrying yourself over a cliff.' But you ignored everything.
The chariot-races, too, once they had exhausted your wealth,
30 sharpened their sword; while the church, despite enjoying your
untimely rage, runs around in every direction in a desire to
snatch you out of their nets.

393   I'm saying these things at this point, not in order to trample
upon someone who's lying down, but out of a desire to make
safer those who are standing; not in order to rip open again
the sores of the wounded, but with the intention of preserving
in secure health those who haven't yet been wounded; not in
order to drown someone who is being tossed about by the waves,
but to teach those sailing with a fair wind how not to end up at
the bottom of the deep. How might this come about? – if we
bear in mind the changeability of human affairs. I mean that, if
this person had been afraid of change, he wouldn't have experi-
10 enced change. Instead, since he didn't improve either of his own
accord or on the advice of others, you, who pride yourselves on
your wealth, are at any rate profiting from this man's disaster.
For nothing is more trifling than human affairs. For that
reason, whatever label one might attach to their inconsequen-
tiality – whether one calls them 'smoke' or 'chaff' or 'a dream'
or 'spring flowers' or anything at all – it would express less
than the truth. They're so perishable and are more worthless
than things that have no value at all. It's clear from this that
they have much of the precipitous about them in addition to
being worthless.

20   After all, who was loftier than this man? Didn't he surpass all
the world in wealth? Didn't he ascend to the pinnacles of the
honours? Didn't everyone tremble before him and fear him?
Yet, see! He has become more wretched even than prisoners,
more miserable even than servants, more needy even than

beggars who are wasting away with hunger. Each day he's gazing
at sharpened swords and the pit and executioners and being led
away to his death. Nor does he enjoy the memory of past
pleasure, nor even perceive sunlight itself. On the contrary, in
30 his enclosed space he's deprived of sight in the very middle of the
day, as if he were in the densest night. Rather, however hard we
try, we couldn't present in words the suffering which he's likely
to be enduring as he expects with each hour that passes to be
executed. But then, what need is there of words from us when
his own affairs are clearly sketched out for us as on an icon?
For when on the previous day they came after him from the
emperor's palace[5] with the intention of dragging him away by
force and he fled towards the sacred vessels, his countenance –
40 as even now – was for once no better than that of a corpse.
His teeth were chattering, and his whole body was rattling
and trembling, and his voice kept faltering, and his tongue
was slack, and his appearance suggested that his heart had turned
to stone.

I'm saying these things, not in order to reproach him nor
trample upon his disaster, but out of a desire to soften your
minds and induce them to pity and persuade them that what
has happened is sufficient punishment. For there are many
50 among us who are so inhuman that they nevertheless criticised us
too because we received him in the sanctuary.[6] I parade forth this
man's suffering from a desire to soften their lack of compassion
with my comments.

Tell me, beloved! Why are you annoyed? 'Because', you say,
'the man who fled to the church is a person who constantly
warred against it.' So, then, we should glorify God on that
account most of all – that God let him fall into such depths
of necessity that he's come to know both the power and the
394 generosity[7] of the church. (He's learnt) its power from the enormous change in circumstance that he's undergone from his
battles against it. (He's come to know) its generosity from the
fact that the church he warred against is now putting forth its
shield, and has taken him under its wings, and has set him in
complete security. Nor has it borne any grudge for past injuries,
but has opened its arms to him with much compassion. For this
is more magnificent than any trophy; this is a manifest victory;
10 this undermines pagans, this shames Jews too; this shows the
church with a radiant face – that it spared its enemy when it
took him captive and that, when everyone else overlooked him

in his isolation, it alone hid him beneath its veils[8] like a compassionate mother, and stood up to the emperor's anger and popular rage and unbearable hatred. This is an adornment for its altar. 'What kind of an adornment is it', someone says, 'to have that accursed, greedy robber clinging to the altar?' Don't say that, since even the prostitute, who was exceedingly abomin-
20 able and impure, touched the feet of Christ (cf. John 12:3); and what happened wasn't accounted to Jesus as a fault, but as a miracle and great anthem of praise.[9] The point is that she who was unclean didn't harm him who is pure. Instead he who is pure and faultless rendered the accursed prostitute pure through the contact.

Don't bear a grudge, fellow![10] We're servants of him who was crucified and who says: *'Forgive them, for they don't know what they're doing'* (Luke 23:34). 'But', someone says, 'he blocked flight here through documents and various laws.' But look, through experience he's learnt what he did and, through what
30 he's done, is the very first to break the law. He has become a spectacle for the world and, though silent, from this experience utters words of advice to all: 'Don't do this kind of thing, in case you experience the same fate!' Through the disaster he's shown himself to be a teacher and the altar emits a great radiance – particularly fearsome at this moment – and shows by this that it holds the lion tied up. After all, in the case of an imperial icon too, considerable ornament occurs not just when the emperor is seated on the throne dressed in purple and wearing a diadem, but also when barbarians with their hands bound behind their backs are lying beneath the emperor's foot with their heads bowed.

40 Through your zeal and racing here together you are witnesses that no persuasive speeches were used. For today our theatre is magnificent and the assembly radiant and I see as great a crowd assembled here now as I saw at holy Easter. Though silent, he has summoned you all in this fashion, through his experiences uttering a voice louder than a trumpet. And you virgins deserted your chambers, and you women your women's quarters, and you men the market-place and all raced together to
50 this spot to see human nature put on trial and the feebleness of worldly affairs exposed and that whorish face (the state of well-being that derives from acts of greed is such that it comes across as more deformed than any old crone with wrinkles) as if by a sponge wiped clean of its rouge and makeup by a change in

circumstance – (a face) which yesterday or a few days ago beamed radiantly.

I say this because such is the strength of this misfortune: it has made him who was bright and illustrious above all appear rather 60 paltry now. Were a rich person to enter, they would derive considerable benefit. For, when they saw the man who used to shake the entire world brought down from such a height and in 395 straitened circumstances, and become more timid than a hare or a frog, and nailed to this column without bonds, and squeezed tight by fear instead of a chain, and filled with fear and trembling, they would check their arrogance, expunge their conceit, and depart, after reflecting upon human affairs in the philosophical way that they should. The scriptures express these thoughts through sayings and teach through experience that: *All flesh is grass, and all human glory is like a grass-flower. The* 10 *grass withers and the flower falls off* (Isa. 40: 6, 7). For example: *They will quickly wither away like grass and will swiftly fall away like green herbs* (Ps. 37:2); or *His days are like smoke* (Ps. 102:3); and similar sayings. In turn, were a poor person to enter and look at this vision, they wouldn't utterly despise themselves nor feel distress at their beggarly state. Instead, they would feel grateful that their poverty affords them a protected place, a wave-free harbour, a secure wall; and, on viewing these things, would choose over and over to remain where they are, rather than to have everything for a brief period and later be at risk of shedding their own blood.

20 Do you see how this man's flight here affords no small benefit for both rich and poor, both lowly and lofty, both slaves and free? Do you see how each person receives medicine and departs from here after being treated by this sight alone? Have I softened your passion and cast out your anger? Have I quenched your inhumanity? Have I drawn you into sympathy? I very much think so – the faces indicate it and the fountains of tears. Come, then, let's now prostrate ourselves before the emperor, seeing that for you the rock has become deep soil and the land 30 fertile (cf. Matt. 13:1–8), and we have also sprouted the fruit of charity[11] and shown that the stalks of sympathy are ripe. Rather, let's ask God, who loves humankind, to soften the rage of the emperor and make his heart gentle so that he'll grant our favour in its entirety. Already there has been no small change since the day on which this person fled here. For,

once he knew that he had run to this inviolate place, in the
40 army's presence, while it was growing inflamed at this person's
misdeeds and was demanding him for slaughter, the emperor
made a long speech and quashed the soldiers' rage. He invited
them to consider not just this person's failings[12] but, if he had
any virtue, to take this into consideration too; and he professed
himself thankful for the latter, while he pardoned the characteristics that were of contrary character as failings that were human.
But when they were inclined again towards revenge for the insult
to the emperor and were shouting, jumping, baying for death,
and shaking their spears, from that point on he let fountains of
50 tears fall from his most gentle eyes and reminded them of the
holy table to which he'd fled, and in this way put an end to
their anger.

396   Even so, let's also add our own advice. For what pardon would
you deserve if you, who've experienced nothing of the kind, were
to display such vehement anger, when the emperor who's been
insulted bears no grudge? How will you touch the mysteries,
when this spectacle is finished, and say that prayer through
which we're commanded to say: *'Forgive us, just as we too forgive
those who are in debt to us'* (Luke 11:4), when you're demanding
a penalty from the one who's in debt to you? Did he wrong
10 you greatly and insult you? There's nothing we can say in reply.
No, at the moment it isn't the time for a lawcourt, but for
mercy. It isn't the time for demanding an account, but for
generosity, not for interrogation but for concession, not for a
ballot and penalty, but for pity and grace. So then, let no-one
get heated or become upset, but rather let's ask God, who
loves humankind, to grant this person an extension of life and
snatch away the threatened slaughter so that he might shed his
misdeeds. Let's also approach the generous emperor and plead
that, for the sake of the church, for the sake of the altar, he
20 favour the sacred table in respect of this one man. If we do this,
both the emperor himself will approve and God, before the
emperor even, will applaud and will give us in return a considerable reward for our generosity. I mean that in the same way as
God hates and turns away a person who's cruel and inhumane,
he admits and loves a person who's merciful and generous.
Whether such a person is righteous, he weaves them crowns
that are more radiant; whether a sinner, he bypasses their sins
and gives them in return this reward for their sympathy towards
30 their fellow slave. *'For I want pity'*, it says, *'and not sacrifice'*

(Hos. 6:6); and everywhere in the scriptures you see him constantly seeking this and saying that this deliverance from sins exists.

By this means, then, shall we too render him merciful, in this way shall we discharge our misdeeds, in this way shall we adorn the church. In this way too the generous emperor will approve, as I said a moment ago, and the entire populace will applaud, and the ends of the earth will marvel at the humanity and gentleness of the city and, when they learn what's happened, people all over the world will cry out our name. So that we may enjoy such blessings, then, let's prostrate ourselves, let's plead, let's request, let's snatch from danger the captive, the fugitive, the suppliant, so that we too may attain the blessings that are to come, through the grace and love for humankind of our Lord Jesus Christ, to whom be the glory and the power now and always, for ever and ever. Amen.

40

ON: 'I OPPOSED HIM TO HIS FACE' (GAL. 2:11)

INTRODUCTION

In the brief extract from this homily we observe the tension which existed at one point in John's life at Antioch between the need to serve his own congregation in the Old Church as preacher and the demands of his bishop. As we learn from the title and John's opening comments, Flavian had recently required John's presence at another church at the same time that he would ordinarily have been preaching before his regular audience. Being replaced by a locum in such a situation was always risky in case a preacher was outshone and the audience transferred its attention and loyalties.[1] In the opening to the homily John gives rein to two of his favourite metaphors – the language of hospitality and of providing a lavish feast in the sermon that is dished up, and the language of navigation. The simile of the relationship between mother and infant is also typical. The New Church of the title is most probably the Great Church, called more familiarly 'new' because of its location in the new quarter of the city, the area which contained the palace and hippodrome and which occupied the island in the Orontes. The date of the homily cannot be determined.

Translated from PG 51,371–88.

TEXT

371-2 *At the previous service he celebrated with the bishop in the New Church. He delivered this homily in the Old Church on the pericope of the apostle: 'When Peter came to Antioch, I opposed him to his face' (Gal. 2:11), and showed that the event was not an opposition, but happened according to the divine plan.*

140

371 I was away from you for just one day, and I ended up so
distressed and beside myself that it was like being separated
10 *a.i.* from you for a whole year. And you know from what you felt
that this is true. When a child at the breast is torn away from
the mother's nipple, it keeps turning around, looking around
for its mother no matter where it's taken off to. So too when I
was taken quite far away from my mother's lap, I kept looking
around me, searching everywhere for your holy assembly. However, I took sufficient consolation from the facts that I was suffering this pain through being obedient to a very loving father,[2]
and that the reward for obedience was keeping at bay the anguish
which had resulted from the separation. This to me was more
372 splendid than any diadem, loftier than any crown – being led
around everywhere with my father. This to me was honour and
security. It was honour, because I'd won him over and drawn
10 *a.i.* him to love me to such an extent that he couldn't bear to appear
anywhere on any occasion without his child. It was security,
because he personally watched our struggle and offered us his
complete support and prayers. The hands of helmsmen, oars
and puffs of wind send a boat safely into harbour. So too will
his goodwill, his love and the help of his prayers, which are
better than a wind, a helmsman and the oars, guide our sermon.
        In addition to these benefits he consoled me on this point too –
373 the fact that at that time you were enjoying a brilliant table, and
that you had secured a distinguished and lavish host. We knew
this not merely from hearsay but also from experience itself, for
there were people who conveyed to us what had been said, and
from the leftovers we were able to make a conjecture about the
banquet itself. Indeed, I praised the host and admired his lavish-
ness and wealth, but I also congratulated you on your goodwill
and your scrupulosity, because you'd retained what was said
10 with such care that you could even convey it to another person.
That's why we'll also gladly discuss the question of your love.
For the person who sows seeds in this place doesn't throw
them *beside the road* (Matt. 13:4), or pour them into the thistles,
or strew them on rocky ground. So fruitful and fertile is your
field, and all the seeds which it receives into its furrows it multi-
plies (cf. Matt. 13:1–8).
        If ever you offered me an enthusiasm and great zeal for listen-
20 ing – as, indeed, you have always offered – I beg you to grant me
this favour today as well. Our sermon isn't about incidentals but
about important affairs. That's why I need your eyes to be

sharply focused, your attention aroused, your mind alert, your thoughts ordered and your soul awake and vigilant. I say this because you've all heard the reading from the apostle, and if someone has paid close attention to what was read out, they know that great struggles and labours lie before us today. 30 *'When Peter came to Antioch'*, it says, *'I opposed him to his face'* (Gal. 2:11).

. . . (the sermon continues for a further 21 paragraphs, in which John treats at length the dispute between Peter and Paul, the character of each of the antagonists and the motivations of each character) . . .

388   In future let's ask the God of Paul and Peter, who bound them fast to each other with the bonds of mutuality of purpose, to 40 bind us tightly too into a more burning love for each other, so that, in possession of that mutuality of purpose which is in accord with God, we may be deemed worthy of seeing those holy men and of finding ourselves among their eternal tents, by the grace and love for humankind of our Lord Jesus Christ, through whom and with whom to the Father and to the Holy Spirit be glory, power, honour and adoration, now and always, for ever and ever. Amen.

ON: 'MY FATHER'S WORKING STILL' (JOHN 5:17) (NEW HOMILY NO. 10)

INTRODUCTION

In this homily, delivered at Constantinople, we are afforded a glimpse of the loyalty of the audience to John and his preaching, regardless of the strength of his criticism of their behaviour. Even allowing for rhetorical exaggeration, it is clear that John is at this point confident of his power over the audience and, despite his avowed embarrassment at their rejection of his venerable colleague at the preceding synaxis, evidently delights in their attachment to his own person. The rare information regarding the protocol to be observed when a bishop visits the see of another bishop and is present at synaxis is significant for understanding the challenges which John faced as a preacher at Constantinople. As in *On Eutropius*, here the allusion to the recent tragic death in the hippodrome demonstrates John's ability to exploit the shock value of local events for pastoral purposes. While it has long been thought that the homily was delivered two Sundays after *Against the games and theatres* on 17 July 399 (Pargoire 1899–1900: 157–9), this is not necessarily the case. In fact, as argued elsewhere (Mayer forthcoming (c)), it is unlikely that the two homilies are connected. In the light of this difficulty it is better to assign the homily generally to the first three or four years at Constantinople.

Translated from PG 63,511–16.

TEXT

511 *The same. About the fact that one should not go to hippodromes or theatres. And because he hurt them, at the service on the Sunday after*

143

*that he allowed a bishop to speak who had arrived from Galatia, and
did not preach (himself). And because he hurt them by doing this too, he
delivered this homily in the Great Church on the text: 'My Father's
working still, and I'm working' (John 5:17).*

Recently I severely upbraided you when speaking about theatres
and hippodromes. That's why I'm happy and joyful, according to
10 the utterance of the apostle which runs: *'Who is there to make me
joyful but the one who was hurt by me?'* (2 Cor. 2:2), because I see
much fruit growing out of this hurt. I mean that drugs too,
which heal sores, bite into the wounds at first and then stop
the putrefaction. So too a sermon which touches the audience
provides a beginning for healing. In the case of our bodies,
once the flesh is dead it doesn't feel incision, or drugs, or cautery.
20 Thus innumerable remedies couldn't restore it to health, because
it's lost the first-principle and starting-point of the cure. But the
flesh which feels both knife and burning and drugs would be
quickly restored to health. So too, then, in the case of souls:
some which are disposed to be unfeeling wouldn't easily be
changed; others which know how to feel shame and embarrassment and pain and suffering at being censured offer us the
greatest proof of quickly recoiling from evil. This is why blessed
Paul, too, who knew this, gladly accepted those who'd been hurt
and was happy in their regard, while those who weren't in that
30 situation he rejected with the words: *'They've become callous and
given themselves up to licentiousness, greedy to practise every kind of
uncleanness'* (Eph. 4:19). For how would the one who doesn't
know pain ever be healed unless they learnt this very lesson
first? Since, then, you've been healed of this sickness, we have
the greatest confidence in the matter of your love: if one address
bit you in this way and made you so anxious that you were
depressed and confused and shaken, it's obvious that, if a
second and a third are added, it will free you from every
weakness.

And in order for you to know that I'm not saying this to
40 flatter you, you have testified to the truth of what we said by the
proof you gave on the previous occasion. I mean that you who
were so bitten, so suffering, so pained and depressed, on the
Sunday following that one made the theatre more splendid for
us, and the assembly more numerous, and the desire greater,
and you were all raised from the ground like swallows' chicks

hanging from the nest, and with your mouth open for our tongue. Then, since in showing respect for our brother who had
50 come from Galatia, both because of that ecclesiastical rule that orders us to receive strangers in this way and because of his illustrious age, we allowed him to speak, you drew back with shouts, complaining loudly of your suffering, as if you had endured
512 famine for a long time, and longed for our tongue which cuts, censures, strikes, makes suffer. You behaved in the same way as a child who's been hit (and) censured won't even in these circumstances be parted from its mother, but follows her, weeping, clutching firmly the sides of the mother's clothes, and trails after her wailing. It's on this account that I'm jumping with excitement and flying under the influence of pleasure and call myself blessed as I struggle (to preach) among so many people who
10 love me, having you hanging like this from my tongue. This is sweeter to me than this sunlight, this is more pleasurable than light, this is life – to have favourable listeners like this who don't simply applaud but wish to be corrected, who are censured and don't recoil, but take refuge in the one who censured them.

That's exactly why I too broach my address to you with greater enthusiasm, and today I wish to give you the leftovers of what I said to you recently, leaving aside now the censure, lest by accusing once more those who don't care we punish the
20 zealous, in that we expend the entire address on refuting the former. For even if nothing is learned from us, what happened yesterday is enough to keep those who are exceedingly crazy and fanatical about the hippodrome from this inappropriate desire. Indeed the murder which occurred yesterday in the hippodrome filled our city with tragedy, attracted bands of women, filled the market-place with much wailing, while the man who had been so pitifully mutilated by the chariots was carried through the middle of the crowd. This man, as I know, was
30 going to light the matrimonial candles the next day, when the bridal chambers were organised and everything was prepared for the wedding.[1] In his role as an official in the bureau of the eparch[2] he was running across down below in the stadium, when the charioteers came upon him and vied with one another; he was cut off in the middle and underwent this violent and pitiful death when his head and limbs were cut off.

Did you see the fruit of the hippodrome? 'And what's that got to do with us who sit up high?' someone asks. It's got to do

with *you* most of all: if *you* weren't keen to join the throng,
40 what came to pass down (in the stadium) wouldn't have
happened. But so that I don't make the homily too tiresome
once more and lacerate the wound, I'll leave these subjects to
your conscience and try to give you the remainder of what I
said to you recently.

So what was it that I said to you recently? I was saying that
Christ was called the foundation-stone (cf. 1 Cor 3:11) because
he bears everything and holds it together and props it up. I
wish to demonstrate this now on the basis of another quotation
from the apostle: he it is who said this, in interpreting that
saying, with the words: '*he reflects the glory and character of his*
50 *nature and bears everything by the word of his power; when he had*
purification of sin through himself, he sat at the right hand of the
majesty on high' (Heb. 1:3). What does *bears* mean? Guiding,
513 governing, managing, controlling, holding together, propping
up. For he hasn't only brought everything into existence from
non-existence (cf. 2 Macc. 7:28; Rom. 4:17), but also provided
for what came about, just as the Father who begot him did.
Thus he made this clear too, when he said: '*My Father's working*
still, and I'm working' (John 5:17). As a result, the Jews tried even
more to kill him, not only because he broke the sabbath, but also
because he called his Father God, making himself equal to God.

Where are the children of the heretics now, who act crazily
10 against their own salvation and cut him off from equality with
the Father? Let them hear the evangelist's words (when I say
the evangelist, I mean Christ, who moves his spirit) – let
them hear and be ashamed, and put a stop to such crazy acts.
I say this because the Jews used to persecute him on this
matter, namely that he called himself equal. And they strangle
themselves in this matter, namely that being taught by him
we refer this excellent saying to him. But, they say, this sentence
doesn't belong to him, nor to the evangelist, but to the Jews.
Certainly, if it did belong to the Jews, this is a huge charge
20 and an extreme accusation against you, because what the
ungrateful Jews realised was proven from the words, you yourself
in your pretended deafness don't see: they didn't deduce these
facts by themselves, but from what Christ said in debating
with them. And so that you may learn that this saying doesn't
belong to the Jews either, but is both the sentence and utterance
of the evangelist (when I say the evangelist, I mean Christ who

moves his mind), examine the words themselves: *'My Father'*. Isn't it clear to everyone, even to one who is exceedingly silly, that that's why he said *'My Father'* in order to show that it belonged to him? Isn't the subsequent addition *is working, and I'm working* of one who is maintaining equality? For he didn't even say 'he's working and I'm assisting', 'he's working but I'm serving', but 'he's *working, and I'm working*'. Do you see how this sentence isn't a declaration by the Jews, but the proof of his words? For if making him equal to God was some erroneous Jewish suspicion and sentence, and he didn't want to be suspect on that account, the Jews would have suspected him of not wanting that, and devised other things than what he wanted to prove. The evangelist couldn't have allowed this to stand uncorrected like that, but would've remarked on it and said it clearly. I say this because it was their custom to do this, both theirs and Jesus'.

I'll try to make it clear to you from one or two examples, that when Christ said something, and said it (again) himself in different words, and the Jews suspected a different meaning, the evangelist sets it right.

   . . . (there follow six paragraphs in which the point is highlighted and argued from numerous scriptural citations) . . .

516   But the refutation of the heretics has a fitting ending: if you wish to know what the work was in which the Father was engaged, and what that of the Son was, I'd say that it was providence with regard to creation,[3] preservation, care. I mean that everything which came into being was created within six days. *And God rested on the seventh day* (Gen. 2:2). But the providence with regard to creation didn't cease. It was this providence, then, that Christ called work, when he said: *'My Father's working, and I'm working'*, being provident, caring, preserving, I mean sustaining, allowing nothing to flow away.

So having received the proof of correct teaching from these words too, let's add a scrupulous lifestyle and one that's congruent with the teachings, in as much as the knowledge of correct teachings alone doesn't suffice for our salvation, but an excellent lifestyle is necessary too, so that when we have sent up glory to God in all matters, we may attain the promised blessings. To him be the glory and the power for ever and ever. Amen.

AGAINST THE JEWS ORATION 1

INTRODUCTION

Delivered at Antioch, as is evident from the references to the cave of
Matrona and other local features, the homily can be assigned with
reasonable certainty to the later months of 386, John's first year as
presbyter. This date is derived from the clear reference in the opening
lines of the homily to the first in the series of sermons which John
preached on the topic of the incomprehensible nature of God
(CPG 4318). The homily is noteworthy for a number of reasons.
In the opening comments regarding the sermon of the previous
Sunday John describes the effect of a well-structured and rhetorically
polished argument upon the audience – they burst into thunderous
applause. As the sermon moves into its topic – the imminent festivals
of the Jewish year – the problems posed for the Christian clergy by
a prominent local Jewish community of long-standing become
apparent.[1] In particular, we gain a rare glimpse of a pastoral engage-
ment between John and two members of the local Christian community as a result of a chance meeting on the street in the Jewish
quarter of Antioch. In general, the festivals and sacred sites of the
Jewish community compete with those of the Christian community
for audience loyalty.

A prominent feature of the homily is persistent exploitation of the
rhetoric of abuse. *Psogos* (invective) was as important a form of speech
for the accomplished orator as encomium (praise). Where the purpose
of the latter is to 'glorify and honor', as exemplified by *Hom. delivered
after the remains of marytrs etc.*, the aim of the former is to 'vilify
and defame' (Wilken 1983: 112).[2] As in the case of encomia, the
exaggerated contents of such speeches should not be taken at face
value or thought to reflect the opinions of the orator, but rather
assessed for their intended effect in relation to the target audience.

John employs the techniques of the *psogos* indiscriminately as long as they help him to achieve his aim. As we have seen, rich women become the target of such invective in *On Colossians hom.* 7, whereas it is the men who are guilty of attending the hippodrome who come under the spotlight in *Against the games and theatres*. The hostile statements against the Jews which recur throughout this homily and John's exploitation of medical and animal imagery in aid of his vilification of the Jews should be read with this point firmly in mind. Translated from PG 48,843–56.

TEXT

843 Today I was wanting with the leftovers of the topic on which I spoke to you recently to complete the payment and to demonstrate more clearly how incomprehensible[3] God is. For last Sunday we spoke on this subject copiously and at great length, when I brought Isaiah and David and Paul as my witnesses. Remember, it was Isaiah who cried out: *'Who'll declare his generation?'* (Isa. 53:8); it was David who gave thanks to him

10 for his incomprehensibility with the words: *'I'll praise you because you're fearfully admired. Admirable are your works'* (Ps. 139:14), and again: *'Knowledge of you is admired by me; it's superior, I can't attain it'* (Ps. 139:6); it was Paul who didn't investigate and pry into the very essence of God, but only into his providence – or rather, he considered a small aspect of that very providence which God showed in calling the Gentiles. Regarding (this small part) as an immense and incomprehensible sea, Paul cried out as follows: *'O the depth of the richness and wisdom and*

20 *knowledge of God! How unsearchable are his judgements, and how inscrutable his ways'* (Rom. 11:33).

And the proof furnished by these witnesses was sufficient, but I wasn't satisfied with the prophets, nor did I stop at the apostles, but I went up to heaven; I showed you the choir[4] of angels saying: *'Glory to God in the highest, and peace on earth to people of goodwill'* (Luke 2:14). Again, did you hear the Seraphim in their amazement and fear shouting: *'Holy, holy, holy Lord Sabaoth. All earth is full of his glory'* (Isa. 6:3). I added the cry of the Cherubim: *'Blessed be his glory from its place'* (Ezek. 3:12 LXX).

844 Below were three witnesses, above were three witnesses, who showed that God's glory couldn't be approached. From there on, the proof was beyond dispute; great applause ensued, the

149

theatre became fervent, the assembly was inflamed. As for myself, I was delighted, not because I was the one being praised, but because my Master was being glorified: that applause and the praise showed the love which you have in your hearts for God.

10 Just as devoted servants, on hearing someone praise their master, become fired with longing for the one who speaks because of the affection they bear for their master, so too did you behave on that occasion: by your lavish applause you demonstrated your considerable goodwill towards your Master.

Therefore today, too, I was wanting to engage in those contests.[5] My reason was that, if the enemies of truth can't have their fill of blaspheming our Benefactor, so much the more is it encumbent on us to be insatiable in praising the God of all (cf. Eph. 4:6). But what am I to do? Another very

20 serious illness bids me to speak in order to cure it, an illness which has sprung up in the body of the church. First we must root it out, then take thought for matters outside; first we must cure our own people, and then concern ourselves with those who aren't our own people.

What's this disease? The festivals of the wretched and miserable Jews are about to approach thick and fast: the Trumpets, the Tabernacles, the Fasts.[6] Of the many in our ranks who go to

30 watch the festivals, who say they think as we do, some will both join in the festivities and take part in the Fasts. This bad habit I want to drive out of the church right now. I mean that my

845 sermons against the Anomoeans can be put off for another occasion, and no harm would result from the postponement. But if we weren't to cure those suffering the Jewish illness now when the festivals of the Jews are imminent and at the door, I'm afraid that through inappropriate habit and great ignorance some will participate in their lawless activities,[7] and consequently what we say about those activities will be a waste of time − if they hear nothing (from me) today, they'll fast

10 with the Jews. So after the sin has been committed, there will be therefore no point in our applying the remedy. That's why I'm in a hurry to stop them beforehand. This is also what doctors do: the diseases that are urgent and acute they check first.

But this fight is intimately related to the former, in that the Anomoeans' impiety is related to the Jews', and our present conflicts are related to our previous one. I mean that the accusation which the Jews make is made by the Anomoeans as well. And

150

what accusation do the Jews make? That he (sc. Christ) called God his own father, making himself equal to God (cf. John
20 5:18). The Anomoeans make this accusation too – I should say that they don't make the accusation, but they even wipe out the phrase (sc. equal to God) with its meaning, even if they do this not with their hand but in their mind.

Don't be surprised if I've called the Jews wretched, for truly they are wretched and miserable since they spurned the numerous blessings which came into their hands from heaven, and they took great pains to throw them away. *The sun of justice* (Mal. 4:2) rose for them in the morning, but they spurned its rays and remain sitting in darkness. We, who were nurtured in
30 darkness, drew the light to ourselves and were freed from the gloom of error. They were the shoots of the holy root, but they were broken off. We had no share in the root, and we picked the fruit of piety. They read the prophets from an early age, and they crucified the one whom the prophets foretold. We didn't hear divine prophecies, and we worshipped the one whom the prophets foretold. On this account they're wretched, because they drove away the blessings that were sent to them, while others seized them and drew them to themselves.
40 Although the Jews were called to adoption as sons, they degenerated into a relationship with dogs; we who were dogs received strength through God's grace to lay aside our former irrational nature and to rise to the honour of being sons. What's the proof of this? *'It's not fair'*, it says, *'to take the children's bread and throw it to pet dogs'* (Matt. 15:26). It was to the Canaanite woman that Christ was speaking when he called the Jews children and the Gentiles dogs.

But see how after that the order was reversed: the Jews became dogs, and we became children. *'Look out for the dogs'*, Paul says of
50 the Jews, *'look out for the evil-workers, look out for mutilation. For we are the circumcision'* (Phil: 3.2–3). Did you see how those who were formerly children became dogs? Do you want to find out how we, who were formerly dogs, became children? *'But to all who received him'*, it says, *'who believed in his name, he gave power to become children of God'* (John 1:12).

Nothing is more wretched than those who in every case run counter to their own salvation. I mean that when they should have observed the law, they trampled it under foot, and now,
60 when the law has ceased, they're eager to observe it. What could

151

be more piteous than those who provoke God not only by transgressing the law but also by keeping it? That's why it says: 846 *'You stiff-necked people, uncircumcised in heart, you always resist the Holy Spirit'* (Acts 7:51), not only by transgressing the law but also by wanting to observe it at the wrong time.

Stiff-necked. And he (sc. Stephen) was right in calling them *'stiff-necked'*, in that they didn't take up the yoke of Christ, although it was agreeable and had nothing about it that was burdensome or oppressive. For he said: *'Learn from me, because I am gentle and humble of heart'*, and *'Take my yoke upon you, because my yoke is agreeable and my burden light'* (Matt. 11:29, 30). But in 10 spite of this, they didn't take it up because of the stiffness of their necks. Not only didn't they take it up, but they broke and destroyed it. *'For long ago'*, it says, *'You broke your yoke, destroyed your bonds'* (Jer. 2:20). It wasn't Paul who said this but the prophet crying out, speaking of the yoke and the bonds as the symbols of rule, because the Jews rejected the dominion of Christ when they said: *'We have no king but Caesar'* (John 19:15). You broke the yoke, you shattered the bonds, you cast yourself out of the 20 kingdom of heaven and subjected yourself to human rule. Please consider how accurately the prophet hinted at their refractory nature: he didn't say 'You put aside the yoke', but *'You broke the yoke'*, which is the shortcoming of skittish[8] animals that refuse to obey the reins and reject being ruled.

But where does this stiffness come from? From gluttony and drunkenness. Who says so? Moses himself. *'Israel ate, and was filled and grew fat, and the darling grew frisky'* (Deut. 32:15). He means that just as when animals feed from a full trough they 30 become corpulent and more obstinate and hard to hold in, and tolerate neither the yoke nor the reins nor the hand of the driver, so too the Jewish people were driven by drunkenness and corpulence to the ultimate evil; they became skittish and didn't accept the yoke of Christ, nor did they pull the plough of his teaching. It was this, then, that another prophet hinted at when he said: *'Like a stubborn heifer, Israel is stubborn'* (Hos. 4:16). Yet another called Israel an *'untamed calf'* (Jer. 38:18 LXX).

40 Such animals, when they're unfit for work, become fit for the slaughter. It was this fate, then, that the Jews suffered: in making themselves useless for work, they became fit for the slaughter. This is why Christ said: *'But as for those enemies of mine, who didn't want me to reign over them, bring them here and*

slay them' (Luke 19:27). You should have fasted then, Jew, when drunkenness was doing those terrible things to you, when gluttony had brought forth impiety – not now. I mean that, as it is, your fasting occurs at the wrong time and is disgusting. Who said so? Isaiah himself when he cried out in a loud voice:
50 *'I didn't choose this fast, says the Lord'* (Isa. 58:6). Why? *Because you fast only to quarrel and fight, and you hit those subordinate to you with your fists* (Isa. 58:4).

But if your fasting was disgusting when you were hitting your fellow servants, does it become acceptable when you've slain the Master? How could that be right? The person who fasts should be restrained, contrite, humbled, not drunk with rage. Do you hit your fellow servants? In the time of Isaiah they fasted only
60 to quarrel and fight, but now they do it for licentiousness and extreme intemperance, dancing with bare feet in the market-place.[9] While their pretext is that they're fasting, their appearance is that of drunks. Listen to how the prophet commands them to fast: *'Sanctify a fast'*, he says. He didn't say: 'Show off your fasting' (but) *'call the assembly, gather the elders'* (Joel
847 1:14). But the Jews gather bands of effeminate men and a great mob of female prostitutes; they drag the whole theatre and the actors into the synagogue: there's no difference between theatre and synagogue. I know that some charge me with audacious speech because I said: 'There's no difference between theatre and synagogue', but I charge them (with audacity) if they don't think like this. The point is that, if my declaration is made on my own initiative, charge me (with audacity), but if I'm repeating the words of the prophet, accept his assertion.

I know that many people respect the Jews and think that their
10 present way of life is honourable. That's why it's urgent for me to tear out this deadly notion by the root. I said that the synagogue is no better than the theatre, and I adduce my evidence from the prophet – the Jews aren't more worthy of belief than the prophets. What, then, does the prophet say? *'You had a prostitute's face; you became shameless before all'* (Jer. 3:3 LXX). Where a prostitute has established herself, that place is a brothel. I should say that the synagogue isn't only a brothel and a theatre, but also a
20 cave of robbers and a resting-place for wild beasts. *'For'*, it says, *'your house has become for me a hyena's cave'* (cf. Jer. 7:11; 12:9 LXX). He doesn't just mean 'of a wild beast', but 'of a filthy wild beast'. And again: *I've abandoned my house; I've forsaken my inheritance* (Jer. 12:7). When God abandons (a people), what

hope of salvation is left? When God abandons (a place), that place becomes the dwelling of demons.

But the Jews will no doubt say that they too worship God. Heaven forbid them to say that! No Jew worships God. Who says so? The Son of God. *'If you knew my Father'*, he says, *'you*
30 *would know me too. But you neither know me nor do you know my Father'* (John 8:19). What sort of evidence can I produce that's more trustworthy than that?

If, then, the Jews don't recognise the Father, if they crucified the Son, if they repulsed the help of the Spirit, who wouldn't be bold enough to declare that (the synagogue) is the resting-place of demons? God isn't worshipped there. Heaven forbid! Therefore it's the place of idolatry. Nonetheless some people are intent on these places, as if they were hallowed.

I'm not making these statements from guesswork, but because
40 I've learned from experience itself. Indeed three days ago (believe me, I'm not lying) I saw an elegant freewoman, well-behaved and a believer. She was being forced by some brutal and unfeeling man, supposedly a Christian (I wouldn't call a person who had the effrontery to do this a sincere Christian) to go into the place of the Hebrews (sc. synagogue) and to swear an oath there about business under dispute with him. Approaching me, the woman called on me for help, and asked me to prevent
50 this lawless violence (she was forbidden to go into that place because she had partaken of the holy mysteries). I was inflamed with indignation and enraged; I was galvanised into action and refused to allow her to be dragged any further into that transgression,[10] and I snatched her away from that unlawful abduction. When I asked the abductor if he were a Christian, and he confessed he was, I stood over him insistently, accusing him of being unfeeling and extremely stupid. I said he was no better than a mule if, while claiming to worship Christ, he
60 dragged off someone to the caves of the Jews, who had crucified him. I spoke to him at length, saying firstly that swearing oaths was absolutely forbidden, and so was forcing someone to swear
848 them. I drew my lesson from the holy Gospels. Then I told him that he was forbidden to subject not only a baptised believer to this compulsion, but also an unbaptised person.

After I'd talked to him at great length and driven out the mistaken notion from his mind, I asked him his reason for dismissing the church and dragging (the woman) to the assembly of the Hebrews. He said that many people had told him that oaths

sworn there were more awe-inspiring.[11] I groaned at these words,
and I was inflamed with rage, and after that I began to smile
10 again: on seeing the devil's mischief, I groaned because he had
the power to mislead human beings; on considering the carelessness of those who were taken in, I was inflamed with rage; on
looking again at the degree and extent of the stupidity of
those taken in, I began to smile.

I have related and explained these events to you because you
are inhuman and hard-hearted towards those who perpetrate
and suffer such actions. Even if you see one of your brothers or
sisters falling into a trangression like this, you deem it someone
else's misfortune, not your own; and you think you have
20 defended[12] yourself against your accusers when you say: 'What's
it got to do with me? What have I got in common with that
person?' In these words you express extreme hatred for humanity
and a cruelty that comes from Satan. What are you saying?
You're a human being and you share the same nature. Rather,
if I'm to speak of a common nature, I should say that you
have one head, Christ. How can you have the effrontery to say
that you have nothing in common with your own members?
How can you then confess that Christ is the head of the
church? It's indeed the nature of the head to join together all the
30 members, to arrange and connect them exactly to each other. But
if you have nothing in common with your member, neither do
you have anything in common even with your brother or
sister, nor do you have Christ as your head.

The Jews frighten you as if you were small children, and you
don't realise it. It's like when many nasty slaves show frightening
and ridiculous masks to children (they're not frightening in
themselves, but appear so because of the simple minds[13] of the
children), and arouse a great deal of laughter. In exactly the
40 same way the Jews scare the more simple-minded Christians, for
how could (their synagogues) be frightening, when they're full of
great shame and ridicule – (the synagogues) of people who have
rebelled, been dishonoured and condemned?

Our (churches) aren't like that, but are truly frightening[14] and
filled with awe. For the place where God is present, possessing
power over life and death, is a frightening place – where homilies
are delivered on everlasting punishments, on rivers of fire, the
50 poisonous worm, chains that can't be broken, external darkness.
But the Jews know none of this, not even in a dream, because
they live for the belly, they have their mouths open for the

things of this world, being no better than pigs or goats by reason
of their licentiousness and their excessive gluttony. They only
know one thing – how to gorge themselves and get drunk, to
be made mince-meat of because of pantomime dancers, to be
wounded because of charioteers.[15]

Tell me, then, are (their synagogues) venerable and awe-
inspiring?[16] Who would say so? Where's your evidence for thinking that they're awe-inspiring, unless someone were to say that
servants who've been dishonoured and have no right of speech
60 and have been deprived of their master's house are awe-inspiring
to those who have influence and the freedom to speak? No, this
isn't the case – it isn't, because inns are not more hallowed than
the emperor's palace. I should say that the spot where the syna-
849 gogue is, is less worthy of honour than any inn. For it's not only
a resting-place for robbers and cheats, but also for demons, which
holds not only for the synagogues but also for the very souls of
the Jews. I'll try to prove this at the end of the homily.

Please, then, remember in a special way what I've said. We
aren't speaking now with an eye to show or applause, but to the
cure of your souls. I mean – what's left for me to say to you when
10 some of you are sick, although there are so many doctors.

The apostles were twelve in number, and they won over the
whole world. The majority of the city is Christian, and still
some suffer the Judaising disease. How would those of us who
are healthy defend ourselves on this point? Surely those who are
ill themselves deserve to be accused. But *we* aren't free of blame
either, because we've neglected them in their ill-health. In other
words, it would be impossible for them still to be sick if they'd
enjoyed constant care from us.

This is why I'm pre-empting you now in what I say, so that
20 each of you may win over your brother or sister, even if you have
to subject them to duress, even if you have to force them and
treat them badly and obstinately, do everything to have them
escape the devil's snare and to be free of fellowship with those
who killed Christ.

Tell me, if you saw someone who'd been justly condemned
being led through the market-place and if you had the power
to snatch them from the hands of the executioner, wouldn't
you do everything to save them from being dragged off? Now
it's your own brother or sister whom you see, who's being
dragged off not by the executioner, but in an unjust and
30 unholy manner by the devil to the pit of destruction. Aren't you

even prepared to do your part so that he or she escapes from his transgression? What excuse could you find? But (you will say), your brother or sister is stronger and more powerful than you are. Show the person to me. I'll choose to lay down my life[17] rather than let them enter the holy doors, should they remain obstinate in their intentions.

(I'll say to them): 'What have you got in common with the free Jerusalem, with the Jerusalem above? You've chosen the one below – remain in slavery with her: indeed, according to
40 the words of the apostle, she'll *"remain in slavery with her children"* (Gal. 4:25). Are you fasting with the Jews? Well, take off your shoes with the Jews too, and walk in the market-place with bare feet, and join in their indecent behaviour and their laughter. But you wouldn't choose to do this, because you'd be ashamed and would blush. Then is it the case that you'd be ashamed to join in with them in the way they dress, but you wouldn't be ashamed to join in with their impiety? What excuse will you have, you who are half-Christian?'

Believe me, I would sooner lay down my life than neglect one
50 of those who suffer from this disease – if I see them. But if I don't recognise them, surely God will forgive me. Let each of you, too, take these matters into consideration, and not think that the issue is of secondary importance. Don't you pay attention to what the deacon calls out continuously at the mysteries? *'Recognise one another'*.[18] Don't you see how he entrusts you with the careful scrutiny of your brothers and sisters? Practise this scrutiny in the case of the Judaisers as well. When you recognise a Judaiser, take hold of them, make the situation plain to them, so that you too don't become party to the danger. I say this because also in the case of army camps outside the country, if someone from the ranks of the soldiers is caught favouring
60 barbarians, that is, being well-disposed towards Persians, not only is he in danger, but so also is everyone who knew his inclinations and failed to point him out to the general. Since, then, you are Christ's army, you must make it your business
850 to investigate scrupulously whether a foreigner has infiltrated your ranks, and you must point them out – not so that we may execute them, as they do in the army, nor so that we may punish them or avenge ourselves on them, but so that we may free them from error and impiety and make them entirely ours. If you're unwilling to do this and knowingly conceal (the person), be assured that you'll be subject to the same penalty

157

10 as they are. For Paul, too, subjects to punishment and penalty
not only criminals but also those who connive with them
(cf. Rom. 1:32). And the prophet for his part brings not only
thieves but also their accomplices to the same judgement (cf.
Ps. 49:18). And this is fair. For the person who's aware of the
criminal's actions and covers for them and conceals them, provides them with more excuse for carelessness and makes them
less afraid in their pursuit of crime.

But we must return again to the sick. Well, then, consider
who it is they've joined with in fasting. It's with the people
20 who shouted: '*Crucify him, crucify him*' (Luke 23:21), with those
who said: '*His blood be upon us and upon our children*' (Matt.
27:25). If some people had been caught rebelling against their
leader and had been condemned, surely you wouldn't dare to
approach them and converse with them? I don't think so. Isn't
it absurd, then, to be assiduous in avoiding contact with
people who've committed a crime against a human being, but
to join up with people who've insulted God himself? (Isn't it
absurd that) those who worship the crucified one join in celebrating with those who crucified him? Isn't this a sign not just of
stupidity but also of extreme craziness?

30   Because there are some people who consider that the synagogue is a holy place, it's imperative to say a few words to
them too. What's the reason for revering that place when you
should despise it, abominate it and leap away from it? 'The
law and the books of the prophets', you say, 'are kept there.'
So what? Surely it's not the case that every place where such
books are found will be holy? Certainly not. For my part this
is the reason above all others that I hate the synagogue and
have an aversion to it: although they have the prophets, they
don't believe in them; although they read out the sacred
writings, they don't accept their evidence – and this is a sign
of people whose ways are quite outrageous.

40   Tell me, if you saw someone venerable, distinguished and
notable being dragged off into a bar or resting-place for robbers,
then outraged there, beaten and subjected to extreme violence,
would you have held the bar or the cave in high esteem because
that great man had been inside it while being subjected to
violence? I don't think so, but for this very reason you would've
had a special hatred for and aversion to the place.

That should be your judgement in the case of the synagogue as
50 well: they brought the prophets and Moses in with them there,

158

not to honour them but to outrage and dishonour them. For when they say that the prophets and Moses didn't know Christ or said nothing about his coming, what greater outrage could they inflict on those holy men than when they accuse them of not recognising their Master, and call them partners in their own impiety? Consequently we must hate both them and the synagogue all the more because they behave offensively with regard to those holy men.

But why am I talking about books and synagogues? In time of
60 persecution the executioners handled the bodies of the martyrs and scourged and beat them. Are their hands then holy because they handled the bodies of saints? Heaven forbid! The hands which handled the bodies of the saints remain unhallowed for the very reason that their handling of them was wicked. And will those who handle the writings of holy men and commit
851 outrage against them, no less than the executioners did the bodies of the martyrs, be venerable on that account? Wouldn't that be the ultimate stupidity? I mean that, if the wicked handling of the bodies not only failed to hallow those who handled them, but even made them more polluted, even more so is it the case that reading out the scriptures without believing in them could never bring benefit to those who read them out. It's precisely because they keep these books on purpose that
10 demonstrates their greater impiety, because they wouldn't have deserved an accusation of such seriousness if they hadn't the prophets in their possession. They wouldn't have been so impure and unhallowed if they hadn't read the books. But as it is, they've been robbed of all pardon because of the fact that, although they have the heralds of truth, they resist with hostility both the prophets and the truth. So on this account they would be all the more unhallowed and impious, in that, while they have the prophets in their possession, they treat them with hostile intent.

So, please, avoid and leap away from their gatherings. The
20 harm they do to your weaker brothers and sisters isn't to be taken lightly; the excuse they give the Jews to act without sense is not to be taken lightly. For when they see that you, who worship the Christ they crucified, are reverently following their ritual, why wouldn't they believe that all the rituals they perform are the best and that ours are worthless, when after worshipping and paying honour at our mysteries you run to the people who

destroy them? '*If someone sees you*', it says, '*a person of knowledge, reclining at table in an idol's temple, wouldn't they be encouraged, if*
30 *their conscience is weak, to eat food offered to idols?*' (1 Cor. 8:10). *I* say: 'If someone sees you, a person of knowledge, walking off towards the synagogue and being a spectator at the Festival of Trumpets, wouldn't they be encouraged, if their conscience is weak, to admire what the Jews do?' The one who falls not only pays the penalty for their own fall, but is punished for tripping others as well. Similarly the person who has stood firm not only is crowned for their own virtue, but is admired for leading others on as well to the same fervour.

Therefore avoid both their gatherings and their places, and let
40 nobody venerate the synagogue because of its books, but let them hate and turn their back on it because the Jews maltreat the holy ones, because they refuse to believe their own words, because they accuse them of the ultimate impiety.[19]

So that you may know that the books don't make a place holy, but that it's the intention of those who come together (in a place) that makes it impure, I'll tell you an old story. Ptolemy Philadelphus[20] collected books from everywhere. When he learned that the Jews had writings which studied God and the
50 ideal state, he sent for men from Judaea and had the books translated by them, and deposited them in the Temple of Serapis (he was a pagan). Up to the present the translations of the books of the prophets remain in the temple. Well, then, will the temple of Serapis be holy because of the books? Heaven forbid! While the books possess their own holiness, they don't communicate it to the place, because those who come together there are defiled. You must, therefore, apply the same argument to the synagogue
852 as well. Even if there isn't an idol installed there, still demons inhabit the place. I'm not saying that only about the synagogue here in town, but about the one in Daphne as well, for there you have a place of perdition that's more wicked, which they call Matrona's. I have heard that many of the faithful go up there and sleep beside the place.

But heaven forbid that I should ever call these people the faithful! To me both the shrine of Matrona and the temple of Apollo[21] are equally impure. If anyone charges me with rashness,
10 I charge them in turn with utter madness.[22] I mean, tell me – isn't the place where demons live a place of impiety even if there's no statue[23] standing there? This is where the Christ-slayers assemble, where the cross is driven out, where God is

blasphemed, where the Father is ignored, where the Son is insulted, where the grace of the Spirit is repulsed. I shouldn't say that, since the Jews themselves are demons, a greater harm comes from the place? I mean that in the pagan temple the impiety is naked and obvious, and it wouldn't be easy to deceive someone and allure them there if they had a brain and were
20 sensible. But in the synagogue, by claiming to worship God, to abhor idols and to possess and honour the prophets, the Jews are preparing a lot of bait by these words, and they catch in their snares the rather simple-minded and the silly when they're off their guard.

So the impiety of the Jews and the pagans is equal, but the deceit practised by the Jews is more difficult to deal with: indeed, in their synagogue there stands an invisible altar of deceit, on which they sacrifice not sheep and calves but the souls of human beings. In short, if you admire their rituals, what have you got in common with us? The point is that, if
30 their rituals are venerable and great, ours are false. But if ours are true, as indeed they are true, theirs are full of deceit. I'm not talking about the scriptures – heaven forbid! – for it was the scriptures that led me by the hand to Christ, but I'm talking about the impiety and the present madness of the Jews.

Now, then, it's time to show that demons live in the synagogue, not only in the place itself but also in the very souls of the Jews. *'When the unclean spirit has left'*, it says, *'it passes through*
40 *waterless places seeking rest. When it doesn't find it, it says "I will return to my house." And when it comes it finds it empty, swept and put in order. And it goes on and brings with it seven other spirits more evil than itself, and they go in to it and the last state of that person will be worse than the first. So shall it be with this generation'* (Matt. 12:43–5).

Do you see that the demons dwell in their souls, and that the Jews nowadays are more difficult to deal with than the ones before them? And this is a very fair statement: in the olden
50 days they acted impiously towards the prophets, whereas now they insult the Master of the prophets himself. Tell me, don't you shudder when you come into the same place as people who are possessed, who have so many unclean spirits, who've been brought up among slaughter and murder? Do you have to join in greeting them, and exchange a scant word? Shouldn't you turn away from them because they are the common corruption and disease of the whole world? Haven't they come to every

kind of wickedness? Haven't all the prophets wasted many long speeches of accusation on them? What tragedy, what manner of
60 transgression haven't they eclipsed by their bloodthirstiness? They sacrificed their own sons and daughters to demons. They ignored nature, forgot the pangs of birth, trampled on child-rearing, overturned from their foundations the laws of kinship; they became more savage than any wild beasts.

853 Indeed, wild beasts often lay down their lives and hold their own safety of no account in order to protect their young. But there was no necessity for the Jews to kill their own children with their own hands in order to pay honour to the avenging demons, which are the enemies of our life. What attribute of theirs would be the first to strike us with astonishment – their impiety or their cruelty or their inhumanity? The fact that they sacrificed their sons, or that they sacrificed them to demons (cf. Ps. 106:37)? Through their licentiousness didn't
10 they eclipse even the most extreme lust of animals? Listen to what the prophet says about their excesses: *'They were lusty stallions. Each one neighed after his neighbour's wife'* (Jer. 5:8). He didn't say: 'Each one lusted after his neighbour's wife', but he expressed the madness which was generated by their licentious-ness most vividly by speaking of it as the neighing of animals.

What else do you want me to tell you? (Shall I tell you about) their acts of plunder, greed, their betrayal of the poor, their theft
20 and cheating? Not even a whole day would be long enough to describe these to you. But do their festivals have something solemn and great about them? They've demonstrated that these, too, are impure. Listen to the prophets – or I should say, listen to God and how vehemently he turned his back on them: *'I've found your festivals hateful, I have thrust them away'* (Amos 5:21).

God hates these festivals, and do you join in them? He didn't say this or that festival, but all of them collectively. Do you want to see that God hates worship that's made with drums and lyres and harps and other instruments? He said: *'Take away from me the*
30 *noise of your song, and to the melody of your instruments I will not listen'* (Amos 5:23). God said: *'Take (them) away from me'*, and you rush to listen to their trumpets? Aren't these sacrifices and offerings abominable? *If you bring me the finest wheaten flour, it is in vain. Incense is an abomination to me* (Isa. 1:13 LXX). *Incense is an abomination*; isn't the place also an abomination? And when was it an abomination? Before they committed the worst of

crimes, before they killed their Master, before the cross, before
the slaying of Christ, it was an abomination. Isn't it much
40 more an abomination now? And indeed what's more fragrant
than incense? But it wasn't the nature of the gifts but the intention of those who bring them that God pays attention to, and so
judges the offerings.

He paid attention to Abel, and then to his gifts. He saw Cain,
and then turned his back on his sacrifices. 'To Cain and to his
sacrifices', it says, 'he paid no attention' (Gen. 4:5). Noah offered
to God sacrifices of sheep and calves and birds. And scripture
says: 'The Lord smelled a pleasing odour' (Gen. 8:21), that is, he
50 accepted the offerings. For God has no nostrils but is a dis-
embodied divinity. Yet what rises from the altar is odour and
smoke from burning corpses, and no odour is more foul than
that. So that you may learn that it's the intention of those bringing the offerings that God pays attention to, and accepts or
rejects it, scripture calls the odour and the smoke a pleasing
odour, but it calls the incense an abomination because the intention of those bringing the offerings reeked with a foul smell.

Do you wish to learn that, together with the sacrifices and the
60 musical instruments and the festivals and the incense, God also
turns his back on the temple because of those who enter it?
He showed this especially through his actions, when he surren-
dered it into the hands of barbarians, and later when he destroyed
it completely.[24] Still, even before its destruction he called out
and said through the prophet: 'Don't trust in deceptive words because
854 they won't help you when you say: "This is the temple of the Lord, the
temple of the Lord"' (Jer. 7:4 LXX). 'It's not the temple which
sanctifies those who gather in it', he says, 'but those who gather
in it who make the temple holy.' If the temple didn't help at the
time when the Cherubim and the Ark were there, this will be the
case much more when they've all been removed, when God's
rejection of it's complete, when the reason for enmity is greater.
How silly and how deranged it would be to take as your partners
in the festivals those who've been dishonoured, who've been
10 abandoned by God, who've provoked the Master.

Tell me, if someone had killed your son, could you bear to lay
eyes on them? Could you bear to listen to their greeting?
Wouldn't you avoid them as you would an evil spirit, as the
devil himself? The Jews killed your Master's Son – do you
have the effrontery to go with them to the same place? The
one who was killed has honoured you to the point of making

you his brother or sister and co-heir, whereas you treat him with
dishonour to the point of honouring those who killed the
Master and crucified the Son, and worshipping in their company
20 during the festivals, and going to their impure places, and entering their unclean doors, and taking part in the table of demons.
(I'm persuaded to call the fast of the Jews 'the table of demons'
because they killed God.) How wouldn't they be worshipping
demons, when they act against God? Are you looking for a
cure from the demons? On the occasion when Christ allowed
them to go into the swine, they plunged immediately into the
sea (cf. Matt. 8:31–2). Will the demons spare human bodies? I
wish that they wouldn't kill human bodies, that they wouldn't
30 plot against them. They expelled human beings from paradise,
they deprived them of honour from above – will they cure
their bodies? These are ridiculous stories. The demons know
how to plot and harm, not to cure. They don't spare souls –
tell me, will they spare bodies? They try to expel people from
the kingdom – will they choose to free them from illness?

How wouldn't you hear the prophet speaking, or, I should say, God
speaking through the prophet? He said that the demons could
do neither good nor ill. Even if they *could* cure, and were willing
40 to do so – which is an impossibility – you shouldn't exchange a
small, ephemeral benefit for a punishment that's eternal and
never-ending. Are you going to cure your body in order to lose
your soul? That's bad business on your part: are you going to
anger God, who made your body, and call on the demon who
plots against you, to cure you?

How wouldn't it be easy for a demon-fearing pagan to woo
you to worship the pagan gods through using medical knowledge? I mean that pagans too often cure many illnesses through
50 their art, and restore the sick to health. Well then, should you
join in with their impiety on this account? Heaven forbid!
Listen to what Moses said to the Jews: *'If a prophet arises among
you, a dreamer of dreams, and gives you a sign or a wonder, and the
sign or wonder which he has told of comes to pass, and if he says to
you the words: "Let's go and worship other gods which our fathers
haven't known", don't listen to the voice of the prophet or to the dreamer
of dreams'* (Deut. 13:2–4 LXX). What Moses means is this. 'If
60 some prophet rises up', he says, 'and performs a sign, either by
raising the dead, or making a leper clean, or curing someone
who's maimed, and after performing the sign calls you to

impiety, don't be persuaded because the sign has come to pass.'
Why not? *For the Lord your God is testing you, to see whether*
855 *you love him with all your heart, and with all your soul* (Deut. 13:4
LXX). From this it's clear that demons don't cure. But if ever
God permitted someone to be cured, as happens with human
beings, his permission is given to test you, not because God
doesn't know you, but in order for you to learn to reject even
the demons who do cure.

And why do I speak of bodily cures? If someone threatens you
with hell unless you deny Christ, don't accept their words. If
10 someone promises you a kingdom if you revolt against the only-
begotten Son of God, turn your back on them and hate them.
Become a disciple of Paul and emulate those words which his
blessed and noble soul exclaimed. *'For I'm sure'*, he said, *'that
neither death, nor life, nor angels, nor principalities, nor powers, nor
things present, nor things to come, nor height, nor depth, nor anything
else in creation can separate us from the love of God, which is in
Christ Jesus our Lord'* (Rom. 8:38–9).

Neither *angels, nor powers, nor things present, nor things to come,*
20 *nor anything else in creation* separated Paul from the love of Christ
– and you hold yourself aloof from curing your body? What sort
of excuse could we find? Indeed we must regard Christ as more
fearful than hell, and we must desire him more than a kingdom.
Even if we're sick, it's better to remain in a state of infirmity
than to fall into impiety through being freed from weakness.
Even if a demon cures you, it's harmed you more than helped
you: it's helped your body, which a short time later is going
30 to die and rot away; it's harmed your soul, which is immortal.
Kidnappers often entice small children by offering them sweets
and cakes and knucklebones and other such objects, and deprive
them of their freedom and their very life. So, too, the demons
hold out the promise of the cure of a limb and completely
sink the soul's salvation.

No, let's not put up with that, beloved, but in every way let's
seek to be free from impiety. Couldn't Job have been convinced
by his wife to blaspheme against God, and to have been freed
40 from the misfortune which beset him? *'Curse God'*, she said, *'and
die'* (Job 2:9). But he chose rather to suffer and waste away, and
to put up with that unbearable blow, rather than blaspheme and
be freed from the evils which beset him. You too must emulate
him. Even if the demon were to promise you countless deliver-
ances from the ills which beset you, don't be convinced, don't

put up with it either, just as the just man wasn't convinced by his wife. But choose to endure your illness rather than to destroy
50 the faith and the salvation of your soul. It's not because God is abandoning you, but it's because he wants to make you more vibrant that he frequently allows you to fall sick. So continue to be patient so that you too may hear the words: *'Do you think that I've dealt with you for any reason other than that you may be shown to be just?'* (Job 40:8 LXX).

I could have said more even than this, but in order not to spoil your memory regarding what I've said, I'll bring the sermon to an end at this point, quoting the words of Moses: *'I call heaven and earth to witness against you'* (Deut. 30:19). If any of you,
60 either those who are present or those who are absent, goes to watch the Trumpets, or rushes to the synagogue, or goes up to the shrine of Matrona, or joins in the fasting, or takes part in the sabbath, or performs any other Jewish rite great or small, I'm guiltless of the blood of all of you. These words will stand by your side and mine on the day of our Lord Jesus Christ. If you're convinced by them, they'll provide you with great
856 confidence. If you disregard them or conceal anyone who has the effrontery to do such things, my words will stand against you like vehement accusers. *For I didn't shrink from declaring to you the whole counsel of God* (Acts 20:27), but I've deposited money with the bankers. It remains for you to increase the deposit and to use the profit from what you've heard for the salvation of your brothers and sisters.

Is it burdensome and oppressive to denounce those who
10 commit these sins? It's indeed burdensome and oppressive to remain silent. For both to you who conceal them and to those people themselves who are escaping notice, this very silence brings destruction by making God your enemy. How much better it is to incur the hatred of your fellow servants for saving them than to provoke the Master's anger against yourselves. For even if your fellow servant is annoyed with you at the present moment, they won't be able to harm you, but will rather be grateful to you afterwards for the cure. God, on the other hand, will exact from you the ultimate penalty, if you curry a harmful favour with your fellow servant and remain
20 silent and conceal them. The upshot will be that by remaining silent you'll make God your enemy, and you'll harm your brother or sister; on the other hand, if you denounce them and show them up, God will be propitious to you and you will help

166

your brother or sister – you'll gain a friend who's crazy about you, who learned by experience how you'd helped them.

Don't think, then, that you're doing your brothers and sisters a favour if you observe them going after something inappropriate and fail to accuse them with every intensity. If you lose a cloak, don't you have the same enmity for not only the one who stole it but also the one who knew about the theft and didn't denounce 30 the thief? Our common mother has lost not a cloak but a brother or sister. The devil stole them and now holds them fast in Judaism. You know who the thief is; you know who was stolen. Do you see me lighting the homily of instruction like a lamp and searching everywhere as I mourn them? And will you stand in silence and not denounce (the perpetrator)? What kind of excuse will you have? How could the church not reckon you as one of her direst enemies and consider you a destructive foe?

Heaven forbid that anyone who hears this advice should ever 40 commit such a sin as to betray a brother or sister on whose behalf Christ died. Christ shed his blood for them – are you holding back from even saying a word on their account? Please don't do this. Instead, straight after you leave here rouse yourselves to undertake this hunt, and let each of you bring me one of those who are sick in this way.

Heaven forbid that there should be so many who are sick! Let two or three of you, or ten or a hundred, bring me one person, so that on that day, when I see that your quarry is inside the net, I'll 50 serve you a more lavish meal.[25] When I see that my advice today has been put to work, I'll tackle the cure of those persons with more purpose, and both you and they will benefit more.

Don't neglect my words. Let the women chase after women, and the men after men, and the slaves after slaves, and the freemen after freemen, and the children after children, and in general let everyone be very scrupulous in chasing after people who are suffering from this kind of illness. Come to the next service with such success that you'll win praise from us, and, before 60 our laudatory words, you'll obtain a great and indescribable reward from God, surpassing in great measure the efforts of those who are successful. May all of us attain this through the grace and love for humankind of our Lord Jesus Christ, through whom and with whom to the Father, together with the Holy Spirit, be glory now and always, and for ever and ever. Amen.

ON 1 CORINTHIANS HOMILY 21

INTRODUCTION

Delivered in Antioch, as explicitly stated by John, the homily details several important aspects of the welfare activities of the church and the provision of pastoral care for the poor and homeless of that city. There is reference to the church dole and to the register of such persons, presumably as a means of controlling the provision and reception of it. There are references also to the necessity for the church to own property that provides an income sufficient to finance such activities, and intimations that the actions and personal ethics of the clergy who administer the programme on behalf of the local church are not above suspicion. The attitude of members of the Christian community not in need towards the different categories of needy persons is likewise detailed. John's angry exhortation to the audience to exercise charity and humility reflects a common pastoral emphasis on caring for one's own soul through observing the command to love one's neighbour. Throughout the homily the Greek term *eleēmosynè* is translated variously by us as mercy, charity and almsgiving, according to the sense of the passage. The date of the homily is unknown.

Translated from Field (1847: 241–58).

TEXT

241 *Aren't I an apostle? Aren't I free? Haven't I seen Jesus Christ, our Lord? Aren't you my work in the Lord?* (1 Cor. 9:1).

... (The homily opens and continues for six paragraphs with an exegesis of 1 Cor. 9:1–12, during which the topics of Paul's self-praise and wisdom are also raised) ...

251 (186) Let's listen to these words too, beloved, so that we don't look down on those who've fallen or *put any obstacle in the way of Christ's Gospel* (1 Cor. 9:12), so that we don't betray our salvation. When your brother or sister has fallen please don't say: 'The occasion of their falling couldn't be prevented', or 'It's permitted.' I'll tell you something more significant – if you see someone is being harmed, even if Christ has permitted it, you must stop what you're doing and not take advantage of the fact that it's been permitted. For Paul too did this: when with Christ's approval he could have taken (his rights), he didn't
B (cf. 1 Cor. 9:12, 15). Indeed, because the Master is generous, he has mingled abundant gentleness with his commandments, so that we perform many actions not only as a result of his injunction but also as a result of our own decision. I mean that, if he hadn't wanted to do that, he could have extended his commandments further and said: 'Let the person who doesn't fast all the time be punished; let the person who doesn't remain a virgin be penalised; let the person who doesn't give away all their possessions pay the ultimate penalty.' No, he didn't do that, giving you the opportunity to aspire to do more if you wished. On that account, both when he was speaking about virginity, he said: '*Let the one who is able to receive, receive*' (Matt. 19:12), and in the case of the rich man he gave some orders, but gave permission for other matters to be left to the man's
C discretion. For he didn't say: 'Sell what you have', but '*If you wish to be perfect, sell*' (Matt. 19:21).

Instead, not only don't we aspire to do more or go beyond his instructions, but we fall far short even of the measure of his commands. Whereas Paul went without food in order not to *put any obstacle in the way of the Gospel*, we haven't the heart even to touch what we've stored up, although we see countless souls being ruined. 'Yes, let the moth munch', they say, 'and let the poor person not munch; let the worm devour, and let the naked person have no clothes; let everything be consumed by time, and let Christ not be nourished even though he's hungry.'
D 'Who was it who said this?', someone asks. Indeed, this is the really serious thing, that these sentiments aren't expressed in words, but in actions. I mean that it would be less serious if

they were expressed in words, than being manifested in deeds. Isn't this what Avarice, the tyrant who's both inhuman and 252 cruel, cries out daily to his captives? Let your wealth be put before both informers, robbers and traitors for extravagance, and not before the poor or the needy as sustenance. Aren't you the ones who create robbers? Aren't you the ones who add fuel to the fire of the envious? Aren't you the ones who create runaway slaves and traitors as you dangle your wealth before them E like bait? What's this madness? (For madness it is and obvious derangement) to fill your chests with clothes, and to overlook the *one made in the image and likeness of God* (Gen. 1:26), naked and shivering with cold and scarcely able to stand upright.

'But', you say, 'this shivering and weakness is a pretence.' And then you're not afraid that a thunderbolt from heaven will be ignited by these words and fall on you? I'm bursting with anger – forgive me. While you're gorging yourself and getting (187) fat, extending your drinking session late into the evening, burying yourself in soft coverings, you don't think that you'll pay the penalty for having used God's gifts in such an unlawful way. (The purpose of wine is not for us to get drunk, nor is the purpose of nourishment for us to gorge ourselves, nor is the purpose of food for us to distend our belly.) The poor person, on the other hand, who's wretched and as good as dead – are you demanding strict accounts from them without being afraid of Christ's lawcourt, which is so awesome and awe-inspiring? And even if they are pretending, they're pretending because of necessity B and want, thanks to your cruelty and inhumanity which require such masks (and) aren't inclined to mercy. For who is so wretched and miserable that, in the absence of a pressing necessity, they would submit to such disgrace, bewail their lot and put up with a punishment of that magnitude for the sake of a loaf of bread?

The upshot is that their 'pretence' does the rounds, announcing your inhumanity. I mean that, since by beseeching, entreating and uttering pathetic words, by lamenting and weeping and walking around all day, they haven't procured even essential nourishment, perhaps they've devised this strategy, which doesn't bring with it as much disgrace and blame to themselves as it does to you. The point is that, while it's right 253 C for them to be pitied because they've ended up in such great need, we deserve countless punishments in that we've forced poor people to undergo such sufferings. If we were inclined to be flexible, they would never have chosen to undergo sufferings like these.

Why do I speak of their nakedness and shivering? I'll tell you something more shocking than this, namely that some people have been compelled to blind their children at an early age, in order for them to touch our insensibility. The point is that, since while having sight and walking around naked they were able to win over the merciless neither on the grounds of their youth nor on the grounds of their plight, the parents added to ills of this magnitude another tragedy which is more painful. Their purpose is to put a stop to their hunger, because they

D think that it's easier to suffer the deprivation of that common light, that sunlight which is given to all, than to struggle with continual hunger and undergo the most pitiful death. I mean that, since you haven't learned to pity poverty but take pleasure in misfortunes, they satisfy your insatiable desire, and both for themselves and for us they kindle a fiercer flame in hell.

And so that you may learn that this is the reason for these and similar happenings, I'll tell you of an incontrovertible proof that nobody can contradict. There are other poor people who are frivolous, and inflated in their minds, and who don't know how to put up with being hungry, but endure everything rather than that. These often came to us with their pitiful gestures and

E words, and when they didn't derive any profit, stopped their supplications and they subsequently outstripped your side-show performers. Some of them chewed the hide of worn-out shoes, some drove sharp nails through their heads, others lay in frozen water with bare torso, still others endured more absurd activities than these, in order to present a sorry spectacle. You, for your part, while this is taking place, stand there laughing and admiring them, making a fine show of other people's

(188) miseries, while our common nature disgraces itself. What more could a savage demon do than this? Next, so that the poor person will perform the act more enthusiastically, you give them a more generous sum of money. And the poor person who prays and calls on God and approaches you modestly, you don't even deign to answer or look in the face, but when they begin to annoy you with constant requests, you say to them harshly: 'Should this person live? Should they breathe at all, or

254 see this sun (of ours)?' Towards the other people, though, you're cheerful and generous, like a judge of the games presiding

171

over that disgraceful spectacle that is ludicrous and a work of Satan.

B This is why it's quite fair to ask the following questions of those who set up those games and give no prizes at all until they see others punishing themselves: 'Should these people live, or breathe at all, or see this sun (of ours), when they transgress against our common nature and insult God?' When God said: 'Give alms, and I'll give you the kingdom of heaven' (cf. Matt. 6:1), you didn't listen; but when the devil shows you a head that's been nailed through, you immediately become generous. The strategy of the evil demon, which carries with it so much harm, has influenced[1] you more than the promise of God, which carries countless blessings. Even if it's necessary to pay

C money so that these things don't happen and you don't watch them happening, it's imperative to do everything and endure everything in order to get rid of this great madness. But so that these things happen and you watch these things happening, you make every effort and busy yourself on every score. Tell me, are you still asking why hell exists? Ask that question no longer, but ask why there's only one hell. How many punishments don't they deserve – those people who approve of that savage and hard spectacle, and laugh at things that both they and you yourselves should weep over? More so you, who've forced them to perform these disgraceful acts.

'But I don't force it', you reply. Tell me, how don't you force it, when you can't even bear to lend an ear to people who are

D quite modest, who weep and call on God, whereas to the others you even provide money lavishly and surround yourself with many who admire them? 'Are we to stop pitying them?' you ask. Is this your command?' No, it's not pity, my good fellow,[2] to exact such severe penalty for a few cents, to command that someone be maimed for the sake of essential nourishment, and to cut their scalp to shreds in such a painful and pitiful

E manner. 'Be quiet', you reply. 'We're not the ones who put nails through those heads.' I wish you were, then the terrible deed wouldn't be so terrible. The point is that the person who kills someone commits a much more serious crime than the person who commands them to kill themselves, which indeed occurs in the case of these persons. For they put up with more piercing pain when they're commanded to become the executors of those evil instructions. And this situation is found in Antioch, where

they were first called Christians (cf. Acts 11:26), where the most
civilised of all people were bred, where the abundant fruit of
255 charity³ grew of old. They didn't send (food) just to the inhabitants, but also to those very far off when a famine was expected
(cf. Acts 11:27–30).⁴

(189)   'What, then, should we do?' you ask. Give up this wild behaviour, convince everyone who's needy that if they behave like
that they'll receive nothing, whereas if they approach people
modestly, they'll enjoy great munificence. If they learn this
lesson, even if they're the most wretched people of all, they'll
never choose to punish themselves in this way – I guarantee it.
Instead, they'll thank you because you've released them from
their ridicule and pain.

But as it is, you would give away even your children for the
sake of charioteers, and you would throw away your very souls
for the sake of pantomime dancers.⁵ But you wouldn't offer
B even the smallest portion of your wealth for the sake of Christ if
he were hungry. Instead, if you give a paltry sum of money, you
feel as if you've spent all you have, because you don't know that
it's not the fact of giving but the fact of giving generously that's
the special point of charity. That's why it's not simply those who
give whom the prophet proclaims and calls blessed, but those who
pour out money unstintingly. I mean that he doesn't simply say:
'He gave', but he speaks about how (the person gave): *'He distributed freely, he gave to the poor'* (Ps. 112:9). For what use is it when
you give as much of your wealth as someone might give a spoon-
ful of water from the ocean, and you don't imitate the widow's
C generosity of spirit? How will you be able to say: *'Lord, have
mercy on me according to your great mercy, and according to your abundant pity blot out my transgression'* (Ps. 51:1), when you yourself
don't show 'great mercy', but possibly not even 'small mercy'
either? Indeed I'm acutely ashamed when I see many of the
rich riding horses with golden bridles, with a train of servants
clad in gold. They have silver couches and an excessive amount
of other ostentation, and when they're asked to give an offering
to a poor person, they become poorer than the extremely poor.

But what's their constant talk? 'He's got the common church
D allowance',⁶ they say. And what's that to you? I mean, if I give,
256 you're not saved; if the church makes an offering, you haven't
blotted out your sins either. For if you don't give on account
of the fact that the church is obliged to give to the needy,
(then) because the priests pray, will you refuse ever to pray?

And because other people are observing the fast, are you going to be continually drunk? Don't you know that God laid down laws about almsgiving not so much for the sake of the poor as for the sake of those very people who make an offering?

So, you're suspicious about the priest? This itself is an especially serious sin. However, I'm not going to go into any details. Do everything by your own hands, and in that way you'll harvest a double reward. The point is that what we're saying on the subject of almsgiving we're saying not so that you'll make an offering to us, but so that you personally will minister by your own hands. If you make an offering to me, you would maybe be caught by conceit, and perhaps being offended you would withdraw because you suspected me of improper conduct; whereas if you do everything by your own hands, you won't be offended or unreasonably suspicious, and your reward will be greater.

No, I'm not making these statements in order to force you to give your money to the church, nor am I annoyed because priests are being badly spoken of. If I *had* to become annoyed and sad, I'd have to be sad about the fact that you speak badly of them. I mean that those who are spoken badly of in a frivolous and idle way will have a bigger reward, but those who speak badly of them will have a sentence and a punishment that's more grievous. No, I'm not making these statements on their account, but because I care and worry about you. After all, why is it surprising if in our generation some people become suspicious, when in the case of those holy men who imitated the angels and possessed nothing that was their own – I mean the apostles – there was a rumour on the subject of the ministry to widows (cf. Acts 6:1) to the effect that the poor were being overlooked – and this *at a time when nobody said that any of the things they possessed were their own, but they had everything in common* (Acts 4:32)?

Let's not put forward those pretexts or think that the fact that the church has a great deal of property is an excuse. When you look at the extent of her property, bear in mind too the crowds of poor people who are on her books,[7] the great numbers of sick people, the countless occasions when money must be spent: investigate this thoroughly, scrutinise it, nobody will prevent you – no, they're even prepared to give you an account.[8] But I wish to go much further. That is, when we've rendered the accounts[9] and shown that the expenses incurred are not less

c than the income but on occasion even exceed it, I'll gladly ask
you this question: 'When we die and approach heaven[10] and
257 hear Christ saying: *"You saw that I was hungry and you didn't feed
me, naked and you didn't clothe me"* (Matt. 25:42, 43), what shall
we say? What will our defence be? Will we produce this
person or that one who didn't obey these commandments, and
some of the priests who were under suspicion? "And what's
that to you?" he'll say. "I'm accusing you of sins which you personally have committed. Your defence should be that you've
washed off your own sins, not that you point to others who've
made the same mistakes as yourself."'

Indeed, it's because of your stinginess that the church is forced
to have such property as it has now: if people acted in every
D respect according to the laws of the apostles, her income would
be your goodwill, which would be both a secure treasury and an
inexhaustible fortune. But as it is, when you lay up a fortune for
yourself on earth and lock up everything in your treasury, while
the church is forced to spend money on the groups of widows,
the bands of virgins, the visits of strangers, the tribulations of
travellers, the misfortunes of those in prison, the needs of the
sick and maimed, and other occasions of this kind, what should
E be done? Turn away from all those people and block up so many
ports? And who'd be able to endure the shipwrecks that would
occur, the tears, laments and wails that would be produced
from every quarter?

Let's not just say, then, what comes into our heads. For now,
as I said a moment ago, we *are* prepared to render to you the
accounts. But even if it were the reverse, and you had teachers
who were corrupt and rapacious and greedy in every respect,
not even in those circumstances would their evil deeds give
you an excuse. I mean that the generous and all-wise only-
begotten Son of God both saw everything and knew the chance
(191) that, over a long period of time and over the whole world, there
would be priests who would be corrupt. In order that the carelessness of those subject to them shouldn't be increased through
the priests' negligence, he removed every excuse for carelessness.
'*The scribes and the Pharisees sat on Moses' seat*', he said, 'so *do and
observe whatever they tell you to do, but don't do what they do*' (Matt.
23:2–3), indicating that even if you have a bad teacher, it won't
help you at all unless you heed what they say. I mean that it's not
on the basis of what the teacher has done but on the basis of what
258 B you heard and didn't obey that God will pass judgement on you.

The upshot is that if you do what you've been ordered, you'll then stand with a great deal of confidence.[11] But if you disobey what you've been told, even if you can point to countless priests who are corrupt, this won't help you at all. Judas was an apostle too, but nonetheless this fact will never be any defence at all for people who commit sacrilege and are greedy. Nor will anybody who's been accused be able to say: 'Indeed the apostle was a thief, committed sacrilege and was a traitor.' No, it's that very point that in particular will punish and condemn us – the fact that not even the wicked deeds of others have brought us to our C senses. That is precisely why they're recorded in writing, so that we may avoid emulating them.

Let's leave this person and that, and pay attention to ourselves: each of us will have to render an account to God for themselves. So that we may therefore render that account with a proper defence, let's compose our own lives and stretch out a hand generously to the needy, in the knowledge that this is our only defence, namely to show that we ourselves have observed the commandments – there's no other defence. If we can offer this defence, we'll escape those unbearable pains of hell and attain the blessings to come. May we all attain them, through the D grace and love for humankind of our Lord Jesus Christ through whom and with whom to the Father, together with the holy and life-giving Spirit, be glory, power, honour now and always, and for ever and ever. Amen.

ON THE ACTS OF THE APOSTLES
HOMILY 3

INTRODUCTION

The homily was almost certainly delivered at Constantinople as suggested by the detailed reflection on the woes of a bishop and on the quality of the persons required for the office, the claim to be speaking from personal conviction, and John's final statement regarding his status as a brother, but the one in charge. Whether it was delivered in the latter half of 400, as claimed by Kelly (1995: 166–7) and Cameron (1987: 344–9), however, is another matter. The homogeneity of the series, which underpins their argument, has yet to be proven. In this extract John details for us the enormity of the problems faced by a bishop in his relations with individuals and the community. The conflicting and irreconcilable demands placed upon him cause him endless anguish. We also learn something of the milieu in which John himself operates at Constantinople – the palace, the sphere of women and the homes of the powerful and wealthy.

Translated from PG 60,33–42.

TEXT

33 *Then the apostles returned to Jerusalem from the mountain called Olivet, which is near Jerusalem, a sabbath day's journey away* (Acts 1:12).

'Then', it says, *'they returned.'* When is *then*? When they heard:
40 *a.i.* 'they wouldn't have put up with it otherwise, unless Christ had promised them to come again'. It seems to me that these events, too, occurred on the sabbath, for (the evangelist) wouldn't have

pointed out the distance in that way with the words: '*From the mountain called Olivet, which is near Jerusalem, a sabbath day's journey away*', unless they had walked a journey of a prescribed length on the day of the sabbath.

> . . . (there follow nine paragraphs in which the text is closely exegeted, up to and including Acts 1:26 – the election of a replacement for Judas) . . .

38 To put it another way: if there were neither prayer nor remark-able men, the election would've had as much force as in the case of Jonah, on account of the fact that it happened through right judgement (cf. Jonah 1:7); but much more in the case of the disciples where it filled the band, completed the ranks. Nor was the other candidate grieved: the apostles wouldn't have hidden shortcomings within their ranks,[1] because they didn't abstain from speaking about their chief apostles on other
50 occasions when they were annoyed with them – and this hap-pened not once, but twice and many times.[2] Let's then imitate them. I'm no longer addressing myself to everyone, but to those who aim at office. If you believe that election comes from God, don't become annoyed: it's God you're annoyed at, it's he whom you provoke; he's the one who's made the choice. But if he made the choice and you dare to be annoyed by this, you're doing the same as Cain (cf. Gen. 4:3–9). For he should have given his approval, but because his brother's sacrifice was preferred, he was hurt, he was annoyed; he should have felt
60 compunction. I don't say this myself, because it's God who knows how to manage things in a fitting manner. Perhaps you're rather modest in your demeanour but aren't suitable. Again your
39 life is blameless and your demeanour confident, but in the church these aren't the only requirements. In other words, the one's con-nected to the other. Don't you see how much divine scripture discussed these matters?

But let me say why the matter has become contentious. It's because we approach it (sc. episcopal office) not as we would an office and the patronage of brothers, but as an honour and a sinecure. After all, if you knew that the bishop is obliged to belong to everyone as he carries the weight of everyone; that while there's pardon for others who've become angry, for him
10 it's nowhere; that when others make mistakes there's lavish pardon, but for him there's none either – you wouldn't rush,

you wouldn't run to the office. Indeed, the bishop is subject to everyone's tongue, to everyone's judgement, both wise and unwise; he's worn out every day, every night, by worry; he has many who hate him, he has many who envy him. Please don't tell me about those bishops who do everything to curry favour, who wish to sleep, who approach the matter as they would a
20 sinecure. I'm not talking about these men, but about those who go without sleep for the sake of your souls, who put the salvation of those they govern above their own salvation. Tell me, if someone who has ten children subject to him and living with him the whole time is forced to take thought for them continually, the one who has the same number who are not subject to him and live with him but obey their own licence – which one wouldn't you be obliged to be?

'But (the bishop) is honoured', you say. With what kind of honour? Beggars with three cents to their name insult him in the market-place. 'Why, then, doesn't he muzzle them?' All
30 right, but you're not talking about the work of a bishop. Again, if he doesn't provide for everyone, both those who don't work and those who have employment, there are countless complaints on every side – nobody is afraid of accusing him or slandering him. This is because fear hangs over those in office, but not at all over the others: fear of God has no sway over them. How could someone describe the worry concerning preaching and teaching? The difficulty in cases of ordination? Perhaps either I happen to be exceedingly weak and pathetic and good for nothing, or the matter is really like this. The priest's soul is
40 no different from a tossing ship – it's punctured on all sides, by friends, by enemies, by his own people, by strangers. Doesn't the emperor rule the whole world, but the bishop only a city? But the latter's worries are so much greater, as much as the difference between river waters moved simply by the wind and the swollen and furious sea. Why, do you suppose? Because in the case of the emperor there are many who support him (in that everything happens according to law and order), but in the case of the bishop there's nothing comparable, nor can he command on the basis of his authority: but if he's exceedingly moved, he's
50 called cruel; if not exceedingly moved, cold. It's necessary for these opposites to come together so that he's neither despised nor hated. In other words, affairs preoccupy him. How many people is he forced to offend, both whether he likes it or not? How many is he forced to strike with terror, whether he likes

it or not? I'm only saying what I really think and feel. I don't think that many of the clergy will be saved, but a far greater number will be lost — the reason is that the business requires a large spirit. I mean that there are many circumstances which force him to act out of character, and he must have countless eyes on every front.

60
40 Don't you see how much is required of a bishop? — that he be a teacher, patient, *holding firm to the sure word as taught* (Tit. 1:9). How difficult is this? He has responsibility even for the sins of others. I will say nothing of the others — if just one person dies without being initiated, hasn't he ruined his own salvation completely? For the loss of one soul carries such a great punishment that no sermon can convey it: if its salvation is worth so much that the Son of God became a human being, and suffered so much, think how great a punishment its loss will bring. If in
10 the present life a person who's the instrument of another's death deserves to die, it's much more the case with the after-life. Please don't tell me that the priest has done wrong, or the deacon. The responsibilities rest with all those who laid their hands on their heads.[3]

I'll tell you something else again. It happens that someone accepts the election of unsound men. They wonder what counsel he should take concerning their previous sins. The point is there are two precipices: he (sc. the bishop) should neither send the candidate away, nor offend the others. So, should he excommunicate the first man? But there's no current pretext for it. Send him away? 'No', you say, 'for it's the responsibility of the
20 person who ordained (him).' What should he do, then? Not ordain him, but not promote him to another rank either? But it'll be clear to everyone that the person is unsound; therefore he'll offend again in another way. But to promote him to a higher rank? This is much worse.

The upshot is that if someone approached the high-priesthood as they would an office,[4] nobody would accept it immediately. But, as it is, we pursue this too in the same way as secular offices, for in order to be given glory, in order to be honoured in the eyes of human beings, we're lost in the eyes of God. What's the
30 benefit of this honour? How can it be proved to be nothing? When you set your heart on the priesthood, set against it hell, set against it the accounts (to be rendered) there (sc. in heaven), set against it the carefree life, set against it limited punishment. But, even if you sin as a private person, you'll suffer nothing like

it; if you're a priest, you're lost. Consider how much Moses put up with, how spiritual a life he led,[5] how much he displayed good qualities, and because he committed one sin only, he was punished harshly (cf. Num. 20:2–12). Rightly so. This involved the punishment of the others. The result was that he was
40 punished more harshly, not because the sin was committed in public, but because it was the sin of a priest. I mean that we don't inflict the same punishment for sins which are committed in public and those which are committed in private: while the sin is the same, the punishment isn't the same – rather the sin isn't even the same. For sinning in private and in secret isn't the same thing as sinning in public. The bishop can't sin in private, for he must be content to be freed of charges when he hasn't sinned, let alone when he has sinned. Even if he's angry, even if he laughs, even if he desires to dream and relax, many
50 people scoff at him, many people are offended, many people lay down the law, many call to mind the bishops of old, and reproach the present one. And they do this not wishing to praise the former, but to sting the latter, as they call to mind the co-bishops, the presbyters. 'War is sweet for the inexperienced', they say.

It's fitting to say this in the present circumstances as well – rather, we'll say it too before engaging in battle: after engaging in battle we aren't even recognisable to many people. Our battle at present isn't directed against those who oppress the poor, nor are we enduring the defence of the flock, but in the manner of
41 those shepherds in the book of Ezekiel (34:2–3), we're slaughtering and devouring. Who of us exhibits such great concern for the flocks of Christ as did Jacob for the flocks of Laban (cf. Gen. 29:15–30)? Who can give a detailed description of the cold at night? Don't tell me about all-night vigils and extended worship. Everything is, in fact, the other way around. Prefects and magistrates[6] don't enjoy as much honour as the one who governs the church. If you go into the palace, who is first? If he's with
10 women, if he's in the houses of the great, no-one else is honoured above him. He's lost everything and has perished. I make these statements not because I wish to put you to shame, but to check your desire. With what kind of conscience do you lobby either for yourself or for another? With what kind of eyes do you regard the one who helped you? What can you offer in your defence? Certainly the bishop, involuntary, forced and unwilling, would have some defence, even if he's the one who

for the most part is deprived of pardon. But apart from this he has some defence. Consider what befell Simon (cf. Acts 8:18–
20 20). For what use is it if you don't give silver, but give flattery in the place of silver, and make many arrangements, and scheme? *'May your silver perish with you'* (Acts 8:20). Peter said this to him, and he'll say it to these people: 'May your lobbying perish with you, because you thought that you could buy the gift of God by human cajolery.'

Nobody is like this? Heaven forbid! – I wish that nothing of what has been said applied to you, but, as it is, we've fallen into these words as a natural consequence. The point is that not even when I'm attacking greed, am I speaking against you, nor against
30 a single person. My wish is that the drugs prepared by us aren't needed. Such are the prayers of doctors: they request nothing other than that, after so much preparation, the drugs be simply thrown away. This is our prayer too, that our words be spoken simply into the air, with the result that they're just words. I for my part am prepared to give my support to everything, in order not to arrive at the necessity of making these statements. But if you wish, we'll be silent; only let it be a silence without danger. For I don't think that there's anyone, not even if they're extremely conceited, who would want simply
40 to put on an oratorical display. We'll concede the teaching to you. This is a greater teaching, which touches through the facts. The best of doctors would wish their friends to be
42 well, even though the illness of the sufferers earns them their livelihood, and we too wish everyone to be well. We wish this not so that we may be approved of, and you disapproved of. If it were possible, I would like the love which I have for you to be obvious from my face: no-one afterwards would bring any accusation against me, even if the sermon had been very harsh, for what is said by friends, even if it's insulting, is bearable. For *the wounds inflicted by a friend are more trustworthy than the spontaneous kisses of any enemy* (Prov. 27:6).

10 Nothing is dearer to me than you, not even this light. I would pray to be blinded a thousand times if in this way I could convert your souls. Thus your salvation is sweeter to me than light itself. What use to me are the sun's rays when the despondency caused by you spreads great darkness over my eyes? I mean that light is good when it appears in a joyful situation, whereas it appears troublesome to a grieving soul. May I never have to prove that
20 I'm not lying! But if ever it happens that one of you sins, you

should stand beside me as I sleep. Let me be damned if I don't seem like the paralytics or the insane, according to the saying of the prophet: *'And the light of my eyes — it's also gone from me'* (Ps. 38:10). For what hope have you got, if you don't make progress? What despondency can there be, if you're in good repute? I have the impression that I'm flying, when I hear something good about you. *Complete my joy* (Phil. 2:2).

I've introduced such a powerful statement into my prayer only because I desire your progress. I strive for this with regard to you all, because I love you, because I hold you close, because you are everything to me — both father and mother, and brothers and children. Don't think, then, that any of what I say is said from hatred; it's said to correct you. *'For a brother who is helped by a brother'*, it says, *'is like a strong city'* (Prov. 18:19 LXX). Don't, then, feel rejected, because I'm not holding what you say in contempt, but I'd like to be corrected by you, I'd like to learn. We're all brothers, we have the one guide. Among brothers too it's the case that one gives orders, and the others obey. Don't feel rejected, then, but let's do everything for the glory of God, because to him is the glory for ever and ever. Amen.

CONCERNING BLESSED PHILOGONIUS

INTRODUCTION

About Philogonius, the subject of this homily, little is known other than that he was bishop of Antioch at the time when the Arian controversy began in the first quarter of the fourth century. He is thought to have died a few months before the Council of Nicaea (EEC 2: 682). According to Theodoret (HE 1.3) he was also responsible for completing the rebuilding of the Old Church that had been initiated by Vitalis. The homily was delivered on the feast day of Philogonius, 20 December, possibly in the year 386. The day and month are confirmed by John's anticipation of the liturgical festival of Christmas, which had only recently been introduced at Antioch (see Intro., Ch. 2), and which he says will occur in five days' time.

The homily is significant for a number of reasons. It alludes to the fact that at this time on major liturgical festivals the audience not infrequently heard more than one person preach. In this case the bishop, Flavian, is to preach immediately following John. John anticipates that Flavian will cover some of the same material but provide more detailed information. Such occasions could also be accompanied by a market day, so that not only was it a special time because of the commemoration of an individual significant in the life of the Nicene (Meletian) church at Antioch, but also because people flooded into the city from the surrounding countryside to ply their produce and wares, and the festival atmosphere extended into the entire city. We are also informed about people's habits when it came to attending the eucharist. Not only did a number of people communicate only once a year on the day of a major festival, but their behaviour at such times tended to be unruly.

Throughout this homily the words *panēgyris* and *heortē* present some difficulty for the translator, since John uses them interchange-

184

ably and because in addition the term *panēgyris* can refer not only to a festival or celebration, but also to a market day. The unusual subtitle to the text (*Homily 6*) refers to the location of the homily in the manuscript tradition as sixth among a series of homilies on the topics of the incomprehensible nature of God and the equality of the Father and the Son, which John preached against the Anomoeans, the majority at Antioch, some at Constantinople.

Translated from PG 48,747–56.

TEXT

747–8 *On blessed Philogonius who, from being an advocate, became a bishop; and on the subject that nothing makes us acceptable in God's eyes to the same extent as taking thought for matters which are conducive to the common good; and that approaching the holy mysteries in a careless way will result in a punishment that cannot be endured, even if we have the effrontery to do this only once a year. The sermon was delivered five days before the birth of Christ.*

747 *Homily 6*

Today too I was preparing myself to strip off in order to wrestle with the heretics[1] and to repay you the rest of my debt. But the day of blessed Philogonius, whose festival we are celebrating now, has invited us[2] to describe his achievements. And of course I'm obliged to accede. I mean that if the person who curses their father or mother will be put to death (cf. Exod.
748 21:17; Lev. 20:9), it's plain that the person who blesses them will indeed have the benefit of life. And if it's essential for our natural parents to enjoy such a degree of goodwill from us, it's much more the case with our spiritual parents. This is especially true when praising them can't make them more distinguished because they're dead, whereas it makes us, the congregation, better people, whether we are preaching or listening. For the saint who's gone up to heaven has no need of acclamation
749 from human beings in order to arrive at a greater and more blessed lot. We, on the other hand, who are meanwhile engaged in matters on earth and crave a great deal of consolation from all quarters, need to hear the saint praised in order to be galvanised to emulate him. This is why some wise person said in encouragement: '*The memory of the just person is accompanied by words of praise*'

185

(Prov. 10:7 LXX). It's not as if those who've passed away derive the greatest benefit from this, but those who utter words of praise. Since, then, such great benefit accrues to us from this
10 course of action, let's be convinced and not dispute it. Indeed, the time is appropriate for a description of this kind. I mean that today blessed Philogonius was translated to the undisturbed life, and brought his boat into an anchorage where in future he couldn't fear shipwreck, nor any dejection or pain. And what's surprising if that place is free of dejection, the place about which Paul spoke to people who were still alive when he said: *'Rejoice always, pray constantly'* (1 Thess. 5:16–17)?

But here on earth there's illness, abusive treatment, premature
20 death, blackmail, envy, dejection, anger, evil desire, countless plots, day-to-day worries, and ills that come thick and fast, bringing countless sufferings from all quarters. (Yet) Paul said it was possible to rejoice always, if a person gets their head above the wave of mundane affairs for a little while and composes their life in the proper way. How much more easily, after our departure from this life, will we achieve what's good, when all those ills are removed – bad health, suffering and the cause of
30 sin, when 'mine' and 'yours' (those cold expressions), as well as everything that introduces horrors into our lives and engenders countless wars, cease to exist.

This is why I'm making a special point of calling this saint blessed, because, even if he's been translated and has left our city, he's nonetheless gone up to the city of God; and while he's left the church here, he's ended up in the church in heaven in which the first-born are enrolled (cf. Heb. 12:23); he's left the feasts on earth, and has moved on instead to celebrating with the angels. That there are city, church and celebration in heaven,
40 listen to Paul when he says: *'You've come to the city of the living God, the heavenly Jerusalem, and to the church of the first-born who are enrolled in heaven, and to innumerable angels in celebration'* (Heb. 12:22–3). It's not only because of the great number of powers in heaven, but also because of the abundance of blessings, and the unbroken joy and gladness, that Paul calls everything there a celebration.

I mean that it's not usual to celebrate for any other reason than that a great number of people have been gathered together and that there's an abundant supply of goods for sale, when wheat
50 and barley and miscellaneous produce of every kind, flocks of sheep and herds of cattle, clothing and other such wares are

186

brought (into town). Some are vendors, some are buyers. 'But', you say, 'what is there of that in heaven?' There's none of that. Heaven's much loftier than that. They don't have wheat and barley and different kinds of produce, but everywhere there there's the fruit of the spirit, love and joy and gladness, peace and goodness, and a great abundance of gentleness. There are no flocks of sheep and herds of cattle, but the spirits of the
750 just who've been perfected and the virtues of souls, and everywhere in heaven you can see their life's achievements. You can't see clothes or coverings, but crowns more precious than solid gold, trophies[3] and prizes, and the innumerable blessings which are laid up in store for those who have achieved (this life).

And the crowd of those who come together (sc. in heaven) is both loftier and larger — it's not composed of men from both towns and countryside, but in one place there are thousands of
10 angels, in another millions of archangels, on one side there is a group of prophets, on another there are bands of martyrs, ranks of apostles, assemblies of the just, various communes of all those who've pleased God. The celebration is something truly wonderful, and greater than all (others) because the one who's king over all this walks around in the middle of the celebration. For when Paul said: '*To the thousands of angels in celebration*', he added, '*and to the judge who is God of all*' (Heb. 12:23). Whoever saw a king appear at a celebration? On earth nobody has ever seen him. But in heaven those present see him continually to the extent that it's possible, as, with his presence,
20 he honours with the brilliance of his own glory all those who've come together. And while these celebrations (on earth) are often finished at midday, the celebration in heaven isn't like that: it doesn't wait for periods of months, or cycles of years, or a number of days, but it takes place continually, and all the blessings it contains don't have an end, it knows no conclusion, it can't be out of date or lose its effectiveness[4] — it's not subject to age or death. There's no clamour there as there is here, no tumult, but everything is well-ordered and has an inherent
30 discipline, just as in the case of a cithera: they send up to the Master of both parts of creation[5] an elaborate rhythmical song sweeter that any other music, while the souls there perform the divine act of celebration as if in secret inner places and divine mysteries.

It's to that saintly lot which isn't subject to death that blessed Philogonius went today. What homily is there that could match

a person who has attained such good fortune? There isn't one.
40 Well, then, tell me — are we to keep silent on that account,
and why have we come together? Shall we say that we won't
be capable of reaching the grandeur of his deeds? It's because
of that very fact that we're obliged to speak, because it's precisely
that topic which is the most important part of our encomium,
when our words can't be made equal to the deeds they describe.
I mean that when people's achievements go beyond our mortal
nature, encomia are clearly also beyond a human tongue. However, our words won't evade us on this account, but they'll
imitate the Master himself: to the widow who deposited just
50 two cents he gave a reward that didn't consist only of two cents
(cf. Luke 21:1–4). Why did he do this? Because it wasn't the
amount of money he paid attention to, but the wealth of her
intention. For if you examine the money, it was a very paltry
sum, but if you disclose her motive for giving, you'll observe a
treasure of generosity that's inexpressible. The upshot is that
even if our words are few and of little value, they're still what
we have to offer; and if they're inferior to the generosity of the
noble and just Philogonius, the very fact that he doesn't reject
our few words but does the same as rich people do would be the
751 greatest proof of his generosity of spirit. For when rich people
receive from poor people small amounts of money which they
have no need of, they add to it from their own money, repaying
those who offered what they could. Similarly when Philogonius
too receives words of acclamation from us which he has no need
of, he'll repay our blessing by his deeds, which we're always in
need of.

Where, then, should we begin our words of praise? Where else
but from the office which the grace of the Spirit entrusted him
10 with. Secular offices wouldn't of course be a proof of the virtue of
those entrusted with them: instead they're often an indictment of
their wickedness. Why? Because it's usually the patronage of
friends, cajolery, flattery and many other activities more shameful than these that procure such offices. But when God appoints[6]
and elects, and that hand touches the holy head, the election is
impartial, the choice is above suspicion, the authority of the
one who makes the appointment would be the indisputable
commendation of the appointee.

20 That it was God who appointed Philogonius is clear from his
very way of life: he was plucked from the middle of the market-
place and brought to this throne. So he demonstrated that his

188

former way of life was chaste and distinguished, since he had a wife and daughter and was engaged in the lawcourt. In this way he eclipsed the sun, such that from that rank he was immediately considered worthy of the priestly office, and he was brought from the tribunal of the lawcourt to the sacred tribunal.[7] Formerly he acted as advocate for people against machinators, making the wronged more powerful than those who wronged them; coming into the church he acted as advocate
30 for people against abusive demons. (In regard to) how substantial the demonstration of his virtue is – in that, by the grace of God, he was considered worthy of such high office – listen to what Christ said to Peter after his resurrection. When he said: *'Peter, do you love me?'* (John 21:16), and Peter answered: *'You know, Lord, that I love you'*, Christ didn't say: 'Throw money away, practise fasting, austerity, raise the dead, drive out demons' – he didn't bring up any of these activities, nor any other signs or
40 achievements, but passing over all of that, he said: *'If you love me, tend my sheep'* (John 21:16). He said this not only because he wanted to show us the most powerful sign of Peter's love for him, but also, in order to show the love which he bore for his sheep, he gave moreover this very powerful demonstration of Peter's goodwill towards him, almost saying: 'The one who loves my sheep, loves me.'

See, then, how much Christ endured for that flock: he became human, he took on *the form of a slave* (Phil. 2:7), he was spat on, he was beaten (cf. Matt. 26:67ff.). In the end he didn't refuse
50 even death, and the most disgraceful death: he poured out his blood on the cross. And so if someone wanted to be high in his esteem, they should concern themselves with those sheep, seek the common good, care for their own brothers and sisters. No achievement is preferable to this in God's eyes. This is why he said on another occasion: *'Simon, Simon, Satan demanded to winnow you like grain, and I have prayed for you so that your faith doesn't desert you'* (Luke 22:31–2). 'Well, then, what will you give me in exchange for that care and forethought?' What kind of thing does he require in exchange? The very same
60 thing that he gave. *'And when you have turned again'*, he says, *'strengthen your brothers and sisters'* (Luke 22:32). Paul too said in
752 like vein: *'Become imitators of me, just as I am of Christ'* (1 Cor. 10:33). How do you become an imitator of Christ? *By pleasing everyone in all respects, and not seeking my own advantage, but that of many, so that they may be saved* (1 Cor. 10:33). And on another

occasion he says: *'For Christ didn't please himself'* (Rom. 15:3), but
many. Indeed, there's nothing that would mark or characterise
the believer who loves Christ, as much as caring for their
brothers and sisters and being concerned with their salvation.

Let all the monks listen to this, both those who occupy the
10 mountain peaks, and those who've crucified themselves to the
world in every respect, so that to the extent they can they may
support the presidents of the churches, (and) encourage them
with prayers, concord, love. Let them know that, even though
they live[8] at a distance, unless in every way they support those
who've been appointed by the grace of God and have taken
upon themselves the worries of so many affairs, the point[9] of
their existence will be lost, and wisdom will be cut off completely. That this is the most powerful demonstration of love
20 towards Christ is clear from the following: let's observe how the
bishop has administered that office. I should say that there's no
need of explanation, nor is there need for our voice, because your
zeal shows his administration for what it is. It's just as someone
who goes into a vineyard and sees that the vines are luxuriant
with leaves, heavy with fruit, walled on all sides with fences
and palings, will have no need of any explanation or other
proof to know the quality of the vine-dresser and the labourer.
Similarly in the case of the episcopal office too, if someone
30 comes in and sees these spiritual vines, and your fruit, they'll
have no need of an explanation and instruction to learn (the
quality of) your president. It's just as Paul also said: *'You yourselves are our letter of recommendation, written and read out'* (2 Cor.
3:2). The river is an indication of the source, and the fruit, of
the root.

I should have spoken about the time when Philogonius was
entrusted with this office – it forms no small part of the encomium, and is rather an extremely fitting indication of the
40 man's quality. There was namely a great deal of discontent at the
time, because the persecution had just finished, vestiges[10] still
remained of that most difficult period of distress, and matters
badly needed rectifying. And again I should have added to that
the fact that the separation of the heretics, which had its beginning at the time of the persecution, was being held in check,
because Philogonius in his wisdom made provision for everything. But, in any case, our homily is running on to another,
unavoidable subject. On this account we'll leave our common

father,[11] who's an admirer of blessed Philogonius, to speak on these subjects because his knowledge of all the historical material
50 is more accurate than ours, and we'll move on to another avenue of discourse. I say this because a feast is approaching which is the most solemn and awe-inspiring of all feasts. If one were to call it the metropolis[12] of all feasts, one wouldn't be wrong. What is it? The birth of Christ according to the flesh.

In this feast namely Epiphany, holy Easter,[13] Ascension and Pentecost have their beginning and their purpose. For if Christ hadn't been born according to the flesh, he wouldn't have been
753 baptised, which is Epiphany. He wouldn't have been crucified, which is Easter. He wouldn't have sent the Spirit, which is Pentecost. So from this event, as from some spring, different rivers flow – these feasts of ours are born. But not only on this account would it be right to give precedence to this day, but also because what happened on it is much more awe-inspiring than all other days. I say this because the fact that Christ died after becoming human was the consequence of that: even if he didn't commit sin, still he assumed a mortal body. And that
10 too was an amazing fact: that, although God, he was willing to become human and to condescend to take so much on himself that not even the imagination can embrace. It's this that's most awe-inspiring, and completely perplexing. Even Paul said in amazement: *'Great indeed, we confess, is the mystery of our religion'* (1 Tim. 3:16). How great? *God was manifested in the flesh* (1 Tim. 3:16). And again he says elsewhere: *'For surely it's not with angels that God is concerned, but with the descendants of Abraham. Therefore he had to be made like his brothers and sisters in every respect'* (Heb. 2:16–17).
20 On this account especially I embrace and love this day, and put my ardent love on show to make you share in my affection for it. On this account I beg and entreat all of you to be present with much zeal and enthusiasm, each having vacated your own house, so that we may see our Master lying in the manger, dressed in swaddling-clothes – that awe-inspiring and miraculous sight. What kind of defence could we have, what kind of excuse, when he came down from heaven for our sake while we
30 can't even leave the house to go to him? (Or) when the Magi, who were barbarians and foreigners, hurried from Persia to see him lying in the manger? But you, a Christian, can't be bothered to travel even a short distance in order to enjoy this blessed

sight? For if we're present in faith we'll certainly see him lying in the manger: this table fulfils the role of the manger.

40 swaddling-clothes as formerly, but attired completely with the Holy Spirit. Those who are initiated know what I'm saying. The Magi merely worshipped him, whereas you, if you approach (to communicate) with a clear conscience, we permit to consume him and go back home. Approach, then, bringing gifts – not gifts like the Magi brought but ones that are much more solemn. They brought gold; you must bring temperance and virtue. They brought incense; you must bring pure prayers, (which are) spiritual incense. They brought myrrh; you must

50 bring humility and a humble heart and charity. If you approach with these gifts, with great confidence you'll enjoy this holy table. For my part, I'm saying this now because I know quite well that on that day many of you will come forward and fall on this spiritual sacrifice. So that we don't do this to the detriment or condemnation of our soul but for our salvation, I'm calling you to witness beforehand, and I'm begging you to approach

60 the holy mysteries after you've cleansed yourselves in every respect.

Please don't let anybody say to me: 'I'm full of shame, I have a

754 conscience crammed with sins, I'm carrying a very heavy burden.' If you're sober, and pray and keep vigil, the appointed period of five days is sufficient to trim away your many sins. Don't look at how short the time is, but consider the point that the Master is loving. The Ninevites were able to beat off (God's) considerable anger in three days, and the time-constraint was no hindrance,

10 but their readiness of spirit captured the Master's generosity and was able to effect everything (cf. Jon. 3). The prostitute, too, coming to Christ in a brief critical moment washed away all her offences (cf. Luke 7). When the Jews made the accusation that Christ had admitted her and had given her so much confidence, he silenced them, and freed her from all evils, and, having approved her enthusiasm, he sent her away. What's the message? That she came with an ardent mind and a burning soul and a fervent faith, and she touched those holy and sacred feet, when

20 she had let down her hair, let tears flood from her eyes, and poured out the perfume.

The objects by which she bewitched people, she used to prepare the drugs of repentance. The objects by which she excited the gaze of the licentious, she used to weep tears. The locks of

192

hair by which she tripped up many people so they fell into sin, she used to wipe Christ's feet. The perfume by which she enticed, she used to anoint his feet. And you too must therefore placate
30 God in turn by using the objects by which you provoked him. Did you provoke him by stealing money? Win him over by giving away what you stole to those who've been unjustly treated, and give other things in addition; say in the words of Zacchaeus: 'I give back four times everything I've stolen' (cf. Luke 19:8). Have you provoked him with your tongue and your abuse, by insulting many people? Propitiate him in turn with your tongue, by sending up pure prayers, by blessing those who abuse you, by praising those who speak badly of you, by
40 thanking those who wrong you. These actions don't require days or the passing of many years, but only right purpose, and they can be accomplished in one day. Keep aloof from wickedness, embrace virtue, desist from evil; promise to commit these sins no longer, and this will be sufficient for your defence. I testify and guarantee that, if each of us who've sinned keeps aloof from their former evil ways and promises God truthfully that they won't touch them any more, God will require nothing else for a substantial defence. I say this because he is generous
50 and merciful, and just as a woman in labour longs to give birth, so he too longs to dispense his mercy – it's our sins that interfere with this.

Let's pull down the wall, then, and right from that time begin the feast, renouncing all activities during these five days. 'Farewell to the lawcourts, farewell to the council chambers – a plague on daily business, with its contracts and transactions. I want to save my soul.' *What does it profit a person if they gain the whole world but forfeit their life?* (Matt. 16:26). The Magi came away from Persia; you must come away from daily business
755 and travel towards Jesus. The distance isn't great, if we're willing. The point is that you don't have to cross the sea, or traverse mountain peaks, but if you sit at home, exhibiting piety and much compunction, you can see the wall being completely broken down, you can remove the obstacle, you can cut the length of the journey. *'For I am a God at hand'*, it says, *'and not a God far off'* (Jer. 23:23), and *'The Lord is near to all who call on him in truth'* (Ps. 145:18).

But as it is, many of the faithful have arrived at such a degree
10 of silliness and neglect that, although they're full of countless evils, and because they take no thought whatsoever for themselves,

they approach this table on feast days in a random and frivolous fashion. They don't know that the time of communion doesn't consist of a feast and a celebration, but of a clear conscience and a life free of reproach. Just as the ordinary person who has nothing on their conscience ought to approach communion every day, so it's unsafe for the person who's overpowered by sin

20 and doesn't repent to approach even on a feast day. For approaching once a year isn't going to free us from reproach, if we approach unworthily; but it's precisely this that damns us all the more, namely that when we approach on that one occasion we're not even then approaching with a clear conscience.

That's why I beg all of you not to touch the divine mysteries in a negligent manner because you have to celebrate the feast. If, however, you're ever going to partake of this holy offering, you must purify yourselves for many days beforehand through repentance and prayer and almsgiving and devotion to spiritual matters, and not *return like a dog to its own vomit* (Prov. 26:11).

30 Isn't it absurd to take so much care over bodily concerns, so that many days before the feast approaches you get your best clothes out of their chests and get them ready, and you buy shoes, and enjoy a more lavish table, and over and above that you take thought for many provisions from all quarters, and in every respect you smarten yourself up and make yourself look good? On the other hand, you take no account of your soul, which is neglected, dirty, squalid, wasted from hunger and still unclean.

40 (Isn't it absurd that) while you bring your smart body to church, you overlook your soul, which is naked and disgraced? Yet whereas your fellow servant sees your body and no harm results

756 no matter how it's dressed, the Master sees your soul and will put in place a most serious punishment for its neglect.

Don't you know that this table is full of spiritual fire, and just as springs gush forth the force of water, so too does the table contain a certain mysterious flame? So don't approach it if you're carrying stubble, wood or dry grass, in case you cause a bigger blaze and you burn your soul as it takes communion. But bring precious stones, gold, silver, in order to make the

10 material more pure, in order to go back home having derived a great deal of profit. If you've got something wicked in you, get rid of it, banish it from your soul. Is it the case that someone has an enemy, and is suffering grievous wrongs at their hands? Let them bring the enmity to an end, let them restrain their inflamed and swollen attitude, so that internally they experience

no tumult or disturbance. I say this because in communicating you are going to welcome a king. But if it's a king coming into your soul there must be abundant tranquillity, abundant silence and a deep peace for your thoughts. But you're suffering grievous wrongs, and you can't stop being angry? Why, then, do
20 you visit much greater wrongs and difficulties on yourself? Whatever the person does, your enemy won't inflict on you the kind of harm you inflict on yourself by not being reconciled with them but rather trampling God's laws under your feet. Did your enemy insult you? Is it on this account, tell me, that you then insult God? Refusing to be reconciled with the one who hurt you isn't so much a sign of taking revenge on them as of insulting God, who laid down these laws.

So don't look at your fellow servant, nor at the magnitude of the wrongs they've done, but when you've put God and the fear
30 of God into your mind, consider the following point. The excessive wrenching that you feel internally when, after countless evil acts, you force yourself to be reconciled with the one who hurt you, will be commensurate with the increased esteem which you will enjoy in the eyes of God, who ordered this course of action. And just as here on earth you'll welcome God with great honour, so too will he receive you in heaven with great glory, as he pays you back ten-thousandfold for your obedience. May all of us attain this through the grace and love for human-
40 kind of our Lord Jesus Christ, with whom to the Father, together with the Holy Spirit, be glory, honour, power and adoration, for ever and ever. Amen.

LETTERS FROM EXILE

INTRODUCTION

All of the surviving letters of John Chrysostom date from the period of his exile (late June 404 to 14 September 407). Of the nine selected and translated below the majority appear to have been written during the space of a few months, towards the end of 404. Delmaire speculates that the letter to Theodora, a member of the nobility at Constantinople, cannot date before the winter of 404/5 (Delmaire 1991: 161). The letter to Studius the Urban Prefect was probably written by John in either September or November 404, but most certainly prior to December 404. The *terminus ante quem* can be fixed because Studius was replaced as Urban Prefect of Constantinople by the pagan Optatus, possibly after the sudden death of the empress Eudoxia on 6 October 404 (Delmaire 1991: 159-60). The letters to Salustius and Theophilus, presbyters of Constantinople, and to Theodore, an aristocrat likewise situated at Constantinople, are located by Delmaire (1991: 157, 162, 168) at the end of November 404. It is probably at this same time that John wrote the letter to Valentinus, another aristocrat resident in Constantinople (Delmaire 1991: 169–70). In constrast, the letter to Diogenes, a dignitary of some standing who lives either in Cappadocia, Armenia or Bithynia, belongs to the year 405 (Delmaire 1991: 124). This can be determined from the allusion to the problems being encountered by the missionaries working in Phoenicia. John penned his letter to Carteria, a member of the aristocracy at Antioch, during the winter of 404/5 as determined by the date of two other letters (Letters 18 and 227) which he wrote to her (Delmaire 1991: 116–17). John probably addressed his only surviving letter to Harmatius, a member of the nobility of Antioch, in September 404 (Delmaire 1991: 111–12).

The letters have been chosen for the breadth of pastoral activity that they record. In them we see John using the letter as a medium for direct care for the soul of individuals (Letters 117, 197), continuing to exercise authority over his clergy out of care both for the individuals in question and for the flock whom they serve (Letters 203, 212), and encouraging lay Christians to use their resources to exercise or support welfare and mission activities on his behalf (Letters 210, 217). We also gain a glimpse of the care exhibited towards John by lay Christians supportive of his person and ministry (Letters 34, 75). It should be borne in mind when reading them that the letters which we present here are not necessarily representative. Letters 203, 210 and 212, for instance, are the only surviving letters in which John concerns himself with the daily duties of his former clergy. Likewise, Letters 117 and 197 are two of only a handful in which he directly exercises pastoral care for the individuals with whom he corresponds. The persistence of mission endeavours in Phoenicia and among the Goths are among his more usual pastoral concerns.

Translated from PG 52,629–30 (Letter 34); 636–7 (Letter 51); 649 (Letter 75); 672–3 (Letter 117); 721–2 (Letter 197); 724 (Letter 203); 728 (Letter 210); 729 (Letter 212); 730–1 (Letter 217).

TEXTS

Care for the souls of individuals

Letter 117 – To Theodora

672 I write to your decorousness infrequently, since I don't readily meet with people to convey what I have written; yet I do not remember you infrequently, but rather constantly: the second
40 *a.i.* lies within our means, while the first is not within our means. That is, we ourselves have control of our uninterrupted memories, while we no longer have the capacity to post our letters. That is why the one activity occurs all the time, the other, whenever it is possible. Whereas the other letters that we sent contained a greeting, this letter contains a request for a favour as well. What is the favour? Something that brings reward to you who grant it rather than to me who receive it, and benefits the giver before the receiver. I say this because it has come to our attention that Eustathius is among those who have offended your

30 *a.i.* worthiness, and that he has been thrown out of your house and banished from your sight.[1] And so, while I cannot speak about the precise nature of the affair, nor about the reason why he has experienced such great anger, this much I do know – that the following words are such as you ought to hear from us, since we keep a firm grip on your salvation.

You know that the present life is nothing. Rather, it imitates the flowers of spring and feeble shadows, and is the deceit of dreams. Whereas the things that are true and fixed and unchanging – those things we shall receive after we depart this life. You have often heard these sentiments from us and, for your

20 *a.i.* own part, are constant in your philosophy. For that reason I do not make the letter long, but have this to say.

If certain persons have acted in an abusive way and have been thrown out[2] unjustly, out of consideration for the nature of justice correct what has taken place. If it has been done justly, again, out of respect for the laws of generosity,[3] do exactly the same. You will harvest a much greater reward from the action than that person. My point is that the slave who asked his fellow servant to return the hundred denarii did not harm him so much as deliver himself a fatal blow, seeing that, through

10 *a.i.* his stinginess towards his co-servant, he revoked the forgiveness of his ten thousand talents (cf. Matt. 18:23–35). In the same way, the person who overlooks the sins of their neighbour mitigates for themselves the accounts (that they will have to render) in the life to come and, the greater the sins they forgive, the greater too the forgiveness they themselves will receive. The difference lies not only in this circumstance, but also in that the one who grants a servile favour will receive a master's gift. Don't tell me, then, that he did this wrong or that. My point is that the worse you show what he did to be, the more compelling you

673 reveal to be the grounds for forgiveness, since you will set aside for yourself in advance a far greater promise of generosity in the future.

For this reason let go your anger, even if it's just. Conquer your rage with wise, rational thought. Offer it up as a sacrifice to God. Grant us, who love you, a favour too and show how even via a brief letter we wield considerable influence. Do yourself a favour also with regard to the significant benefits which I have mentioned – namely serenity, the eviction from the soul of the confusion that stems from this world, and, as a result, the

10 utterly confident request of God, who loves humankind, for entry

into the kingdom (of heaven). I say this because kindness towards one's neighbour is truly a great purifier of sins. *'For if you forgive people their transgressions'*, it says, *'your heavenly Father will also forgive you'* (Matt. 6:14).

So then, consider all these points and send us a letter that shows that our writing has had some effect. For the part which is ours is accomplished and we have done what it is within our power to do. We have encouraged, we have entreated, we have asked a favour, we have given the advice that we should.
20 Henceforth, all of our attention[4] is focused on you. I say this because the reward for this encouragement will be set aside for us, whether anything does or does not happen further – one can receive payment even for words. Instead our entire effort is that your decorousness also benefit through this action and that, as a result of your present achievements, you will reap the future, immortal blessings with considerable ease.

Letter 197 – To Studius the Urban Prefect

721 I know, even before I read what you have written, that, because you are intelligent and experienced in philosophy, you will bear mildly the departure of the blessed brother of your magnificence. For I would not call it death. But since it is essential that we too contribute what we can, I ask, most magnificent master, that your excellency show your character at this time too. I don't ask that you do not grieve (that is impossible, since you are
10 *a.i.* human and intertwined with flesh, and are missing a brother of such quality), but that you impose a limit on your grief. For you know the perishable nature of human affairs, and that events mimic the flowing waters of a river, and how one should consider blessed only those people who with firm hope dismiss the present life. For they do not go to meet death, but move from the contests to the prizes, from the wrestling bouts to the victors' crowns, from the raging sea to the tranquil harbour.

With these points in mind, then, console yourself, since,
722 although we too are affected more than is usual by grief, we have a considerable comfort for our distress – the virtue of the man – which I know brings you also considerable consolation. My point is that if the dead man had been a wicked person and full of evil, it would have been proper to howl and wail for that reason. But since he was of such quality and lived his life, as the whole city

knows, with propriety and with goodness; since he always
honoured justice; since he used the appropriate boldness, freedom
and courage; since he placed no value on the present, but was a
10 stranger to worldly care, you should rejoice and congratulate
both him and your excellent self. This is because you have sent
ahead[5] such an excellent brother who from now on keeps in an
inviolate treasury the blessings that were in his possession
when he departed.

So then, consider nothing unworthy of yourself, my most
excellent master, shattered as you are by sorrow. Yet show
your character at this present time also and be so kind as to disclose to us that you have derived some benefit from what we have
written, so that we too, who are situated at so great a distance,
20 may pride ourselves that we have been able to cut away much of
this despondency by a simple letter.

Continuing concern for his clergy

Letter 203 – To Salustius, presbyter

724 I was more than usually upset when I heard that both you and
Theophilus the presbyter have lapsed. I say this because it has
come to my knowledge that the one of you has preached five
homilies up until the month of October, while the other (has
preached) not a single one. That fact is more grievous to
30 me than the isolation here. If this report is false, then please
make it clear to me. If it's true, get things in order and galvanise
each other. (I ask this) because you have the capacity to grieve me
exceedingly, even though I love you exceedingly to distraction.
And yet what is worse is that you also invite a severe judgement
against yourselves from God by spending your lives in such
idleness and indolence and not making your own particular
contribution. For what pardon could you possibly receive when,
while others are being persecuted, exiled and harassed, you con-
40 tribute neither the enthusiasm evoked by your physical presence
nor (the zeal) of your preaching to the storm-tossed population?

Letter 212 – To Theophilus, presbyter

729 I was exceedingly upset when I heard that both you and Salustius
the presbyter attend worship[6] irregularly, and this news caused
me greater than usual sorrow. And so, please, if this report is

untrue, be at pains to make it clear to me that you have falsely
10 been informed against. If it's true, correct this particular carelessness. I say this because, while a very large reward awaits you,
especially if you demonstrate the appropriate courage during
the present time, similarly you will experience a more severe
than usual judgement, if you're indolent and avoid responsibility
and don't make your own particular contribution. For you know
what the servant who buried the single talent suffered. When
there was no other charge against him, he was punished for
that action alone and paid an implacable penalty (cf. Matt.
25:14–30). Be at pains, then, to free me swiftly from this worry.
20 For it will bring me much consolation and comfort when I hear
that you are enthusiastically supporting the entire storm-tossed
population. Similarly, when I learn that some are being careless,
I'm more than usually upset over the very people who are being
careless. For the grace of God supports that most beautiful flock
every day, just as you too know through actual experience. On
the other hand, those who through carelessness desist from
their duties accumulate by virtue of that carelessness no small
judgement against themselves.

The administration of care through others

Letter 217 – To Valentinus

730 I know your eager character, the ardent love that you have for
731 opportunities to assist[7] the poor and the desire that you constantly exhibit for this fine undertaking, and how you make provision and do so with pleasure, and how you double and render
more radiant for yourself the crown of generosity, both through
your generous giving and through the disposition from which
indeed the generous giving arises. Since, then, the most worthy
presbyter Domitian, who has the supervision of the widows and
10 virgins there, has revealed to us that they are all but in a state of
famine, we flee to your hands as to a harbour, that you might put
a stop to this famine-induced shipwreck. And so I ask you, and I
ask you strenuously,[8] to send for the presbyter, in so far as it is
possible, and be so kind as to give aid. For the charitable assistance that is provided now offers a much greater return than that
which is provided at another time, to the extent that those who
are asking to receive are situated in a more severe storm and
upheaval and do not enjoy their accustomed abundance. Since

you therefore understand the advantage that accrues to the matter and the assistance that arises from the moment in time,
20 be so kind as to do what you can. For we need say nothing more when writing to a person who is so generous and utterly civilised. I say this because you know that you in fact owe us salary payments.[9] Nonetheless, on account of those matters I absolve you in regard to this. Be so kind as to write to us too to tell us that you assent to our request, and to give us positive news about your health and about your entire blessed household.

Letter 210 – To Theodore

728 I was astonished at how I learned about the carelessness of
20 Salustius the presbyter from others. For in fact it was made known to me that he has preached barely five sermons up until the month of October, and that both he and Theophilus the presbyter – the one through indolence, the other through timidity – are not attending worship. While I have sent a rather strong letter to Theophilus, upbraiding him, I am writing to your worthiness on account of Salustius, since I know that you are an extreme admirer of his. Indeed I am extremely happy and pleased about that fact. I am upset too at your worthiness for not making this circumstance clear to me, since, although you ought to have set (him) straight as well, you pursued neither
30 of these two courses of action. So then, please, now grant both yourself and us the most enormous favour and give him an extremely rude awakening, and don't allow him to sleep on the job or be idle. My point is that, if he doesn't demonstrate the appropriate courage now in the storm and upheaval of these affairs, when are we to require him (to act) in this way? When it becomes calm and there is peace? Please, therefore, do what is appropriate to your position and arouse both him and everybody to the enthusiasm for and support of the storm-tossed population – which I am quite sure that you are doing from
40 your own initiative and of your own accord even before you receive what we have written.

Letter 51 – To Diogenes

636 After writing the previous letter, I observed that the most worthy and prudent Aphraates was nailed to our side and couldn't bear to leave here and was threatening that he wouldn't accept

letters from us, unless I took back what you had sent. I have (therefore) put my seal on the matter, indicating my extreme gratitude to your nobility and relieving your diligence. When

10 *a.i.* you learn this from him, command him to be a servant of this fine administration. For you know how great the reward for this enterprise will be, both through this man's presence in Phoenicia and through the liberality of your magnificence. You will reap the reward for both these things, seeing that you demonstrate such great largesse[10] concerning those in Phoenicia who are instructing the pagans in the faith and who have been at pains concerning the building of churches, and seeing that you have set in place such a capable man and have sent him for

637 their comfort (especially now when they are in so very difficult a situation and embattled by many). Bearing in mind, then, the difficulty of achieving success, don't let him put it off by even a little. Rather, get him in a position to undertake this journey without delay, since, by means of this fine zeal, my most excellent master, you set aside for yourself in advance a considerable reward from God who loves humankind.

Care exhibited towards John by others

Letter 34 – To Carteria

629 This too is a mark of your love, of your caring person who is vehemently devoted to us, that you didn't just send the polyarchium[11] but also reflected on how it might be useful and you might add to it both spikenard extract and sweet olive oil, which

10 *a.i.* is a corrective to the dryness it suffers from the long journey. And this circumstance in particular made us astonished about your disposition towards us – that you actually prepared it yourself and didn't entrust it to others, and that your priority was not that it be produced in haste, but that it turn out to be of high quality. It's for this reason that we express our thanks to you, offering just one criticism – that you didn't send in writing what was very much desired by us, namely positive news about your health. Since we are at present in a state of anxiety, not knowing how things stand with your ill-health, it would

630 gratify us enormously were you swiftly to send us a letter announcing to us that the traces of your illness had disappeared. Since you now know how earnestly we desire to learn that you

have indeed been brought back from that poor health, favour us with this pleasure, which would be no small comfort to us in this extremely harsh isolation and siege situation.

Letter 75 – To Harmatius

649 What's this? You have granted a great deal of authority so that with indemnity we may instruct the people attached to you in whatever we might require, yet you have deprived us of that
10 which we require most, namely your letters informing us about your state of health. Don't you know that this news above all is craved and longed for by particularly genuine friends, as is precisely the case with us too now? If, therefore, you wish to gratify us, my most worthy master, cease commanding your people to serve us in respect of our physical needs (we require none of these things – rather, everything flows to us as if from springs). Grant us by means of a little paper and ink an enormous favour, which indeed we desire most particularly to enjoy. That favour is
20 that you write to us constantly about your health and your entire household. I ask this because, if it were possible, we would certainly be in each other's company, even though I have displaced you from your home, even though I am in the position of having asked a major favour, that is, to see before my very eyes you who are so ardent an admirer of us. But since fear of the Isaurians prevents this, provide us generously with the comfort at least that comes from your letters, and we would call everything quits.

NOTES

1 JOHN'S LIFE AND TIMES

1 For the arguments which support this date see Kelly (1995: Appendix B, 296–8). The detail provided in this chapter of the Introduction is derived from Kelly's biography unless otherwise stated. For a view of John's life from a different perspective see Allen and Mayer (forthcoming)

2 For an outline of the period and the developments which occurred see Cameron and Garnsey (1998).

3 Regarding this phenomenon and its causes see Brown (1988).

4 For further detail see the now classic Delehaye (1933) and more recently Brown (1981).

5 Throughout the Introduction and notes and introductory comments and notes to the translated texts we refer to all texts other than those translated in this volume by their Latin titles (as per CPG). We do this so that the reader can readily distinguish between texts that are available to the reader in translation in this volume and ones that must be accessed elsewhere.

6 Rather, he tended to exploit the connections and finances of those with whom he came into contact in the course of his work: Mayer (1999). By contrast, the bishop of Antioch, Flavian, sponsored the care of itinerants from his private wealth, using his family property for the purpose (see Intro., Ch. 6).

7 See Bingham (1834: III. v. 'Of Lectors and Readers'); van de Paverd (1970: 100–1). The precise status of this office in the Meletian church at Antioch and whether at this juncture a person was ordained or appointed to it are uncertain. 'Appointment' is employed here as a term that is neutral.

8 The death of the emperor Valens in August 378 led to Arian Christianity being suppressed in favour of Nicene Christianity, the version promoted by both the emperor in the west, Gratian, and Valens' successor in the east, Theodosius. See Kelly (1995: 36–8).

9 Palladius, *Dial.* 5 (ACW 45: 36). For the literature which John produced during his diaconate see Kelly (1995: 40–54).

10 The extent to which John is likely to have been involved in pastoral activities as a deacon or aide to Meletius is an area that has yet to be

studied adequately. Kelly (1995: 39–40), probably correctly, speculates that at Antioch deacons played a significant role as administrators and as mediators between the bishop and laity in the provision of pastoral care. Because of the preponderance of evidence for John's activity during his time as presbyter and bishop we concentrate on those periods here. It is further assumed that at Antioch preaching was an activity undertaken only by persons of the rank of presbyter or higher.

11 This opinion had earlier been expressed by von Bonsdorff (1922: 69).
12 See Mayer (1997a: 71–2). The second sermon *De diabolo tentatore* (CPG 4332), in which John says that Flavian, desiring to hear him preach, has made the effort to come to where he is located (PG 49,257 2–10), supports this point of view.
13 For the argument that far fewer of the sermons can be distributed between Antioch and Constantinople with certainty than has previously been thought see Mayer (1996).
14 Frans van de Paverd (1991: 205–33) convincingly argues that the so-called *Ad illuminandos cat. 2* (CPG 4464) belongs with the other twenty-one homilies *De statuis* (CPG 4330).
15 For a thorough account of the event itself, its causes and consequences see van de Paverd (1991: 15–159).
16 Van de Paverd (1991: 161–87). For a table of the precise days on which John preached the twenty-two sermons see *ibid.* (1991: 363–4).
17 Soc., HE 6.2. For a brief discussion of the various motivations imputed to Eutropius see Kelly (1995: 105).
18 For a discussion of the factors leading to John's alienation of each of these groups see Liebeschuetz (1984; 1990: 195–222). Regarding his relations with Eudoxia, Marsa, Castricia and Eugraphia in the context of his interaction with other women see further Mayer (1999). The character of the ascetic men and women encountered at Constantinople is best described by Dagron (1970); Liebeschuetz (1990: 210–14). See further Mayer (1998a).
19 According to Downey (1961: 358) in 341 the dedication of the Great Church at Antioch attracted over ninety bishops.
20 E.g., *De statuis hom. 13* (PG 49,136 1–7 *a.i.*); *hom. 14* (PG 49,151 56–152 5); *hom. 18* (PG 49,187 30–8).
21 Wilken (1983: 36) states that the Jews constituted 'a sizeable, well-organized, and visible part of the city's life', while John himself places the number of Christians at approx. 100,000 (*In Matt. Hom.* 85/86: PG 58,762 59–763 2). On the difficulty of quantifying the spread of 'paganism' in Antioch at this time see Wilken (1983: 16–26), where he points out that the boundaries between what constituted a Christian or a 'pagan' lifestyle were constantly shifting.
22 Regarding the cultural and political paganism that permeated the upper levels of civic life see Dagron (1974: 380–5).

2 THE LITURGICAL SETTING

1 Kelly (1995: 3) posits that there were three or four parish churches in addition to the Great Church, but there is no evidence to confirm their existence.

2 See the detailed and careful argument put forward by Martha Vinson (1994: 181–8). She locates the construction of the church within the early reign of Theodosius (c.380).

3 Regarding the probable dates of initiation and completion see Downey (1938). For a description of the site and dimensions see Lassus (1938).

4 Downey (1938: 46 n. 10); Lassus (1938: 37–8). Before coming to rest in the church dedicated to him, Babylas' remains had been translated no less than three times – from the common cemetery outside the Golden Gate to Daphne; from Daphne back to the cemetery; from the cemetery to the Church of St Babylas. Meletius, who was responsible for the construction of the church, died unexpectedly in 381 while attending the Second Ecumenical Council in Constantinople (Soc., HE 5.8–9). His remains were most probably interred in the Church of the Apostles of that city as a temporary measure, before eventually being returned to Antioch (Mayer forthcoming (a): n. 56). The fact that the sarcophagus discovered in the archaeological excavations was purpose-built for a double burial suggests that Meletius had from the beginning intended to be buried in this church alongside Babylas.

5 See Soz., HE 5.19; De s. Babyla (PG 50,532 21–51).

6 See In s. Julianum (PG 50,672 366ff.); De s. Droside (PG 50,683 19–34, 684 21–3, 685 12–16); In s. Ignatium (PG 50,595 7–8). In De s. Droside (PG 50,683 29–34) John speaks of a number of martyria, each containing a cluster of burials. He also mentions that the martyrs' coffins are situated towards the rear beyond other undefined remains (PG 50,685 17–19). In In s. Julianum he indicates that the martyrium which contains Julian's remains is located in a pleasant situation which affords opportunities for picnics after the service beneath shady fig trees and grape vines (PG 50,673 46–9).

7 Soz., HE 5.19. Although the remains of Babylas were removed by order of Julian, the other remains which had been interred there by the Christians were left undisturbed.

8 Van de Paverd (1970: 10), however, locates it in the main martyrium in the cemetery on the road to Daphne.

9 In ascensionem (PG 50,441 12 a.i.–442 3 a.i.). Cf., however, De coemeterio et de cruce (PG 50,393 1–36), which appears to refer to a tradition that the Good Friday service is held in the martyrium in the cemetery on the road to Daphne. Either both martyria formed part of the network of churches used on liturgical festivals at Antioch or the usual identification of the site is mistaken.

10 See also De ss. martyribus (PG 50,648 31–9), where he indicates that visits to martyrs' tombs on the part of his audience have often had a more sobering effect than his sermons.

11 See also In s. Ignatium (PG 50,595 7–12); De ss. Bernice et Prosdoce (PG 50,640 44–60).

12 At least, a larger number are known to us. Even if there existed other urban churches at Antioch that were used regularly for worship, there is no evidence that John preached in other than the churches listed. At Constantinople, by contrast, a larger number of churches receive mention in relation to his episcopal activities. At both cities there were, in addition, urban churches in the possession of alternate Nicene Christian

factions – at Antioch, the Paulinians/Eustathians; at Constantinople, the Novatians.

13 The bulk of the Goths at Constantinople, particularly those in the army, were Arians. John had been instrumental in the emperor refusing the general Gainas' request for a local church in which he and his fellow Arians might worship (Soz., HE 8.4; Theod., HE 5.32; Soc., HE 6.6).

14 Soc., HE 6.6; Soz., HE 8.4: the site of a meeting between Arcadius and the Gothic general Gainas.

15 Severian of Gabala, *In ascensionem* (CPG 4187) (PG 52,775 22–5); Soc., HE 7.26.

16 Mocius and Acacius are the only indigenous martyrs who seem to have been commemorated *in situ*. As observed, the remains of Paul were returned to Constantinople in 381, but placed in an already extant building.

17 Vanderspoel (1986: 248–50) suggests that the remains are those of two western martyrs Sisinnius and Martyrius and their companions, which Vigilius, bishop of Tridentum, had promised to send to Constantinople. Holum (1982: 56 n. 35) dates the event to after 9 January 400 and before 10 January 402.

18 It is argued that Gregory of Nazianzus introduced the festival to Constantinople in 379 or 380 (P. Gallay, SC 358, Intro., 11–15), but the evidence is not conclusive. Higgins (1952) points to evidence that the birth of Christ was celebrated in the city on Epiphany in 602, which does not discount the introduction of the 25 December feast in the interim, but suggests that, even if it had been introduced at some earlier date, its place in the local calendar was only temporary.

19 Although the majority of John's festal sermons reflect the situation at Antioch, the major liturgical festivals at Constantinople can be established from the sermons preached there by his locum, Severian. See Datema (1988: 109–13).

20 See Palladius, *Dial.* 9 (ACW 45: 64), where those baptised during the night before Easter Sunday in 404 are said to have numbered 3,000. This may be an exaggeration, but still indicates that relatively large numbers were involved.

21 E.g., the festival of the Maccabees, All Saints.

3 JOHN AS PREACHER

1 E.g., *De statuis hom. 16* (PG 49,163 31–4); *De eleemosyna* (PG 51,261 1–2); *Laus Diodori* (PG 52,763 9–11). See also Mayer (1997b: 110–12).

2 For an excellent discussion of this form in relation to the preaching of John Chrysostom and the orations *Against the Jews* in particular see Wilken (1983: 112–23).

3 In the following paragraphs only a few of the more common techniques are outlined. For more detailed discussion on this topic see Ameringer (1921) and Wilken (1983: 106–12).

4 There is considerable argument about the status of the homilies which belong to the exegetical series. In particular, there is much dispute as to whether what survives is a much edited version of the original and

whether many of them were even preached or are simply written in the style of an orally delivered sermon (see, e.g., Baur 1959: 286–300; Olivar 1991: 907–10, 929–30; Kelly 1995: 92–4; Hill 1998). Moreover, although it is assumed by many scholars that such series were nonetheless preached more or less sequentially (e.g., Aubineau 1992: 537, Cameron 1987: 348–51), in certain instances this was clearly not the case (see Allen and Mayer 1994; 1995).

5 Cf. A.M. Devine (1989: 112) in relation to the 'rough' recension of the homilies on Acts: 'Preoccupied with his other concerns, Chrysostom, instead of preparing a finished text, extemporized from personal notes, and the text as we have it was drawn up by an unskilful editor from a transcript taken by a tachygrapher during the actual preaching. This transcript . . . the preacher himself never had the opportunity to revise.'

4 JOHN'S AUDIENCE

1 We are indebted to Susan Ashbrook Harvey for this suggestion.

2 So in Palladius (*Dial.* 14; ACW 45: 90) we learn that at Constantinople a large number of bishops, in the vicinity of twenty-two or more, were seated with John in the Great Church on one particular occasion.

3 For exceptions see *Sermo 6 in Gen.* (PG 54,605 1 and 36–9) and *Sermo 8 in Gen.* (PG 54,616 10–18 *a.i.*). John may be referring obscurely to the senior clergy in the audience in *In Heb. hom. 15* (Mayer 1997b: 113).

4 Dorys, a fellow-presbyter under Flavian, donated various sections of the mosaic pavement which adorned the church of St Babylas (Lassus 1938: 39–40, fig. 33).

5 *De baptismo Christi* (PG 49,365 5–14); *In kalendas* (PG 48,957 37–8); *Ad illuminandos cat. 2* (PG 49,237 23–8).

6 Mayer (1997a: 74), citing *In Heb. hom. 15* (PG 63,121 54–6 and 122 42–3) and *In 2. Thess. hom. 3* (PG 62,484 11–24). In the first case it is a number of women who are seated, in the second a wealthy male.

7 On the significance of being seated in the presence of social inferiors see Mayer (1997b: 109–12).

5 JOHN AS SOUL-CARER

1 Cf. the night-time processions for which John gained imperial support (Soc., HE 6.8; Soz., HE 8.8), which were instituted to the same end.

2 If the Constantius who is so heavily involved in the management of these activities is identical with the Constantius who is a prominent presbyter of Antioch (Palladius, *Dial.* 16; ACW 45: 101–2). See Delmaire (1991: 120–1).

3 Including wealthy aristocratic women at both locations. Regarding Constantinople see Mayer (1999: 9–10). The allusion to the difficult personal history of Chalcidia in an individual letter to her (*Ep.* 105: PG 52,664) may also be indicative of long-term private care. That Chalcidia is an

NOTES

inhabitant of Antioch (Delmaire 1991: 119) suggests that as a presbyter, if not earlier during his years as a deacon, John was likewise involved in this aspect of pastoral care.
4 This point is made in part in Mayer (1999).

6 PASTORAL CARE AND DAILY LIFE

1 For the social changes which influenced this development see Miller (1985: 69–74); Brown (1992: 78–103).
2 According to Theodoret (HE 5.19), Theodosius' first wife Flacilla used to do the rounds of the *xenōnes* attached to the city's churches and assist personally in giving the clients their meals.
3 Miller (1990: 107) speculates that both the Sampson *xenōn* and the *orphanotropheion* at one time belonged to the Great Church.
4 *Dial.* 5 (ACW 45: 39): said to be for the benefit of travellers who had fallen ill.
5 On her refusal to marry a second husband of Theodosius' choice the property was initially confiscated and placed under the administration of the *eparch* of the city, Clementinus. Theodosius later relented and it was placed under her control. *Vita Olymp.* 2–5; Palladius, *Dial.* 17 (ACW 45: 113–14).
6 *Vita Olymp.* 14; Palladius, *Dial.* 17 (ACW 45: 115).
7 Even without family however, absolute control of disposal of assets on welfare ventures was difficult, particularly for women. Even after she recovered control of her property from the state, Olympias was taken to task by Chrysostom for bestowing her largesse indiscriminately (Soz., HE 8.9).
8 *Vita Olymp.* 14; Palladius, *Dial.* 17 (ACW 45: 115).
9 *In Eph. hom. 13* (PG 62,98 3–38): the women are below the age of twenty. Whether John is speaking here from Constantinople or from Antioch is uncertain.
10 Miller (1984: 111–12; 1985: 80–2). See also Soz., HE 4.27.
11 See John's comments in *In Matt. hom. 85/86* (PG 58,761 53–6).
12 Olympias and Eugraphia are the best-known examples. See Mayer (1999: 11–12). While the *Dialogue* of Palladius and the *Vita Olympiadis* are selective in their evidence, describing only bishops as the beneficiaries of their hospitality, given her reputation it is unlikely that Olympias housed only individuals of high status.

GENERAL INTRODUCTION TO THE TEXTS

1 Greek philosophers of the fourth century promoted the concept as a counterpart to the Christian notion of *agapē*. For an excellent and still valuable discussion of the range of meanings which could attach to the word see Downey (1955). See further Brown (1992: 82–4).

210

2 Regarding the Field edition and the problems inherent in each of the various editions of these series of homilies see Goodall (1979: 1–5).

3 The translations of the homilies which appear in LNPF are likewise based upon the Field text. In the cases where the text was unavailable to the original translator, the editors have revised the translation and added useful footnotes accordingly.

ON EPHESIANS HOMILY 11

1 For a detailed argument concerning the probable Constantinopolitan provenance of this homily see Mayer (1996: 345–51).

2 The number rose to some forty or more in the period immediately preceding the Synod of the Oak (Palladius, *Dial.* 8; ACW 45: 52).

3 They could also preside at the liturgy at John's request (Palladius, *Dial.* 14; ACW 45: 91).

4 If one accepts that John returned to Constantinople shortly after Easter 402. The chronology of Cameron (1987), on which Kelly (1995: 165–73) relies, rests on a dubious assumption regarding the homogeneity of John's fifty-five homilies on the book of Acts. Even so, the location of the journey to Ephesus in 402 may well be correct.

5 Although we follow the text of Field, we here observe the punctuation in Montfaucon for the sake of clarity.

6 Paul, a bishop of Antioch in the third century, is thought to have taught that Christ did not 'come down from heaven' but was 'from below'. See Grillmeier (1975: 164–5).

7 The Field text is difficult to interpret at this point and we here revert to that of Montfaucon.

8 I.e., the Last Judgement.

9 Lit. 'Gehenna'.

10 He is still addressing the women at this point.

ON COLOSSIANS HOMILY 7

1 I.e., behaves in an arrogant fashion by taunting the losers. There has been some hesitation about the text at this point, Montfaucon preferring a passive verb rather than the active *epēreazē*. The active makes sense, however, and there is no need to seek an alternative reading.

2 We follow Montfaucon in this instance, where the addition of the negative particle makes better sense of the text.

3 We follow the Montfaucon text in this instance, for the sake of clarity.

4 There is a discrepancy here in the Greek between the single demonstrative and the plural antecedents.

5 John here refers to the riot of 387 and its consequences. See the introduction to *On the statues hom. 17.*

6 Probably Laodicea.

7 At this point in the Field text there is a *kai* which is untranslatable.

8 See Herod., *Hist.* 5.119 and 7.27, 31.
9 Unable to be located within the scriptural canon. The only other identifiable occurrence of this citation is in a text falsely attributed to Chrysostom (*Ecloga 6*: PG 63,605–16), where unfortunately the passage in which the citation occurs is clearly excerpted from the concluding paragraphs of *On Col. hom.* 7.
10 Gr. *charis*. It has the sense of both personal charm and influence. John is saying here that, since he is doing his duty, each person is responsible before God for their decision either to ignore his injunctions or respond to them.
11 Unable to be located within the scriptural canon. Also cited in Ps. Chrysostom, *Ecloga 6* (see n. 9).

HOMILY DELIVERED AFTER THE REMAINS OF MARTYRS ETC.

1 Lit. 'chorus'.
2 Gr. *diadēma*.
3 Gr. *diadēma*.
4 An allusion to the trade in martyrs' remains. See Intro., Ch. 2.
5 John 12:36; 1 Thess. 5:5.
6 Lucifer, i.e., Venus.
7 An indeterminate metal, considered in antiquity to be the hardest.
8 Gr. *basileian*, rendered elsewhere by us as 'kingdom', when not used in this technical sense. John refers here to Eudoxia's status as an Augusta and to the clothing that signified that status.
9 Gr. *prostatin*, lit. 'patroness'. The same feminine form of the noun is used in association with Phoebe and occurs in the citation from Romans.
10 An allusion to Abraham receiving the three angels in his tent in the desert (Gen. 18), a favourite Chrysostomic exemplum of hospitality.
11 In the context of Constantinople, the term usually signifies the local community of Goths.

A HOMILY ON MARTYRS

1 For a description of the drinking and revelry at Antioch that was associated with this festival see *In kalendas* (PG 48,953–62). For more complete details of the festival at this time in general see Asterius of Amasea, *hom. 4* (Datema 1970: 38–43, 228–31).
2 We differ here from the punctuation in Montfaucon.
3 Gr. *archōn*.
4 Gr. *pankratiazein*. The *pankration* was a contest which involved both boxing and wrestling.
5 Gr. *philosophia*.

ON HIS RETURN

1 L. 'Here begins the homily of saint John Chrysostom, when he returned to Constantinople from Asia.'
2 Lit. 'of such quality and such extent'.
3 Gr. *tropaion*. According to LSJ a monument of the enemies' defeat, usually consisting of shields, helmets and other equipment removed from the enemy, either fixed on upright posts or frames or hung from trees.
4 See n. 2.
5 L. 'constructing idols and staging rebellions'.
6 Gr. *philosophia*.
7 Retrieved from the Latin.
8 L. 'Moses, in a fit of anger, upbraided Aaron on account of the people's rebellion and took him to task for acquiescing to their will'.
9 Gr. *enkōmia*. The homily *Delivered after the remains of martyrs etc.* is an excellent example of this rhetorical genre.
10 Gr. *stephanous*. Here used in the sense of the wreaths, woven of olive or laurel, awarded the winners in athletic contests.
11 Lit. 'the sicknesses'. The allusion is to the charges of simony brought against the bishop of Ephesus and the bishops in the surrounding sees.
12 L. 'But I received no command of this kind. And when little by little I fell ill, your absence didn't cause me anxiety; rather, with every confidence in you, I awaited treatment for my ill health.'
13 L. 'the grace of God'.
14 L. 'What shall I do? How shall I indicate the exultation of my mind? I call in witness your conscience, which I see is filled with joy at my arrival. That joy is my crown and praise.'
15 L. 'I, however, see not one Joseph, but all of you in his likeness.'
16 Play on Gr. *paradeisos* (paradise) – essentially a cultivated garden, usually private. The church is more often referred to in homiletic literature as a meadow (*leimōn*), than as a garden.
17 The Latin text replaces 'and what's astonishing . . . them' with 'in that Garden every single kind of seed persists in its own condition; but in this garden, if . . .'
18 Gr. *diadēmatos*.
19 These first two statements are missing in the Latin text.
20 I.e., at the Last Judgement.
21 L. 'how your voices penetrated heaven with joy?'
22 L. 'For there is great happiness for a mother when her sons rejoice and immense joy for a shepherd when the sheep of his flock rejoice.'
23 Retrieved from the Latin text.
24 L. 'are my joy, my proud boast, my crown'.
25 Missing in the Latin text.
26 Chrysostom here exploits the two strands of meaning inherent in the term 'Pascha', which can refer, on the one hand, to the Paschal festival (i.e., Easter); on the other, to the Paschal feast (i.e., the eucharist).
27 I.e., 'on Easter Sunday'.
28 L. 'don't be doubtful about the grace, because it's God's gift'.

29 Gr. *hiereus* – in Chrysostom, a generic term which covers both presbyter and bishop.

30 Acts 8:26–40; 16:25–33; Luke 23:39–43. L. 'Beloved, don't then be in any doubt, for God's grace has been perfected. The location is no hindrance, whether you baptise here, or on a ship, or on a journey. Philip baptised on the road, Paul in prison, on the cross Christ (freed) the thief from his wound and earned the right to open at once the door of paradise.'

31 L. 'I'm not present but your mercy is – your mercy which led me there and conceded more than I deserved.'

32 L. (adds) 'For so great is your trustworthiness and love that you provoke everyone else into copying you.'

33 L. 'For, while I was in Asia for the purpose of correcting the churches, people coming from all over the place would report to us, saying . . .'.

34 L. 'increased Paul's confidence for preaching'.

35 L. (adds) 'prayer made the sterile woman fertile'.

36 L. 'That the God of glory on receiving your prayers grant me a sermon on the tip of my tongue, by which I might instruct the people entrusted to me for their salvation, through Christ our Lord to whom, together with God the Father and the Holy Spirit, be honour, glory and power for ever and ever. Here ends (the sermon) about this same person's return from Asia.'

ON THE STATUES HOMILY 17

1 Concerning the characteristic bold speech of the philosopher and the wealth of associations which John exploits in this homily see Brown (1992: 65–7).

2 Van de Paverd (1991: 64–76) comes as close as is possible, given the available evidence, to determining the role of the monks in what actually occurred.

3 Gr. *archontas.*

4 Gr. *asphaleia.*

5 Lit. 'heads'.

6 Gr. *philanthrōpia*, translated elsewhere by us as 'love for humankind'.

7 Gr. *philosophia.*

8 John plays here on the name of the philosophers known as Cynics (Gr. *kynikos* = 'dog-like'). As increasingly became the case with their Christian counterparts – monks and ascetics – pagan philosophers adopted a distinctive mode of appearance and dress.

9 Gr. *pollēn parrhēsian.*

10 Lit. 'in a rural way'.

11 I.e., Constantinople.

12 Gr. *stratopedon.* I.e., in the audience hall of the imperial palace in Constantinople.

13 Gr. *parrhēsia.*

14 See n. 12.

15 Gr. *sōphrosynē*, elsewhere translated by us as 'common sense'.

NOTES

16 Lit. 'orchestra'.
17 Lit. 'obols'.
18 A city designated as a metropolis had the status of a provincial capital and was ranked above every other city in its administrative district. Hence the long-term loss of its metropolitan status would have been a major economic blow to Antioch as well as a blow to its civic pride. Regarding the latter in relation to this same historical episode see *On Colossians hom. 7*.
19 Gr. *parrhēsia*.
20 This same episode from Antioch's past is adduced by John in *On 1 Cor. hom. 21*.
21 Gen. 23:4; Ps. 39:12; Heb. 11:13.
22 Gr. *philanthrōpos*.
23 Gr. *philanthrōpos*.

AGAINST THE GAMES AND THEATRES

1 Pargoire (1899–1900) locates the homily more precisely on 3 July 399, but as is argued in Mayer (forthcoming (c)) his reason for placing it on precisely that day is questionable. Pargoire's argument up to that point is impeccable, however.
2 As in modern sporting venues today the seating ranged from the expensive members' boxes and seats towards the top of the various tiers to cheap standing-room-only areas at ground level. For a description of the Constantinopolitan hippodrome in general and of the disposition of seating within it see ODB II 934–5 s.v. Hippodromes, and further, Dagron (1974: 327). For an illustration of the seating arrangement see Dagron (1974: Plate VII).
3 Gr. *hypophētēs*, i.e., a priest through whom God speaks. John here presumably refers to one of the three apostles whose remains were buried in the Church of the Apostles (Andrew, Luke or Timothy).
4 He here refers to the audience.
5 Lit. 'obol'.
6 Lit. 'Gehenna'.
7 John is exploiting medical imagery here, alluding to the cutting out of the diseased part and the cauterisation of the resultant wound to prevent the spread of infection.
8 Montfaucon notes that there is a problem here with the Greek text. He would prefer it to read: 'It's much better for you to be pained here and snatched away . . .' or 'It's much better for me to cause (you) pain and snatch (you) away . . .'.

BAPTISMAL INSTRUCTION 8

1 Gr. *diatheseōs* – the goodwill that arises from repayment of the debt.
2 Gr. *ergōn*, elsewhere translated by us as 'deeds'.

3 With regard to the liturgical furnishings of rural Syrian churches, what John means here by 'bema' is difficult to determine. For a discussion of the peculiarities which could attach to the interiors of non-episcopal churches in this region see Taft (1968). Van de Paverd (1991: 259) understands the term to refer in this instance to the pulpit or location from which the rural monk-presbyter preached.

4 Gr. *philosophon*.

5 A further reference to the distinctive appearance and mode of dress affected by pagan philosophers. See *On the statues hom. 17*.

6 Gr. *philanthrōpia*.

7 Gr. *synaxis* (lit. 'gathering'), elsewhere translated by us as 'service'.

ON EUTROPIUS

1 Gr. *symposia*. An all-male affair, usually held after dinner and lasting until well into the small hours of the morning.

2 An indication of extreme expense and debauchery. Wine was usually watered down.

3 The Greek text in Montfaucon reads *karpos* (fruit). The Latin translator evidently read *kapnos* (smoke), which is more consistent with the verb (*dieluthē*) and is a metaphor more typically employed by John when he wishes to highlight the ephemeral qualities of human possessions.

4 John refers here to the practice of acclamation – in this case, the shouting or chanting of short slogans in support of or demonstration against bene-factors and members of the upper echelons of the imperial and civic administration. See Brown (1992: 14, 149–50) and Roueché (1984).

5 Lit. 'the imperial halls'.

6 Gr. *bēma*. John here refers not to the ambo, but to the enclosure in front of the synthronon which contains the altar.

7 Gr. *philanthrōpia*.

8 John here refers to the curtains which enclosed the altar.

9 Lit. 'hymn'.

10 Lit. 'O human being'.

11 Gr. *eleēmosynē*, elsewhere translated by us as 'almsgiving'.

12 Gr. *hamartēmata*, usually used by John in the technical sense of 'sins'.

ON: 'I OPPOSED HIM TO HIS FACE'

1 In John's case, at least in his later years, the effects were usually felt by the other preacher. See *On: 'My father's working still'*, which follows.

2 I.e., Flavian.

ON: 'MY FATHER'S WORKING STILL'

1 For an outline of the rites observed at this period see ODB III 2193–4 s.v. Wedding.

2 I.e., the urban prefect (*eparchos tēs poleōs*), the official responsible for organising the chariot-races at Constantinople. See ODB I 705 s.v. Eparch of the City.

3 Lit. 'existing things'.

AGAINST THE JEWS ORATION 1

1 For further detail see Intro., Ch. 1, 'The cities of Antioch and Constantinople'.

2 For a brief, but excellent discussion of the history of the *psogos* and John's exploitation of this medium in relation to the series of homilies to which *Against the Jews or. 1* belongs see Wilken (1983: 112–23).

3 John refers to *De incompr. dei nat. hom. 1*. The Anomoeans taught that because God is *agennētos*, his essence is completely comprehensible by human beings (Kelly 1993: 249).

4 Gr. *choros*, elsewhere translated by us as 'band'.

5 I.e., against the Anomoeans (see Intro., Ch. 1, 'The cities of Antioch and Constantinople'.

6 Regarding the festivals celebrated in this latter part of the year see ODJR s.v. Fasts, 251; Rosh Hashanah, 590 (= Trumpets); Sukkot, 659–60 (= Tabernacles); Yom Kippur, 751 (= Day of Atonement).

7 Gr. *paranomias*. Throughout the homily John plays on the fact that the Jews claim to be under the law.

8 Gr. *skirtōntōn*, elsewhere translated by us as 'jumping with excitement'.

9 The reference is to the custom of the Antiochene Jews on Yom Kippur (the Day of Atonement).

10 Gr. *paranomian*, on other occasions translated by us as 'lawlessness'.

11 Gr. *phoberonterous*. The adjective *phoberos* conveys both the idea of inspiring fear and of inspiring awe.

12 Gr. *apologeisthai*. In *On his return* we translated this verb and its cognates as 'justify', 'justification'.

13 Lit. 'the low capacity of their mind'.

14 Gr. *phobera*.

15 John makes exactly the same criticism of his own parishioners in *On 1 Cor. hom 21*. Cf. *Against the games and theatres* and *On: 'My father's working still'*.

16 Gr. *phobera*.

17 Lit. 'head'.

18 The formula is spoken after the doors have been closed against the catechumens and the others who are ineligible to partake of the eucharist. See van de Paverd (1970: 239–40, 250).

19 I.e., that they didn't know about Christ and his coming.

20 Ruler of Egypt 282–246 BC and keen supporter of the library at Alexandria. For further detail see OCD 1272 s.v. Ptolemy II Philadelphus.

21 I.e., at Daphne. At the time that John was speaking it was in a state of disrepair and no longer functioning.

22 Gr. *manian*, also translated by us as 'craziness'.

23 Gr. *xoanon*. The term refers to the cultic image of the god which stood in a shrine or temple. It was often carved of wood and decorated with paint, gilding and/or ivory.

24 I.e., in 587 BC and AD 70, respectively.

25 Lit. 'table', i.e., instruction.

ON 1 CORINTHIANS HOMILY 21

1 Lit. 'bent'.

2 Lit. 'O human being'.

3 Gr. *eleēmosynē*, elsewhere translated by us as 'almsgiving'.

4 The same episode from Antioch's past is adduced by John in *On the statues hom. 17*.

5 The same accusation is directed by John towards the local Jews. See *Against the Jews or. 1*.

6 On the church allowance see Rentinck (1970: 315–21).

7 Rentinck (1970: *loc. cit.*); Brown (1992: 98).

8 Gr. *logon*.

9 Gr. *euthunas*.

10 Lit. 'depart for there'.

11 Gr. *parrhēsia*.

ON THE ACTS OF THE APOSTLES
HOMILY 3

1 Gr. *ta oikeia elattōmata*.

2 Cf. Matt. 20:20–4; Mark 10:35–41.

3 I.e., ordained them.

4 Gr. *prostasia*.

5 Gr. *ephilosophēson*.

6 Lit. 'Hyparchs and toparchs'.

CONCERNING BLESSED PHILOGONIUS

1 The reference is probably to the Anomoeans. Cf. *Against the Jews or. 1*.

2 Lit. 'our tongue'.

3 Gr. *brabeia*. The term refers to the symbols of athletic, not military, success.

4 Lit. 'grow old or die away'.

5 I.e., heaven and earth.

6 Gr. *cheirotonē*. The verb can mean both to appoint and to ordain.

7 Gr. *bēma*. John exploits the technical juridical and liturgical meanings of the term for the sake of producing a pun.

8 Lit. 'sit'.

9 Lit. 'head'.
10 Gr. *leipsanōn*, elsewhere translated by us as 'leftovers'.
11 I.e., Flavian.
12 I.e., the one that takes precedence over all others. For the status of a metropolis *vis-à-vis* surrounding cities in a province see *On the statues hom. 17.*
13 Lit. 'the sacred Pascha'.

LETTERS FROM EXILE

1 Lit. 'that he has fallen out of your household and is gone from sight'.
2 Gr. *exebalon* (active).
3 Gr. *philanthrōpias.*
4 Gr. *spoudē*, elsewhere translated by us as 'zeal'.
5 Gr. *proepempsas.* The verb may be used here in the double sense of sending the brother ahead of him to heaven and of escorting the body during the funeral procession.
6 Gr. *synaxin.*
7 Gr. *tas prostasias*, lit. 'the supervisions', 'the assistances'.
8 Gr. *sphodra*, translated by us elsewhere as 'exceedingly'.
9 Gr. *sportoula.* The precise meaning of the term is difficult to determine. John may be referring to fees owed for services rendered by him in the episcopal court (*audientia episcopalis*). Regarding the technical use of the term in succeeding centuries see ODB III 1993 s.v. Synetheia.
10 Gr. *dapsileian*, elsewhere translated by us as 'generous giving'.
11 Gr. *polyarchion.* According to LSJ a medicinal salve named after Polyarchus, the physician who invented it.

BIBLIOGRAPHY

TEXTS OF JOHN CHRYSOSTOM

PG 48,747–56 (*De b. Philogonio*); PG 48,843–56 (*Adv. Iudæos or. 1*); PG 49,171–80 (*De statuis hom. 17*); PG 50,661–6 (*Hom. in martyres*); PG 51,371–88 (*In illud: In faciem ei restiti*); PG 52,391–6 (*In Eutropium*); PG 52,629–30 (*Ep. 34*); PG 52,649 (*Ep. 75*); PG 52,672–3 (*Ep. 117*); PG 52,721–2 (*Ep. 197*); PG 52,724 (*Ep. 203*); PG 52,728 (*Ep. 210*); PG 52,729 (*Ep. 212*); PG 52,730–1 (*Ep. 217*); PG 56,263–70 (*Nov. hom. 7: Contra ludos et theatra*); PG 60,33–42 (*In Acta apost. hom. 3*); PG 61,169–80 (*In 1 Cor. hom. 21*); PG 62,79–88 (*In Eph. hom. 11*); PG 62,343–52 (*In Col. hom. 7*); PG 63,467–72 (*Nov. hom. 1: Hom. habita postquam reliquiae martyrum*); PG 63,511–16 (*Nov. hom. 10: In illud: Pater meus usque modo operatur*).

Field, F. (1847) *Sancti patris nostri Ioannis chrysostomi archiepiscopi Constantinopolitani interpretatio omnium epistolarum Paulinarum per homilias facta*, II, continens homilias in epistolam ad Corinthios priorem, Oxonii (*In 1 Cor. hom. 21*).

Field, F. (1852) *Tou en hagiois patros hēmōn Iōannou archiepiskopou Kōnstantinoupoleōs tou chrysostomou hypomnēmata eis tas pros Galatas kai Ephesious epistolas*, Oxford (*In Eph. hom. 11*).

Field, F. (1855) *Tou en hagiois patros hēmōn Iōannou archiepiskopou Kōnstantinoupoleōs tou chrysostomou hypomnēmata eis tas pros Philippēsious kai Kolossaeis kai Thessalonikeis epistolas*, Oxford (*In Col. hom. 7*).

Wenger, A. (1961) 'L'homélie de saint Jean Chrysostome «à son retour d'Asie»', *Revue des Études byzantines* 19: 110–23 (*De regressu*).

Wenger, A. (1970) *Jean Chrysostome: Huit catéchèses baptismales inédites*, 2nd edn, Paris: Éditions du CERF (SC 50bis), 247–60 (*Cat. 8*).

TRANSLATIONS

The following translations have appeared in English prior to our own. The abbreviation LNPF = P. Schaff (ed.) (1886–90) *A Select Library of the Nicene and Post Nicene Fathers of the Christian Church*, New York: The Christian Literature Company.

On Eph. hom. 11. W.J. Copeland, rev. G. Alexander (1889) LNPF 13, 102–8.
On Col. hom. 7. J. Ashworth (1889) LNPF 13, 288–93.
On the statues hom. 17. C. Marriott, rev. W.R.W. Stephens (1889) LNPF 9, 452–8.
Baptismal instruction 8. P.W. Harkins (1963) *St. John Chrysostom: Baptismal Instructions*, New York: Newman Press (Ancient Christian Writers, 31), 119–30.
On Eutropius. W.R.W. Stephens (1889) LNPF 9, 249–52.
Against the Jews or. 1. P.W. Harkins (1979) *Saint John Chrysostom: Discourses against Judaizing Christians*, Washington, D.C.: The Catholic University of America Press (The Fathers of the Church, 68), 1–34.
On 1 Cor. hom. 21. H.K. Cornish and J. Medley, rev. T.W. Chambers (1889) LNPF 12, 118–25.
On Acts hom. 3. H. Browne, rev. G.B. Stevens (1889) LNPF 11, 17–25.

OTHER TEXTS AND TRANSLATIONS

Bidez, J., and G.C. Hansen (1995²) *Sozomenus. Kirchengeschichte*, Berlin: Akademie Verlag (Die griechischen christlichen Schriftsteller der ersten Jahrhunderte, N.F. 4).
Canivet, P., and A. Leroy-Molinghen (1977) *Théodoret de Cyr. Histoire des moines de Syrie. «Histoire Philothée» I–XIII*, Tome I, Paris: Les Éditions du CERF (Sources Chrétiennes, 234).
Datema, C. (1970) *Asterius of Amasea. Homilies I–XIV*, Text, Introduction and Notes, Leiden: E.J. Brill.
Foerster, R. (1903–13) *Libanii Opera*, 7 vols, Leipzig: B.G. Teubner.
Hansen, G.C. (1995) *Sokrates. Kirchengeschichte*, Berlin: Akademie Verlag (Die griechischen christlichen Schriftsteller der ersten Jahrhunderte, N.F. 1).
Jeffreys, E., M. Jeffreys, and R. Scott with B. Croke, J. Ferber, S. Franklin, A. James, D. Kelly, A. Moffatt and A. Nixon (1986) *The Chronicle of John Malalas: A Translation*, Melbourne: Australian Association for Byzantine Studies (Byzantina Australiensia, 4).
Malingrey, A.-M. (1968) *Jean Chrysostome. Lettres à Olympias*, seconde édition augmentée de la *Vie anonyme d'Olympias*, Paris: Les Éditions du CERF (Sources Chrétiennes, 13bis).
Malingrey, A.-M., with P. Leclercq (1988) *Palladios. Dialogue sur la vie de Jean Chrysostome* I–II, Paris: Les Éditions du CERF (Sources Chrétiennes, 341–2).
Meyer, R.T. (1985) *Palladius: Dialogue on the Life of St. John Chrysostom*, New York: Newman Press (Ancient Christian Writers, 45).
Moreschini, C., and P. Gallay (1990) *Grégoire de Nazianze. Discours 38–41*, Paris: Les Éditions du CERF (Sources Chrétiennes, 358).

Parmentier, L., and G.C. Hansen (1998^3) *Theodoret. Kirchengeschichte*, Berlin: Akademie Verlag (Die griechischen christlichen Schriftsteller der ersten Jahrhunderte, N.F. 5).

Wright, W.C. (1913) *The Works of the Emperor Julian*, 3 vols, London: William Heinemann (The Loeb Classical Library).

REFERENCE WORKS

Berardino, A. Di (ed.) (1992) *Encyclopedia of the Early Church = Dizionario Patristico e di Antichità Cristiana*, 2 vols, trans. from the Italian, Cambridge: James Clarke & Co. (Institutum Patristicum Augustinianum).

Hornblower, S., and A. Spawforth (eds) (1996) *The Oxford Classical Dictionary*, Oxford: Oxford University Press.

Kazhdan, A.P. *et al.* (eds) (1991) *The Oxford Dictionary of Byzantium*, New York and Oxford: Oxford University Press.

Liddell H.G., and R. Scott (1983) *A Greek–English Lexicon*, with supplement, rev. and augm. H.S. Jones with R. McKenzie, repr. from 9th edn, Oxford: Clarendon Press.

Werblowsky, R.J.Z., and G. Wigoder (eds) (1997) *The Oxford Dictionary of the Jewish Religion*, New York and Oxford: Oxford University Press.

SECONDARY LITERATURE

Allen, P. (1996) 'The Homilist and the Congregation: A Case-study of Chrysostom's Homilies on Hebrews', *Augustinianum* 36: 397–421.

Allen, P. (1997) 'John Chrysostom's Homilies on I and II Thessalonians: The Preacher and His Audience', *Studia Patristica* 31: 3–21.

Allen, P., and W. Mayer (1993) 'Computer and Homily: Accessing The Everyday Life Of Early Christians', *Vigiliae Christianae* 47: 260–80.

Allen, P., and W. Mayer (1994) 'Chrysostom and the Preaching of Homilies in Series: A New Approach to the Twelve Homilies *In epistulam ad Colossenses* (CPG 4433)', *Orientalia Christiana Periodica* 60: 21–39.

Allen, P., and W. Mayer (1995) 'The Thirty–Four Homilies on Hebrews: The Last Series Delivered by Chrysostom in Constantinople?', *Byzantion* 65: 309–48.

Allen, P., and W. Mayer (forthcoming) 'John Chrysostom', ch. 45 in P. Esler (ed.), *The Early Christian World*, London: Routledge.

Ameringer, T.E. (1921) 'The Stylistic Influence of the Second Sophistic On the Panegyrical Sermons of St. John Chrysostom: A Study in Greek Rhetoric', diss., Washington, D.C.: Catholic University of America.

Attwater, D. (1939) *St John Chrysostom: Pastor and Preacher*, Milwaukee (repr. (1959) London: Harvill Press.

Aubineau, M. (1992) 'Restitution de quatorze folios du codex hierosolymitain, Photios 47, au codex Saint-Sabas 32. Prédications de Chrysostome à Constantinople et notamment à Sainte-Irène', *Journal of Theological Studies* NS 43: 528–44.

Baur, C. (1929–30) *Johannes Chrysostomus und seine Zeit*, 2 vols, Munich: Hueber = (1959–60) *John Chrysostom and His Time*, Sr M. Gonzaga (trans.), 2 vols, Westminster, Md.: Newman Press.

Bernardi, J. (1995) *Saint Grégoire de Nazianze. Le Théologien et son temps (330–390)*, Paris: Les Éditions du CERF.

Bingham, J. (1834) *Origines Ecclesiasticae; or the Antiquities of the Christian Church*, 8 vols, rev. R. Bingham, London: William Straker.

Bonsdorff, M. von (1922) 'Zur Predigttätigkeit des Johannes Chrysostomus, biographisch-chronologische Studien über seine Homilienserien zu neutestamentlichen Büchern', diss., Helsingfors: Mercators Tryckeri Aktiebolag.

Broc, C. (1993) 'Le rôle des femmes dans l'Église de Constantinople d'après la correspondance de Jean Chrysostome', *Studia Patristica* 27: 150–4.

Brown, P. (1981) *The Cult of the Saints: Its Rise and Function in Latin Christianity*, Chicago: University of Chicago Press.

Brown, P. (1988) *The Body and Society: Men, Women, and Sexual Renunciation in Early Christianity*, New York: Columbia University Press (Lectures on the History of Religions, NS 13).

Brown, P. (1992) *Power and Persuasion in Late Antiquity: Towards a Christian Empire*, Wisconsin: University of Wisconsin Press.

Cameron, Alan (1987) 'Earthquake 400', *Chiron* 17: 343–60.

Cameron, Averil, and P. Garnsey (eds) (1998) *The Cambridge Ancient History*, XIII: *The Late Empire A.D. 337–425*, Cambridge: Cambridge University Press.

Carroll, T.K. (1984) *Preaching the Word*, Wilmington, Del.: Michael Glazier (Message of the Fathers of the Church, 11).

Cunningham, M., and P. Allen (eds) (1998) *Preacher and Audience: Studies in Early Christian and Byzantine Homiletics*, Leiden: Brill.

Dagron, G. (1970) 'Les moines et la ville. Le monachisme à Constantinople jusqu'au concile de Chalcédoine (451)', *Travaux et Mémoires* 4: 229–76.

Dagron, G. (1974) *Naissance d'une capitale. Constantinople et ses institutions de 330 à 451*, Paris: Presses universitaires de France (Bibliothèque Byzantine, 7).

Datema, C. (1988) 'Towards a Critical Edition of the Greek Homilies of Severian of Gabala', *Orientalia Lovaniensia Periodica* 19: 107–15.

Deichmann, F.W. (1972) 'Das Oktogon von Antiocheia: Heroon–Martyrion, Palastkirche oder Kathedrale?', *Byzantinische Zeitschrift* 65: 40–56.

Delehaye, H. (1933) *Les origines du culte des martyrs*, 2nd rev. edn, Brussels: Société des Bollandistes (Subsidia Hagiographica, 20).

Delmaire, R. (1991) 'Les «lettres d'exil» de Jean Chrysostome. Études de chronologie et de prosopographie', *Recherches Augustiniennes* 25: 71–180.

Devine, A.M. (1989) 'The Manuscripts of St. John Chrysostom's *Commentary on the Acts of the Apostles*: A Preliminary Study for a Critical Edition', *Ancient World* 20: 111–25.

Devreese, R. (1945) *Le Patriarcat d'Antioche depuis la paix de l'église jusqu'à la conquête arabe*, Paris: Libraire Lecoffre (Études Palestiniennes et Orientales).

Downey, G. (1938) 'The Shrines of St. Babylas at Antioch and Daphne', in R. Stillwell (ed.), *Antioch-on-the-Orontes*, II: *The Excavations 1933–1936*, Princeton, N.J.: Princeton University Press, 45–8.

Downey, G. (1955) 'Philanthropia in Religion and Statecraft in the Fourth Century after Christ', *Historia* 4: 199–208.

Downey, G. (1961) *A History of Antioch in Syria from Seleucus to the Arab Conquest*, Princeton, N.J.: Princeton University Press.

Eltester, W. (1937) 'Die Kirchen Antiochias im IV. Jahrhundert', *Zeitschrift für Neutestamentliche Wissenschaft* 36: 251–86.

Franchi di Cavalieri, P. (1928) 'Il *koimētērion* di Antiochia', *Studi e Testi* 49: 146–53.

Gignac, F.T. (1987) 'The New Critical Edition of Chrysostom's *Homilies on Acts*: A Progress Report', in J. Dummer, J. Irmscher, F. Paschke and K. Treu (eds), *Texte und Textkritik. Eine Aufsatzsammlung*, Berlin: Akademie Verlag (Texte und Untersuchungen, 133), 165–8.

Goodall, B. (1979) *The Homilies of St. John Chrysostom on the Letters of St. Paul to Titus and Philemon: Prolegomena to an Edition*, Berkeley, Los Angeles, London: University of California Press (University of California Publications in Classical Studies, 20).

Grillmeier, A. (1975) *Christ in Christian Tradition, I: From the Apostolic Age to Chalcedon (451)*, 2nd rev. edn, trans. J. Bowden, Atlanta: John Knox Press.

Higgins, M. (1952) 'Note on the Purification (and Date of Nativity) in Constantinople in 602', *Archiv für Liturgiewissenschaft* 2: 81–3.

Hill, R.C. (1998) 'Chrysostom's Commentary on the Psalms: Homilies or Tracts?', in P. Allen, R. Canning, L. Cross (eds) with B.J. Caiger, *Prayer and Spirituality in the Early Church*, Brisbane: Centre for Early Christian Studies, Australian Catholic University, 301–17.

Holum, K.G. (1982) *Theodosian Empresses: Women and Imperial Dominion in Late Antiquity*, Berkeley, Los Angeles, London: University of California Press (The Transformation of the Classical Heritage, 3).

Janin, R. (1969) *La géographie ecclésiastique de l'empire byzantin, première partie: La siège de Constantinople et le patriarchat oecuménique: III. Les églises et les monastères*, 2nd edn, Paris: Centre National de la Recherche Scientifique.

Jones, A.H.M., J.R. Martindale, and J. Morris, *The Prosopography of the Later Roman Empire*, (1971) I: *A.D. 260–395*; (1980) II: *A.D. 395–527*, Cambridge: Cambridge University Press.

Kelly, J.N.D. (1993) *Early Christian Doctrines*, repr. 5th edn, London: A&C Black.

Kelly, J.N.D. (1995) *Golden Mouth: The Story of John Chrysostom – Ascetic, Preacher, Bishop*, London: Gerald Duckworth.

Krautheimer, R. (1983) *Three Christian Capitals: Topography and Politics*, Berkeley, Los Angeles, London: University of California Press.

Lassus, J. (1938) 'L'Église cruciforme. Antioche–Kaoussié 12-F', in R. Stillwell (ed.), *Antioch-on-the-Orontes*, II: *The Excavations 1933–1936*, Princeton, N.J.: Princeton University Press, 5–44.

Lassus, J. (1977) 'La ville d'Antioche à l'époque romaine d'après l'archéologie', *Aufstieg und Niedergang der Römischen Welt* 2/8: 54–102.

Leyerle, B. (1994) 'John Chrysostom on Almsgiving and the Use of Money', *Harvard Theological Review* 87: 29–47.

Leyerle, B. (1997) 'Appealing to Children', *Journal for Early Christian Studies* 5: 243–70.

Liebeschuetz, J.H.W.G. (1972) *Antioch: City and Imperial Administration in the Later Roman Empire*, Oxford: Clarendon Press.

Liebeschuetz, J.H.W.G. (1984) 'Friends and Enemies of John Chrysostom', in A. Moffatt (ed.), *Maistor: Classical, Byzantine and Renaissance Studies for Robert Browning*, Canberra: Australian Association for Byzantine Studies (Byzantina Australiensia, 5), 85–111.

Liebeschuetz, J.H.W.G. (1990) *Barbarians and Bishops: Army, Church, and State in the Age of Arcadius and Chrysostom*, Oxford: Clarendon Press.

MacMullen, R. (1989) 'The Preacher's Audience (AD 350–400)', *Journal of Theological Studies* NS 40: 503–11.

Mango, C. (1986) 'The Development of Constantinople as an Urban Centre', in A.D. Caratzas (ed.), *The 17th International Byzantine Congress: Main Papers*, New Rochelle, N.Y.: Aristide D. Caratzas, 117–36.

Mango, C. (1990) 'Constantine's Mausoleum and the Translation of Relics', *Byzantinische Zeitschrift* 83: 51–61.

Mathews, T.F. (1977) *The Early Churches of Constantinople: Architecture and Liturgy*, University Park and London: The Pennsylvania State University Press.

Mayer, W. (1996) 'The Provenance of the Homilies of St John Chrysostom: Towards a New Assessment of Where he Preached What', diss., Brisbane: University of Queensland.

Mayer, W. (1997a) 'John Chrysostom and His Audiences: Distinguishing Different Congregations at Antioch and Constantinople', *Studia Patristica* 31: 70–5.

Mayer, W. (1997b) 'The Dynamics of Liturgical Space: Aspects of the Interaction between John Chrysostom and his Audiences', *Ephemerides Liturgicae* 111: 104–15.

Mayer, W. (1998a) 'Monasticism at Antioch and Constantinople in the Late Fourth Century: A Case of Exclusivity or Diversity?', in P. Allen, R. Canning, L. Cross (eds) with B.J. Caiger, *Prayer and Spirituality in the Early Church*, Brisbane: Centre for Early Christian Studies, Australian Catholic University, 275–88.

Mayer, W. (1998b) 'John Chrysostom: Extraordinary Preacher, Ordinary Audience', in M. Cunningham and P. Allen (eds), *Preacher and Audience: Studies in Early Christian and Byzantine Homiletics*, Leiden: Brill, 105–37.

Mayer, W. (1998c) 'The Sea made Holy: The Liturgical Function of the Waters Surrounding Constantinople', *Ephemerides Liturgicae* 112: 459–68.

Mayer, W. (1999) 'Constantinopolitan Women in Chrysostom's Circle', *Vigiliae Christianae* 53: 1–24.

Mayer, W. (forthcoming (a)) 'Cathedral Church or Cathedral Churches? The Situation at Constantinople (*c.*360–404 AD)'.

Mayer, W. (forthcoming (b)) 'Female Participation and the Late Fourth Century Preacher's Audience'.

Mayer, W. (forthcoming (c)) '"Les homélies de s. Jean Chrysostome en juillet 399": A Second Look at Pargoire's Sequence and the Chronology of the *Novæ homiliae* (CPG 4441)'.

Miller, T.S. (1984) 'Byzantine Hospitals', *Dumbarton Oaks Papers* 38: 53–63.

Miller, T.S. (1985) *The Birth of the Hospital in the Byzantine Empire*, Baltimore and London: The Johns Hopkins University Press (The Henry E. Sigerist Supplements to the Bulletin of the History of Medicine, NS 10).

Miller, T.S. (1990) 'The Sampson Hospital of Constantinople', *Byzantinische Forschungen* 15: 101–36.

Olivar, A. (1991) *La predicación cristiana antigua*, Barcelona: Biblioteca Herder (Sección de teología y filosofía, 189)

Pargoire, J. (1899–1900) 'Les homélies de s. Jean Chrysostome en juillet 399', *Échos d'Orient* 3: 151–62.

Paverd, F. van de (1970) *Zur Geschichte der Messliturgie in Antiocheia und Konstantinopel gegen Ende des vierten Jahrhunderts*, Rome: Pont. Institutum Studiorum Orientalium (Orientalia Christiana Analecta, 187).

Paverd, F. van de (1991) *St. John Chrysostom, The Homilies on the Statues: An Introduction*, Rome: Pont. Institutum Studiorum Orientalium (Orientalia Christiana Analecta, 239).

Petit, P. (1955) *Libanius et la vie municipale à Antioche au IV*e *siècle après J.-C.*, Paris: Libraire orientaliste Paul Geuthner (Institut Français d'Archéologie de Beyrouth. Bibliothèque archéologique et historique, 62).

Rentinck, P. (1970) *La cura pastorale in Antiochia nel IV secolo*, Rome: Università Gregoriana Editrice (Analecta Gregoriana, 178; Series Facultatis Historiæ Ecclesiasticæ, sectio B, 29).

Roueché, C. (1984) 'Acclamations in the Later Roman Empire: New Evidence from Aphrodisias', *Journal of Roman Studies* 74: 181–99.

Stephens, W.R.W. (1880) *Saint John Chrysostom: His Life and Times*, London: John Murray.

Taft, R. (1968) 'Some Notes on the Bema in the East and West Syrian Traditions', *Orientalia Christiana Periodica* 34: 326–59.

Vanderspoel, J. (1986) 'Claudian, Christ and the Cult of the Saints', *Classical Quarterly* 36: 244–55.

Vinson, M. (1994) 'Gregory Nazianzen's Homily 15 and the Genesis of the Christian Cult of the Maccabean Martyrs', *Byzantion* 64: 166–92.

Wilken, R.L. (1983) *John Chrysostom and the Jews: Rhetoric and Reality in the Late Fourth Century*, Berkeley, Los Angeles, London: University of California Press (The Transformation of the Classical Heritage, 4).

Woods, D. (1991) 'The Date of the Translation of the Relics of SS. Luke and Andrew to Constantinople', *Vigiliae Christianae* 45: 286–92.

INDEX

INDEX

Philogonius, bishop of Antioch
 184–5, 187–9
Phoenicia 45, 196–7, 203
Pityus 11
Plutarch, governor of Antioch 48
polyarchium 203
presbyter 5–7, 12, 17, 24, 26, 31–3,
 37, 43–6, 48, 52, 73, 105,
 110–11, 181
Ptolemy Philadelphus 160

Rome 4, 8, 11, 14, 112

Salustius, presbyter 196, 200, 202
Sampson, monk 48
Saturninus 9
Second Ecumenical Council 4, 6
Serapion, archdeacon 9
Severian of Gabala 9, 59
Sisinnius, bishop 60
Socrates, church historian 6, 30
Sozomen, church historian 6, 30, 35,
 46, 48
Stagirius 48

Studius, urban prefect 44, 196, 199
temple of Apollo, Daphne 12–13,
 19, 160
Theodora 44, 196–7
Theodore 202
Theodoret of Cyrrhus 5, 184
Theodosius I 4, 14–15, 20–1, 48,
 105
Theodosius II 86
Theophilus of Alexandria 9–10,
 51
Theophilus, presbyter 196, 200,
 202
Thrace 9

Valens 11, 18
Valentinus 196, 201
Vitalis 184

Wenger, A. 98, 126

Yakto mosaic 47

Zotikos 48